W9-AOS-890

Toxic Water, Toxic System

The publisher and the University of California Press Foundation gratefully acknowledge the generous support of the Ralph and Shirley Shapiro Endowment Fund in Environmental Studies.

Toxic Water, Toxic System

ENVIRONMENTAL RACISM AND
MICHIGAN'S WATER WAR

Michael Mascarenhas

UNIVERSITY OF CALIFORNIA PRESS

University of California Press
Oakland, California

© 2024 by Michael Mascarenhas

Library of Congress Cataloging-in-Publication Data

Names: Mascarenhas, Michael, author.
Title: Toxic water, toxic system : environmental racism and Michigan's
    water war / Michael Mascarenhas ; with We the People of Detroit.
Description: [Oakland, California] : University of California Press,
    [2024] | Includes bibliographical references and index.
Identifiers: LCCN 2023032335 (print) | LCCN 2023032336 (ebook) |
    ISBN 9780520343863 (cloth) | ISBN 9780520343870 (paperback) |
    ISBN 9780520975217 (ebook)
Subjects: LCSH: Water rights—Michigan—Detroit—21st century. |
    Liability for water pollution damages—Michigan—Detroit—21st
    century. | Water—Pollution—Law and legislation—Michigan—
    Detroit—21st century. | Water-supply—Government policy—
    Michigan—Detroit—21st century. | Environmental justice—
    Michigan—Detroit—21st century.
Classification: LCC KFM4646 .M37 2024 (print) | LCC KFM4646 (ebook) |
    DDC 363.6/109774—dc23/eng/20231002
LC record available at https://lccn.loc.gov/2023032335
LC ebook record available at https://lccn.loc.gov/2023032336

Manufactured in the United States of America

32   31   30   29   28   27   26   25   24
10   9   8   7   6   5   4   3   2   1

Contents

Illustrations

TABLES

Preface

Water will be the issue of your lifetime. It just will be.

—Monica Lewis-Patrick, We the People of Detroit

Water, activists tell me, is the last weapon to move you off your land.

Access to sufficient, safe, potable, accessible, and affordable water for personal and domestic use is recognized by the United Nations as a human right. Both governmental and nongovernmental agencies around the world have issued directives to bring water to people who do not fully enjoy this right. A recent poll taken in the state of California, where I currently live, listed the state's water supply as residents' number one environmental concern.[1] So when the state of Michigan revoked the right to safe and affordable water in Detroit, Flint, Benton Harbor, and other majority-Black cities in the state, many asked how this could happen in a country that prides itself on being a champion of human rights and where access to water remains a leading public concern.

Between 2014 and 2016, the city of Detroit, under the direction of a state-appointed manager, launched a massive water shutoff program, cutting the water supply to more than one in six Detroit households.[2] The numbers are staggering. Water was shut off in more than 80,000 homes and buildings in Detroit alone. Local activists estimate that the water shutoffs adversely harmed nearly half of the city's residents—upward of 300,000 people, mostly Black and poor. Water shutoffs have also been linked with the hepatitis A outbreak in the Detroit area. Since the beginning of the outbreak in August 2016, 610 cases of the disease have been reported in Michigan, including 20 deaths.

Speaking at an environmental justice summit I attended in the fall of 2018, Monica Lewis-Patrick, CEO and cofounder of the community-based grassroots organization We the People of Detroit, explained:

> As we are seeing austerity play out all across the country, Detroit was the beta test. As they were ceasing assets in Detroit, they poisoned Flint. Out of the 126 municipalities, and the 4.3 million Michiganders that drink from Detroit's well, there are only two municipalities that have their water shutoff because they can't afford it [Flint and Detroit]. If you look at it, in Detroit over the last 12 years, water rates have gone up 125%. That's not right, and it's not affordable. What we know is that as Flint got sicker and sicker, cover-ups and collusion happened. This is also taking place in Detroit.

Most people are now all too familiar with the Flint tragedy, at least in terms of its data: 100,000 residents intentionally poisoned, including 9,000 children. Two hundred confirmed cases of lead poisoning. Ninety cases of Legionnaires disease, of which at least twelve have died. Given that Legionnaires bacterium causes fever and other flu-like symptoms, the number of people adversely impacted by Flint's untreated water system could actually have been much higher than officially reported. A *Frontline* investigation found that the death toll from contaminated water to be 119, much higher than state health officials had acknowledged.[3] Researchers also found a substantial decrease in fertility rates and a "horrifyingly large" increase (58%) in fetal death rates in Flint during the water switch. As Claire McClinton, cofounder of the Flint Democracy Defense League, observed, "our nightmare began with the poisoning of the people" in Flint. This was possible, she continued, only when "the emergency manager signed the order to go to the Flint River. . . . So what the State of Michigan has done is [to] dismantle democracy." McClinton described how the city was forced to change its water supply to appease bondholders and other investors. "The type of people that are running our state, over our health, and our well-being" are crooks and criminals, McClinton professed, and "we've got . . . to evidence and expose these criminal activities."[4]

McClinton and Lewis Patrick are not alone in recognizing how racism and anti-Blackness work through diverse environmental conditions, including austerity, debt, and the seizure of local government. This pattern of racialized harm suggests that lead poisoning and water shutoffs are not simply the manifestation of poor decisions or elected officials' dereliction of duty, but the result of the mundane and taken-for-granted workings of austerity policies that use colorblind administrative mechanisms, such as the state's emergency manager law, to strip away Black assets and democratic autonomy for the benefit of white political and economic elites. The neoliberal playbook has been rewritten to spread beyond "the tyranny of tight budgets" toward "a profound restructuring of the institutions of urban governance."[5]

Toxic Water, Toxic System builds on an already voluminous literature on what has been called the Flint-Detroit Water Crisis to offer a holistic framework that extends far beyond the realm of water to reveal how specific methods and foundations of white supremacy erode the public infrastructure of these predominantly Black cities, including housing, education, collective bargaining, and Black political power more broadly. This social regime is akin to what Boaventura de Sousa Santos has described as "financial fascism," whereby the power of financial markets and recklessness of casino capitalism have led to particularly severe forms of exclusion.[6] In this book I pay particular attention to the role of *racialization* in this prevailing social regime. Racialization provided the political hegemony—the grease—that allowed white elites to justify the rhetoric of municipal financial ruin in majority-Black cities in Michigan. Without racialization, polices of emergency management, health care and pension reform, and amendments to constitutional revenue sharing would not have occurred, because they could not have been justified by economic principles alone. For austerity to "get done" in places like Flint and Detroit, a pluralism of white elites has developed elaborate explanations as to why the urban poor got what they deserved. Racialization has been used strategically not only to feed on suburban white insecurities but also to mobilize white censures against Black leadership. Racialization was also employed to conjure the irrationality of Black pathology, which served to push a neoconservative agenda deeper into liberal institutions, interweaving policies regarding housing, employment, education, and urban development more generally into the very fabric of urban renewal in Michigan.

In the analysis that follows, I describe how particular groups of people worked collectively to craft a set of state polices to *realize* what is arguably one of the most extreme examples of environmental racism in this country. And, while we focus on the harmful effects of water precarity, we must remember that these cruel inequities are the result of years of careful planning and forethought, underscoring Michigan's deep class interests and ongoing commitment to racial inequality. It is this pluralist strategy and formation that makes this form of financial fascism so vicious. This strategy began with federally subsidized racial projects of redlining, suburbanization, and white flight, which concentrated people of color in urban environs. The resulting metropolitan segregation that occurred in cities like Detroit and Flint was then rationalized as a threat to white suburban interests, justifying new forms of state-sanctioned racism under the guise of fiscally responsible governance. This new phase of austerity-driven ethnic and racial environmental injustice is consistent with a long history of white possessiveness in this country.[7] However, the ways in which state, corporate, and civil society actors operationalize the ostensibly colorblind, mundane, and taken-for-granted workings of urban austerity in normalizing new patterns of environmental racism in majority-Black cities needs further examination.

Contemporary notions of environmental and social justice largely hinge on who has access to clean, safe, and affordable water. This is particularly true for the residents of Flint and Detroit, who are linked at the hip, both racially and hydrologically. But in addition to Flint and Detroit, we can add lead poisoning and other forms of water precarity in Washington, DC, Newark, Pittsburgh, Milwaukee, Chicago, Baltimore, Benton Harbor (Michigan), New Orleans, Denmark (South Carolina), and Jackson (Mississippi), to name but a few recent cases, all of them majority-Black and -brown cities. To the list of cities, we could add the fact that in California alone, more than 1 million people lack access to safe and affordable drinking water. Also, an investigation published in June 2018 found that at least 6 million Californians were served by water providers that have been in violation of state standards at some point since 2012. Today, an estimated 11.6% of the US population lives without water security. And a study conducted by researchers at Michigan State University found that as much as 36% of the US population will not be able to afford their water bills by 2022.[8] Exposure to toxic waters is a condition of one's citizenship, race, and class in this country. While this is especially true for predominantly Black and brown urban communities, it is not limited to them. The US government and corporations have been poisoning Navajo lands, for example, for decades, leading to obscene levels of water contamination in many Navajo lands, communities, and bodies. Water may flow to where food grows in California's agricultural heartlands, but the largely Latinx labor force can't drink the water because it is unsafe.[9] Moreover, governments and corporate enterprises are poised to repeat this vicious practice of exclusion, exposing millions of Americans of color to unsafe drinking water for decades to come.[10]

In writing this book, I have put front and center the words and actions of people living with water contamination and dispossession in Flint and Detroit: water activists, citizen scientists, professionals, scholars, and local politicians, all of whom witnessed this environmental racism firsthand. These communities have worked tirelessly, sometimes together, other times at odds, to secure access to safe and affordable water. I have watched and learned from pastors, community leaders, artists, and organizations, such as We the People of Detroit and the People's Water Coalition, that are not only resisting this vicious form of vulture capitalism but also giving us practical lessons in environmental justice and democracy. These people and groups are asking hard and pressing questions about the responsibilities of governments, scientists, and the academy, demanding that they create more meaningful and rigorous social justice research and praxis in the face of widening economic disparity and environmental injustice. I have also drawn heavily from scholars and leaders immersed in the Black radical tradition. I have revisited the words of Audre Lorde, Martin Luther King Jr., and James Baldwin, and the scholarship of W. E. B. Du Bois, Frantz Fanon, and Patricia Hill Collins, among others. In effect, I have tried to recenter critical race theory, including anti-Black genocide theory, and Black feminists' studies of how we think about the making of environmental racism *today* in Black and brown cities like Flint and Detroit. In rooting my analysis here, I caution against a consistent refrain in environmental justice literature that recenters whiteness and its possessive logics even while assessing and seeking to understand environmental racism and racial capitalism.

In revisiting the writings of anti-racist and anti-colonialist organizers and theorists, I was struck by the language they had directed at the injustice and violence of their day. James Baldwin highlighted (the social construction of) whiteness and examined its all too real consequences for Black lives. Franz Fanon underscored the violence embedded in the post-colonial condition. Martin Luther King Jr. pointed out a double standard in both the enforcement of and the respect for law, calling laws passed for "the Negro's benefit" a mockery. To paraphrase Malcolm X, racism is like a Cadillac because they make a new model every year; and the racialization of place, George Lipsitz argues, makes American whiteness one of the most systematically subsidized identities in the world. As the brilliant poet and writer Audre Lorde has advised, we should try to learn from the 1960s, learn from those who came before us. The environmental justice movement may have been forged from an intersection between the anti-toxic movement and the civil rights movement. But, as I explain in following chapters, while we (in the academy) have invoked an arsenal of language, metrics, and measures to better articulate the toxic conditions with which people of color still suffer in this country, we have not pursued King's inclusive civil rights vision, a vision, to quote William Julius Wilson, inspired by "activist social movements fighting poverty, racial injustice, and wealth disparities, as well as calls for fundamental redistributive policies" everywhere.[11] We continue to describe a woefully unequal world instead of trying to change it.

Michigan's water wars also tell a cautionary tale. Speaking to an audience in upstate New York, Lewis Patrick of We the People of Detroit warned that the dangers of unsafe water are

> not going to stop at poor Black folks' door. Waterborne diseases won't stop at just my house. It's going to come to your house. . . . So don't think you can buy your way out of this. This is at the heart of it, this is vulture capitalism. There is no other word for it. There is no other phrase for it. Wealthy people never have enough. They never have enough. So we must decide that our children and we deserve a better existence, because we do. We do. . . . I will not leave this disaster to my children. I love them too much. And if you love yourselves and the children that you may have in the future, you better get involved in this work. Water will be the issue of your lifetime. It just will be.

After more than a century of massive public investment, approximately 85% of the people in the United States receive their water from a publicly owned water utility. This public good is now under serious threat as old water infrastructure crumbles and governments continue to cut public spending while undertaking massive welfare reform on behalf of corporations and elite classes. This is the warning that activists like Monica Lewis-Patrick are trying to bullhorn. Public water services in the United States have potential annual revenues estimated at $90 billion.[12] Detroit's water infrastructure alone has been estimated to be worth between $6 billion and $8 billion.[13] With public water infrastructure worth this much, schemes to privatize have been diverse and pervasive. A recent investigation by CBS News and the Weather Channel found that New York hedge fund investors were "snapping up Colorado River water rights, betting big on an increasingly scarce resource." In 2021, Matthew Diserio, the cofounder and president of New York–based investment firm Water Asset Management, "called water in the United States 'a trillion-dollar market opportunity.'"[14]

Flint and Detroit offer one multisited case study to learn from. Michigan's planned urban collapse illustrates how fights for environmental justice, local governance, collective bargaining rights, citizen participation in public health debates, public ownership of water, and democracy itself are all inextricably interconnected. Lewis Patrick recalls the words of Detroit mayor Coleman Alexander Young, "one of the greatest mayors that the city ever had, one in which [even] the racism press in Michigan had to admit he was a great man: 'When you find a good fight get in it.' And I tell you this water struggle is a fight worth getting in."

THE ACTIVISTS

It has been more than five years since I began my ethnographic research in Flint. I remember clearly sitting in the living room of Flint residents Jan Worth-Nelson and Ted Nelson and a group of friends and activists they had invited to help explain to me what the Flint water crisis meant to them. In the following years many people in Flint have taken time out of their daily life to talk to me about the Flint Water Crisis and how it affected them. I also began to spend time with water activists in Detroit, people who continue to be at the forefront of a desperate struggle against the city's water shutoff policy. I am very much indebted to them, as are we all for their efforts to achieve water access and environmental justice. As I write, we are amid a pandemic. COVID-19 and the recent murders of unarmed Black people by white police officers are laying bare the multiple and interconnected ways in which the color of one's skin determines one's fate in life. The devastating health impacts of the coronavirus pandemic on Black and brown people are not the result of pre-existing conditions but rather negative environmental conditions brought on by unequal laws, regulations, and policies that disproportionately expose communities and people of color to harm. Whether it's the streets we walk down, the location of our neighborhoods, or the places we work, learn, pray, or play, racism permeates every aspect of American society and culture.

Water, activists tell me is the last weapon to move you off your land. The only question I have for readers is, Are we listening?

I am truly indebted to all the activists who took the time to share their stories and their lives with me. Special mention goes to Jan Worth-Nelson and Ted Nelson, who in addition to providing me with important historical and political information, introduced me to many people in Flint who's experiences helped shaped the direction of this ethnography. They made time for me and opened their house to me when I was doing fieldwork in Flint. I learned so much from Monica Lewis-Patrick and Debra Taylor with We the People of Detroit.[15] Both Lewis-Patrick and Taylor are leaders and inspirations. Lewis Patrick has been described as a "water warrior."[16] She was born into a family that believes deeply in service, as Mike McGonigal has written in a feature article about the water warrior (fig. 1). As a child, Lewis Patrick was taken to organizing meetings by her mother; as an adult, she has helped to organize against corporate sponsorship of local elections, school charters, and emergency management law in Michigan. Other groups I had the privilege of learning from include the Genesee County Hispanic Latino Collaborative, Raise It Up, the People's Water Board Coalition, and the Flint Democracy Defense League.[17]

Figure 1. Monica Lewis-Patrick. Photo by Jacob Lewkow, *Detroit Metro Times.*

THE ETHNOGRAPHY

I undertook ethnographic fieldwork and archival research to tell this story, translating the perspectives and experiences of community members, activists, and alliances who have challenged these discriminatory urban projects. In the chapters that follow, I present a synthesis of the multiple strands of racial capitalism that produced the profound and, activists argue, genocidal injustices in Flint's and Detroit's water landscape.

I first found out about the Flint water crisis from friends and extended family in the summer of 2014. The story hadn't broken in the national news yet, but many in Flint were using their extended networks to get the word out. At the time, I was an associate professor at Rensselaer Polytechnic Institute. It just so happened that I was mentoring three graduate students with close ties to Flint and Detroit: Michael Lachney, Ellen Foster, and Robb Lauzon. Collectively we were deeply concerned about what we were hearing from people in Flint. We met several times to discuss how we might assist those we knew. At the request of several close friends and family, we decided to go to Flint in an effort to support them as they fought state authorities to provide clean water to the city's residents. We all had personal reasons to be there. Michael Lachney's aunt had taught in southeastern Michigan for more than a decade and connected us with some of her colleagues who were doing work in Flint at the time. Friends of Robb Lauzon in Flint's music and art scene would become valuable voices for this project. Robb also had deep personal networks in Detroit. Jan Worth-Nelson, at the time the editor of Flint's *East Village Magazine*, is good friends with Ellen Foster's mother. It was Ellen's mother who introduced our research team to Jan. One of our first meetings was a group conversation with various community members in Jan and Ted's house. I, too, have deep connections and commitments to the area. I lived in East Lansing for five years during my doctoral studies. We also have family in the greater Detroit area. (It was during my fieldwork that we lost my partner's uncle, a lifelong Detroiter, to leukemia.)

METHODS AND POSITIONALITY

We began interviews in the spring of 2016, and my last interview of record was conducted in the fall of 2019. Sixty-one individual and group interviews were transcribed verbatim. These interviews were in-depth, ranging from one hour to over three. We also had numerous other informal conversations and meetings that were not formally transcribed but were added to the extensive field notes that inform this manuscript.

Interviews took place in participants' homes, church basements, coffee shops and restaurants, the offices of local politicians and government agencies, land banks, local colleges, and community organizations. Participants included pastors, local journalists, labor historians, local artists, early-childhood educators, city planners and administrators, emergency managers, Genesee County Land Bank employees, local activists, and academics.

During the time of my fieldwork, local, regional, and national news outlets were regularly reporting on the Flint Water Crisis and the Detroit water shutoffs. I leaned heavily on the reporting of the American Civil Liberties Union of Michigan. Other mainstream news sources, including *The Guardian*, the *Detroit Free Press*, the *Detroit Metro Times*, *Crain's Detroit Business*, and the *Detroit News*, were central to the archival record that supported this ethnography. The less mainstream archive included *Aljazeera America*, *Demos*, *Ebony*, *Workers World*, and the *Voice of Detroit*. In addition, archival sources—including published scholarship, public news sources, and government records—were referenced in the writing of this book.

In my capacity as an activist scholar, I invited Monica Lewis-Patrick and Debra Taylor of We the People of Detroit and Michael Stampfler, former emergency manager of Pontiac, Michigan, to be keynote speakers at a symposium at Rensselaer Polytechnic Institute in the fall of 2016.[18] The symposium was part of an effort to raise awareness among the mostly disaffected academy and its student body of the water crises in Flint and Detroit and of the perils of emergency management in the state of Michigan. Also part of this effort were the meetings I had with Dr. Agustin Arbulu, executive director of the Michigan Department of Civil Rights. Over the span of several conversations, I communicated to Dr. Arbulu the concerns of people I had spoken with and described the unjust conditions they faced due to the decisions of state-appointed emergency managers. On September 8, 2016, I gave expert testimony at the third public hearing on the Flint Water Crisis before the Michigan Civil Rights Commission.[19]

In September 2018, Monica Lewis-Patrick and Flint water warrior Claire McClinton, together with scholars Ben Pauli (Kettering University), Stephen Gasteyer (Michigan State University), and myself, presented on a panel to discuss research ethics, environmental justice and community empowerment at the third annual summit of the Michigan Environmental Justice Coalition. Other noteworthy events that shaped my fieldwork experience included the Emergency Manager Law Research Forum, hosted by Mary Schulz and Eric Scorsone from Michigan State University on September 22, 2016; the Community Driven Research Day, held October 11–12, 2017; and the Healthy Flint Research Coordinating Center symposium on March 9, 2018.

In 2019, at the annual meeting of the Society for the Social Studies of Science, I copresented a paper with Ben Pauli, Flint resident, scholar, and author of the book *Flint Fights Back*. In the presentation, titled "But Is It 'Safe'?: Water Quality Regulations, Citizen Science, and Power in the Flint Water Crisis," we brought some local perspective to the controversy surrounding citizen science performed during the Flint Water Crisis. At the time, there was much debate about the behavior and actions of a credentialed scientist involved in the citizen science efforts in Flint. On May 10, 2018, residents of Flint wrote to the scientific and engineering community requesting an investigation.[20] The letter was signed by sixty residents and more than thirty nonresident supporters. Not a single scientific organization or engineering association took up the residents' request. In July 2019, I and eleven other academics sent a follow-up letter affirming Flint residents' rights to be heard from the institutions and organizations that received their complaint.[21]

In these and other actions I engaged in while conducting fieldwork for this book project, I hope to have generated knowledge both about the environmental injustices created by policies of racialized urban austerity and about pedagogies that bolstered local forms of resistance against the racialized oppression and economic violence that these policies continue to create.

Acknowledgments

I view this research as truly collaborative and community based, and while I acknowledge the collective making of this manuscript, I also want to concede that for a book like this to be written, I cannot celebrate just those named in this book. I first need to acknowledge the collective leadership of the people who made tremendous contributions to the social justice efforts described in this book. The organized rally in Detroit on Friday, July 18, 2014, became a hallmark of collective mobilizing and organizing efforts against water shutoffs in the city. Those participating in this massive protest included the Canadian Federal of Nurses Unions, the Coalition of Labor Union Women, Color of Change, Detroit Active and Retired Employees, Detroiters Resisting Emergency, Detroit Eviction Defense, the Detroit Public Schools Education Task Force, the Detroit Water Brigade, Food and Water Watch, the Franciscan Action Network, the Health Global Action Project, the Metropolitan Detroit AFL-CIO, the Michigan Nurses Association, the National Action Network–Michigan, National Nurses United, National People's Action, the People's Water Board, We the People of Detroit, the Michigan Election Reform Alliance, the Student Global AIDS Campaign, and many other groups. Residents stood side by side with local, national, and international organizations that day to call for a moratorium on water shutoffs in the city.

I owe much gratitude to Monica Lewis-Patrick and Debra Taylor of We the People of Detroit. They taught me more about local activism and collaborative research than I have read in any qualitative research handbook. The three of us acknowledge this research has been a collaboration in thought and praxis. Activists like Lewis Patrick and Taylor helped cultivate connections to particular leaders in the community, underscoring both those leaders' roles and responsibilities in movement organizing and execution. With this training, I was better positioned to appreciate the different levels of expertise that come to bear when you have fruitful collaboration between a community and scholars.

Fieldwork in Flint was made possible through the generosity of Jan Worth-Nelson and Ted Nelson. They not only welcomed us into their community but also offered us accommodation in their home. It was Jan and Ted who first organized a talking circle in their house and continued to connect us with other Flintstones during my numerous visits. Many people in Flint need to be acknowledged. I do so here anonymously to protect their identity.

I also want to acknowledge the contribution of investigative journalists and reporters who put together the archival record that I assembled while researching and writing this book. They include Curt Guyette, Diane Bukowski, Tawana Petty, Steve Neavling, Tom Perkins, Anna Clark, and many others, some of whom risked their careers to speak truth to power.

At the time I began this research, I was mentoring three graduate students at Rensselaer Polytechnic Institute who held deep connections to southeastern Michigan and joined the project. Michael Lachney was concerned about the impact on educational achievement from lead poisoning but believed in the potential for educators to provide lasting mentoring and training. Michael is currently an assistant professor in the Department of Counseling, Educational Psychology, and Special Education at Michigan State University. Ellen Foster was interested in makerspaces in Flint and Detroit. She is now a postdoctoral researcher at Purdue University. Robb Lauzon has been involved in Flint's arts and music scene since 2006 and sought to help amplify his friends and fellow residents' voices during this time of crisis. He is now an assistant professor of strategic communication at Juniata College in Huntingdon, Pennsylvania. All three colleagues helped to expand the depth and breadth of this research.

I also have much gratitude to the graduate students at the University of California, Berkeley, particularly in the Critical Environmental Justice Lab, who read many draft versions of the manuscript. Their comments and support got this book to the publishing finish line. I am also equally indebted to the editorial team at the University of California Press. Naomi Schneider took over from Stacy Eisenstark as the editor for the manuscript during its review. And editorial assistant Aline Dolinh became a lifeline in prepping the manuscript for publication.

To my partner Kelly Grindstaff, for her optimistic outlook and encouragement in my processing and writing about what, at times, has been difficult subject matter—social and environmental injustice: thank you.

Introduction

Was the Flint water crisis a case of environmental racism? The question has been examined by numerous scholars, journalists, lawyers, and government committees. And the answer, at least according to the Michigan Civil Rights Commission, was an unreserved and undeniable "yes." Similarly, water shutoffs in Detroit have been denounced by the United Nations for contravening basic human rights to water and shelter. But, while most people agree that racism was a factor in these water crises, there remains only a superficial understanding of how these two unprecedented cases of environmental racism were put into practice. One of my aims in writing this book was to offer readers a holistic framework that spans far beyond the realm of water to include white supremacist attacks on the public infrastructure of these predominantly Black cities, including housing, education, collective bargaining, and Black political power more broadly. This reframing departs from the dominant narrative that continues to blame these cities' problems on their residents. A key objective of this reframing is to challenge the notion that what happened in Flint and Detroit was somehow inevitable, the result of years of disinvestment and the loss of industry. I argue instead that what troubled Flint and Detroit was not their passive response to global economic trends but rather the

1

intentional actions and strategic plans devised and maintained by white elites. This reframing brings into account the actions not only of government but also of powerful foundations and other nonprofits, political organizations, media outlets, and prominent individuals and groups.

Environmental justice activists and scholars conceive of the environment broadly as the surrounds in which we live, work, learn, play, and pray, including the places where we are hospitalized, housed, and imprisoned. The environment, from this perspective, is not a people-free biophysical system but rather the ambient and immediate surroundings of everyday life activities and relationships linking people across deeply stratified social systems and uneven institutional arrangements. These include, but are not limited to, residential, working, and recreational. Originally forged from a synthesis of the civil rights movements, antitoxics campaigns, and environmentalism in the 1960s, environmental justice has focused on the class and racial inequalities of pollution. Today, hundreds of studies have substantiated the degree to which unequal laws and policies discriminate against people of color, the poor, indigenous and immigrant populations, and other marginalized communities.[1]

Given the robust history of environmental justice theorizing and movement organizing in this country, popular explanations of *what* environmental racism is and *how* it unfolded in Flint and Detroit are strikingly unsophisticated. For example, in "A Question of Environmental Racism in Flint," *New York Times* reporter John Eligon asked, "If Flint were rich and mostly white, would Michigan's state government have responded more quickly and aggressively to complaints about its lead-polluted water?"[2] While this is a reasonable question, the journalist seems to assume that Black and white communities had equally safe water supplies until the lead pollution in Flint was "discovered" and complained about. Decades of research has consistently shown that race is a predictor of where hazardous waste is located in this county. Yet leading newspapers like the *New York Times* continue to ignore this history of racialized environmental discrimination. Moreover, the explanations typically offered in the press and in social media rest on a narrow understanding of what racism is—that is, bigotry rooted solely in the prejudice and discrimination of individual actors, in this case Governor Rick Snyder. Similarly, government reports documenting the Flint water crisis are equally problematic in the way their authors understand environmental racism. For example, the report by the governor-appointed Flint Water Advisory Task Force concluded that "the Flint water crisis is a story of government failure, intransigence, unpreparedness, delay, inaction, and environmental injustice."[3] In effect, the report reduced the Flint water crisis to a series of government failures, a series of unfortunate "mistakes" by individuals and the agencies in which they work.

ENVIRONMENTAL JUSTICE SCHOLARSHIP

Recent scholarly work examining the Flint water crisis (FWC) and the Detroit bankruptcy, by contrast, is much more substantial than media and government reports, as one can imagine. In his book *Flint Fights Back*,[4] Flint resident and political scientist Ben Pauli offers a systemic critique of the roots of the FWC, although it is grounded more deeply in the political dimensions of the anti-democratic emergency management structures and processes that besieged the iconic city. As a scholar and resident deeply involved in the city's struggle for safe and affordable water, Pauli presents a firsthand perspective of the struggle against anti-democratic measures imposed by the state of Michigan and its allies. Anna Clark's *Poisoned City*, though not an academic text, examines the historical and structural racism at the heart of the Flint water crisis.[5] Likewise, Katrinell Davis's book *Tainted Tap: Flint's Journey from Crisis to Recovery* contextualizes the crisis within Flint's long and troubled history and identifies the conditions and factors determining Flint's attempts to transition from crisis to recovery.[6]

More critical environmental justice scholarship highlights racial capitalism and the illiberal state as antagonists in the Flint water crisis. Malini Ranganathan, in "Thinking with Flint: Racial Liberalism and the Roots of an American Water Tragedy,"[7] analyzes the colorblind, illiberal discourses of race and property that legitimated the environmental racism exposed in the Flint water crisis. Esteemed critical environmental justice scholar Laura Pulido labels the FWC "a powerful example of both environmental racism and the everyday functioning of racial capitalism,"[8] the latter becoming salient when the lives of the mostly Black residents were subordinated to the city's financial health. For Pulido, the poisoning of Flint residents was a deliberate act, a culmination of conscious decisions by elected officials and state agencies. Pulido, like other critical environmental justice scholars, affirms that because people of color are viewed as threats to white supremacy, they are deemed expendable by the state and legal system.[9] This "racial expendability," David Pellow argues, undergirds and supports a particular form of white supremacy whereby the white power structure profits from the environmental peril of people of color, not only in localities such as Flint and Detroit but all over the world.[10]

What is missing from this scholarship is a deep dive into how particular actors, groups, and social networks mobilized both racial capitalism and white supremacy in operationalizing the state's austerity-driven reforms. *Toxic Water, Toxic System* makes explicit the racial, ethnic, and gendered forms of environmental injustice that culminate from the collective, intersecting, and multiscale consequences of a seemingly anonymous authoritarian state willing to maintain white supremacy at any cost.

WHITE SUPREMACY AND ENVIRONMENTAL JUSTICE

The doctrine of white supremacy, as Martin Luther King Jr. described it in 1968, was nothing more than a rationalization that gave legitimacy and moral sanction to a profitable but deeply immoral system. Those concerned with matters of environmental justice, to paraphrase James Baldwin, have to question the intent of the state as it continues to be "collapsed into—become identical with—whiteness."[11] From this perspective, the real foundation on which the multiple and interlocking injustices imposed on nonwhite lives and livelihoods are forged are the state's legal, economic, and political institutions. This is why Black activists in Detroit charge genocide—a topic I develop later in the book.

The only thing unique about the Trump presidency, I would add, is that he enthusiastically stepped out from operating behind the curtain of white supremacy. This former president pushed an unabashed brand of white supremacy, labeling Mexicans criminals, drug dealers, and rapists and calling Haiti and African countries "shitholes." To this racist affront we can add the fact that within two months of Barak Obama taking office, white protesters, backed by predatory monied interests, began a concerted racist campaign against the country's first Black president. Journalist Jane Mayer writes that at rallies "Obama's face was plastered on posters making him to look like the Joker from the Dark Knight films, his skin turned chalk white, his mouth stretched almost to his ears, and his eye sockets blackened, with a zombielike dead gaze, over the word 'Socialism.'"[12] Photoshopped images of Obama as a primitive African witch doctor with a bone stuck through his nose also started to be circulated by white supremacy groups.[13]

Similarly, the US Justice Department's investigation into the Ferguson, Missouri, police department after the murder of Michael Brown, an unarmed Black teenager, on August 9, 2014, revealed the extent to which white supremacy is central to police enforcement in this country. The investigation found that the consistency and magnitude of police and court practices—enforcement, citations, outstanding warrants—impose a disparate impact on Black versus white individuals that itself violates the law. Everyday places that whites take for granted—sitting in their car, playing in the park, walking down the street—became environments for public lynchings of Black people. Let's call it what it is. But in addition to the overwhelming statistical evidence, the investigation uncovered direct communications by police supervisors and court officials, so-called public servants, that revealed the degree to which racial bias and white hate drive this type of white supremacy. For example, an email from police, city, and court officials, including a former Ferguson police captain and a former police sergeant, depicted President Barack Obama as a chimpanzee. Another email thread circulated among public officials implied that Barack Obama would not be president for very long because "what Black man holds a steady job for four years." Other email messages and interviews with court and law enforcement personnel expressed discriminatory views and intolerance about race, religion, and national origin. The report concluded that the "content of these communications is unequivocally derogatory, dehumanizing, and demonstrative of impermissible bias."[14] The doctrine of white supremacy has not only devalued African American lives but also justified their unjust environmental burdens, as well. In failing to recognize how unjust environmental outcomes are a "structural part of the culture,"[15] *white culture*, we turn a blind eye to the ways in which white identity and white supremacy produce particular and every-day environmental harm in this country.

This book reveals, first, how white supremacy is reproduced every day in this country not only through acts of hate and aggression, as carefully documented by (among others) historian Carol Anderson in her brilliant book *White Rage: The Unspoken Truth of Our Racial Divide,* but also structurally and institutionally, by a racialized social machinery of rules, laws, and norms. In the United States white lives are made better and easier, every single day, simply by the way society is organized. Whites live longer, have better access to health care and better education, own more, and enjoy greater social status than do nonwhites. This privilege cuts across class: as Malcolm X so succinctly reminded us, a Black doctor in the United States is still first and foremost a Black person. This form of white supremacy is rooted in the multiple ways by which white people can access resources, spaces, and places—environments—that are simply off-limits to people of color. Home ownership, investment in white suburbs, subsidized water rates, exclusive schools, clean parks, and opportunities for recreation offer just a few examples of exclusively "white first" access. Or as a recent US president liked to phrase it: "American first." These forms of white supremacy are the consequences of years of structural adjustments maintained and reinforced by what George Lipsitz has coined the "possessive investment in whiteness."[16] In other words, environmental racism and other forms of environmental injustice are the results of strategic investments in whiteness by government and other powerful actors, not their failures.

Ignoring white supremacy, traditional environmental justice scholarship has tended to focus on the measurement of environmental disproportionality (a landfill here, a toxic waste site there), substantiating environmental prejudice (abnormally high cancer rates or asthma rates in poor communities of color) and then advocating for better government policies. This substantial body of research has not been without merit, effectively forcing the hand of federal and state governments to write environmental justice laws and regulations, regardless of whether they intend to enforce them. Business, too, has adopted a lexicon of environmental justice in its corporate image, but seldom does the discourse translate into meaningful action. But the strategy of bringing about environmental justice via the state has proved to be largely hegemonic in that it ignores the integral role that government plays in producing unequal lives and segregated spaces in the first place. Moreover, this quantitative effort overlooks the multiple and intersecting ways in which racial oppression is foundational to and deeply ingrained in US history. When I asked my esteemed colleague Michael Omi what motivated him Howard Winant the write their pioneering book *Racial Formation in America*,[17] he replied that *racial formation* was largely a response to the naïve way in which sociology was using race, as a simple variable to be measured or compared to something else, in an otherwise nonracialized society. This reductionist strategy, I suggest, has also served to limit incidents of environmental injustice to disparate events, occurring here and there, diverting attention from the larger social machinery under which environmental inequality is produced, structured, and normalized. This book seeks to advance racial formation theory beyond its focus on the state's role to also include the primary role of nonstate actors and networks in creating and constantly maintaining the system of racial oppression that took hold in Flint and Detroit.

Second, I suggest that environmental justice scholarship has generally undertheorized contemporary processes of racialization in mobilizing white neoconservative policies. Sociologist Herbert Gans suggests that racialization is best understood as a social process.[18] In particular he argues that racialization is a "socially agreed upon construction with a number of participants," including "individuals, organizations, agencies and institutions that help bring about and benefit economically and otherwise from racialization." A key toward understanding this process, Gans suggests, is to reveal which set of dominant actors set it in motion. Because white male elites are usually the official initiators, we need to examine which elites do what. This requires careful analysis, "distinguishing between experts, including scholars, as well as elected and appointed public officials."[19]

Toxic Water, Toxic Systems reveals how the careful racialized deployment of urban problems—finance, infrastructure, foreclosures, and so forth—have provided the necessary condition for Republican-led austerity policies to acquire legitimacy in Michigan. Among these austerity reformers, the term *urban* has become a dog whistle among whites to mean African American people specifically and people of color more generally. In some ways *urban* has become synonymous with segregationist policies of the past. Today, new fiscal reformers are rehabilitating the urban as a new frontier for profit and control, employing code words like *illegality, foreclose,* and *crime,* often but not always conjugated with the modifier *Black,* to push forth their racist policies. In fact, racist tropes were repeatedly used in both Flint and Detroit to legitimate economic and political decisions that contributed to the reproduction of racial inequality. For example, Virginia Tech professor Marc Edwards referred to actions of residents who opposed his claims about the safety of their water as reflecting their "tribalism." Likewise, activists resisting emergency management in Detroit have often been referred to as CAVE people, using an acronym that stands for "citizens against virtually everything." The same racist tropes would never be used by so-called citizen scientists working in predominantly poor white communities. Nor would the same racial character flaws be evoked by state government to remove the authority of locally elected officials from white city councils. In fact, white cities in Michigan, such as Lapeer, that were also on the brink of bankruptcy were never threatened by emergency management or stigmatized for their financial transgressions. It is for this and other reasons, I argue, that racialization is inscribed into the very fabric of urban austerity in Michigan.

Third, environmental justice scholarship can do more to emphasize the multiple and intersecting ways in which environment racism decenters people's lives. These experiences are often hidden from most, and so we have no idea what people of color go through in this country. In Flint and Detroit, poisoned water and water shutoffs cleave families apart as some people relocate, finding temporary relief and shelter elsewhere. Remaining families live in fear that welfare authorities might take their children from their homes for lack of water. Days are lost from working and children miss school days as families navigate new environs or try to figure out how to survive in what Ruth Wilson Gilmore has referred to as "forgotten places."[20] Entire swaths of Detroit and Flint are left abandoned without water, leaving people unable to cook, unable to clean, anxious about bathing or showering, and terrified to nurse their infant children. Living precariously from one bottled water to the next means facing a rising tide of personal despair and indignity and having to ask for help and handouts from family, friends, and charity. For many, mortgage foreclosures stemming from the subprime mortgage debacle have led to homelessness as entire generations of accumulated Black and brown wealth were forcibly taken, leaving homeowners homeless. In other words, we need a real accounting of the multiple and intersecting burdens—health, family, economic, political—that austerity-driven reforms impose.

Fourth, environmental justice scholarship needs to acknowledge the particular role of women of color, who have inspired much of the grassroots anti-racist mobilization and environmental movement in Michigan and elsewhere. I am struck by the resilience and tenacity of these local networks and communities that refuse to accept this new racial formation, offering care and love in the presence of greed and racism. Women of color continue to be the catalysts of major social movements both in the United States and across the globe. This is true in the case of Idle No More, Me Too, and Black Lives Matter. In Flint and Detroit, women have led the efforts of We the People of Detroit, the Genesee County Hispanic Latino Collaborative, Raise It Up, the People's Water Board Coalition, and the Flint Democracy Defense League. Yet the leadership roles of African American and other women of color continue to be obscure in environmental justice scholarship and organizing. For example, African Americans (men and women) occupy a paltry 4.6% of leadership positions in environmental organizations; Hispanics/Latinos, 2.3%.[21] Similarly, Black females account for 2% of full-time college and university faculty, and Hispanic females hold no more than 1% of full-time professorships. Scholars and activists who work in environmental justice can ignore this blatant omission of women of color scholars and organizers only at their own peril.

In insisting that the personal is political, women of color have cultivated a distinctive standpoint that has proven not only to be life saving but also to be a formidable challenge to elite white male interests and their egotistical worldviews.[22] It is this standpoint that challenges the legitimacy of citizen scientists who continue to ignore the citizen in *their* science. It is this standpoint that challenges the unfairness of urban austerity in Michigan and elsewhere. The experience of constantly being targeted by a "machine which orchestrates crisis after crisis" has helped to cultivate in these women of color a distinctive standpoint from which to witness how these latest rounds of racist policies impact themselves, their neighborhoods, and other communities they love. "Four hundred years of survival as an endangered species," poet, writer, and activist Audre Lorde suggests, "has taught most of us that if we intend to live, we had better become fast learners."[23] Women of color have cultivated vital networks in their neighborhoods to counter what one woman called the "reptilian practices"—cold-blooded and lethal—"of shutting off water in the city of Detroit." Women organized talking circles in Flint; women collaborated with pastors to mobilize humanitarian efforts; women were behind the citizen science efforts in Flint and Detroit, working with professors, doctors, lawyers, and think thanks to collect, analyze, and disseminate data in order "to set the record straight." It was We the People of Detroit that brought the United Nations to their city to document the water shutoffs. It was We the People of Detroit that helped to document the city's hepatitis A outbreak, the largest in US history.

For African American women like Monica Lewis-Patrick and Debra Taylor of We the People of Detroit, the knowledge gained at the intersecting oppressions of race, class, and gender has provided the stimulus for social thought and collective action consistent with the Black radical tradition.[24] This praxis of collective intelligence is designed not only to analyze institutional racism but to resist it as well. History has shown us, Lewis Patrick insists, "that when 'we the people' stand up, they [elites] stand down." This critical perspective counters the dominant narrative of urban decay that plagues Black cities like Flint and Detroit. "If you start looking at the cities across the country," Lewis Patrick asks me, "where they are targeting with these egregious policies of water shutoffs? They are places like where? Boston, Philadelphia, St Louis, Detroit, Flint, and Benton Harbor." Black cities. "That is why we are mapping it and digitizing it. . . . Because when we say it," she continues, "we come across as these passionate ignorant activists that don't know anything. . . . We're just angry, mad, and pissed off at everybody."

It is women like Monica Lewis-Patrick who have borne witness to the slow and, for them, not-so-subtle violence of urban austerity in Michigan, and who have invoked the Black radical tradition of care, ingenuity, and guts. Denied the help of sound or trusted government and surpassed by deep monied interests, these communities of color have nurtured a beloved community, working together to ensure the welfare of individuals in their own neighborhoods. For many in the community the simple fact that knowing others genuinely care has provided an inspiring antidote to the violence of urban austerity. Mutual care, African American and American literature scholar Saidiya Hartman has observed, is the antidote to this state-sanctioned violence.[25] Similarly, James Baldwin wrote, in a book addressed to his nephew, "If we had not loved each other" in an otherwise loveless world, "none of us would have survived."[26] We have seen this love and friendship in Flint, where neighbors provided safe drinking water to one another when governmental entities failed to do so, and where citizen groups joined ranks with experts to assemble the evidence necessary to show that residents were being poisoned by the very people who were supposed to protect them. We saw similar examples of care in Detroit, where residents surveyed their neighborhoods to assess the extent of water shutoffs, set up water stations, helped to pay the water bills of those who couldn't afford to, and collaborated with researchers to document the harms. In the absence of government services, the well-being of citizens in Michigan and elsewhere depended on the creative caring strategies and local coalition building of the grassroots organizations featured in this book. Activists learned from their experiences how to bring these issues together: water poisoning and water shutoffs, emergency management and democracy, foreclosures and land banks, science and trust, and poverty and profit. We should pay attention to their efforts.

MUCH MORE THAN NEGLECT

I now circle back to the notion of neglect and failure often put forth to explain incidents of environmental discrimination. This emphasis not only reduces environmental racism to particular incidents or cases but also erases how particular episodes of environmental disproportionality are already embedded in deeply racialized historical processes. What is required instead, to paraphrase Paul Gilroy, is an analysis that would reveal the changing patterns in racist ideology and racialized practices, as well as the manner in which these patterns "fit into the transformation" of state institutions "and political culture at a time of extensive social and economic change."[27] In his instructive book *Clean and White: A History of Environmental Racism in the United States,* historian Carl Zimring traces the intersecting histories of race, waste, and work in the United States from Thomas Jefferson's bucolic idealism to the Memphis Public Workers strike of 1968.[28] Whereas in the first half of the twentieth century, Jews, Italians, and other new immigrants were racialized as less than white, after World War II, Zimring observes, these new European settlers were raced as white or "white ethnics." "The years after World War II," Zimring writes, "saw millions more Americans achieve white identity than had before the war."[29] In 1940, the Immigration and Naturalization Service began designating these groups as white instead of using racial categories found on previous immigration records.[30] These new white ethnics began to enjoy the privileges of white society, which included access to home loans, affordable mortgage insurance, GI Bill benefits for returning veterans, and good education and stable employment, while their nonwhite counterparts were largely denied these benefits. Provisions in New Deal legislation exacerbated and catalyzed unprecedented segregation between the end of World War II and 1980. In every office of the federal Home Owners Loan Corporation (HOLC), Zimring wrote, maps were available to clearly and quickly identify the "red," that is, undesirable, areas in any local vicinity. "These maps allowed the HOLC and Federal Housing Administration (FHA) to efficiently grant insured mortgages to white people living in racially exclusive developments."[31] These generously funded federal government programs not only created new, expansive *all-white* suburban developments but also legitimized racial discrimination and urban segregation—in other words, environmental racism by design.

During the decades preceding World War II, historian Andrew Highsmith argues, "a potent combination of private discrimination, federal housing and development initiatives, corporate practices, and municipal public policies converged to make Flint one of the most racially segregated cities in the United States."[32] To receive Federal Housing Administration (FHA)–approved mortgages, Highsmith confirms, villages had to invest millions of dollars into new infrastructure improvements, including sidewalks, paved roads, drinking water, sewers, and other utilities. In complying with these requirements, suburbs abandoned the conventional "'pay as you go' financing and enacted new taxes to support" the newly forming suburbs. Nowhere was this form of racialized suburban infrastructure more pronounced than in Flint as new residential developments began to spring up all over rural towns in Genesee County, including Fenton, Flushing, Davison, and Grand Blanc. White elected officials, keen to take advantage of the FHA's master plan, passed new building codes and restrictive zoning regulations, recruited new businesses, constructed new schools and roads, expanded fire and police departments, and built new public facilities such as libraries, parks, and recreation centers.[33] By the mid-1950s, Highsmith writes, rural and semirural townships throughout the country followed the Genesee County model, raising taxes and fees in response to FHA strictures that protected white suburban property values, thereby effectively regulating racial and economic segregation throughout the country.[34] New homeowners also participated in redlining white suburbs, creating neighborhood associations, block clubs, PTA groups, and other community organizations that protected white property values and reinforced racial segregation.[35] In postwar Detroit, historian Carol Anderson asserts, police, city, and court officials were all too willing to indulge white aggression against "uppity" Blacks wanting to invade white neighborhoods.[36] In effect, government-supported white supremacy in this country contributed not only to the racialization of space but also to the creation of white identity.

Moreover, as racial categories hardened during Jim Crow, many of the newly designated whites, some of them now fully assimilated, second-generation Americans, enjoyed dramatic socioeconomic mobility. State-sanctioned and private housing discrimination through redlining and restrictive covenants continued through the 1960s, as did anti-miscegenation laws in several states. What these new white ethnics had in common was that they were no longer racialized nonwhite, and being racialized white had significant advantages for "where one lived, where one worked, and what one's social experiences were."[37] While the notion of environmental justice was not yet posited, a clear racialized map of race, place, work, and waste was rapidly being drawn in American cities at the directive of major government programs and agencies. Moreover, this unequally racialized landscape was also reinforced by the participation of ordinary "whites' active, determinative, and continuing position as racial oppressors and exploiters."[38] What these new white ethnics also shared was a rags-to-riches story—their American dream—which became part of their shared American experience. This white identity served to galvanize the growing white apathy and opposition to the mounting nonwhite struggles and civil rights movements that demanded the same privileges for nonwhite citizens. Having fully subscribed to the doctrine of white supremacy, these new white ethnics chose rather to believe in enduring assumptions of Black and brown inferiority, inability, and illegality and to support racist polices that contributed to their newly designated whiteness.[39]

Countering this dominant narrative, Martin Luther King Jr. called out the multiple and intersecting ways in which white supremacy was normalizing environmental racism as a natural feature of the postindustrial American city. "Problems of education, transportation to jobs and decent living conditions are all made difficult," Dr. King reasoned, because of government-sanctioned housing segregation.[40] Moreover, King asserted, the massive investment and rapid expansion of suburbs and migration from the South had worsened big-city segregation. "The suburbs are white nooses around the necks of the cities," he wrote. "Housing deteriorates in central cities; urban renewal has been Negro removal and has benefited big merchants and real estate interests; and suburbs expand with little regard for what happens to the rest of America."[41] The effect of this ongoing history is apparent in Flint, Detroit, and other majority-Black and -brown cities today, that is, if one wants to look. Dr. King claimed that nothing short of "a radical restructuring of the architecture of American society" would bring about environmental justice in the face of "the ingrained white racism of American society." In such an affluent country, King insisted, "it is morally right to insist that every person have a decent house, an adequate education, and enough money to provide basic necessities for one's family."[42]

This deeply historical and anti-racist pursuit first established by Dr. King and others in the civil rights movement has all but fallen off the pages of most environmental justice analysis and scholarship. In contrast to King's formula, traditional environmental justice scholarship has also remained rather conservative, avoiding the use of more controversial language to describe environmental wrongs for fear that it is too alienating, too risky, and not scholarly enough. For example, many citizens fighting today for environmental justice and recognizing its historical meaning use the framework of environmental genocide, not environmental justice. Toward this effort, in chapter 9, I address the history of anti-Black genocide in the United States and its congruence with urban austerity policies in Michigan. We in the academy should give this framing serious consideration.

Today, environmental and social justice groups are also questioning the role of the university, challenging notions of expertise and power in this otherwise academic pursuit. The position paper "Mapping the Water Crisis. The Dismantling of African-American Neighborhoods in Detroit" is one fruit of this social justice effort. Advanced by We the People of Detroit Community Research Collective in collaboration with community activists, academics, researchers, and designers, this report documents the consequences of austerity policies and emergency management law in Detroit, focusing in particular on the racial inequity of these policies.[43] Citizens' groups in Flint and Detroit continue to challenge conventional ideas about expertise, power, and voice in their citizen science efforts. Their collaborative activism, research, and organizing were crucial in exposing the Flint water crisis for what was, and in drawing attention to the largest hepatitis A outbreak in US history.

MAKING THE NUMBERS ADD UP

In the chapters that follow, I posit that Michigan's urban austerity project took the form of a postpolitical, Samaritan-like intervention, as lawmakers insisted that their structural adjustments were simply about balancing the books in these embattled cities. In so doing, they strategically substituted racial inequity for economic incompetence and imposed draconian autocratic measures under the guise of benevolent economic reform. Michigan's road to recovery, then–Michigan governor Rick Snyder infamously declared, would be steered by an accountant, not a politician. This now-popular narrative implied that government works best when run like a business. The belief in running government as a business also implies that no prior public service experience is required; in fact, experience in government is often seen as political baggage. This accountant-turned-politician argued that he could "help more people when the numbers add up." "Michigan was once the engine that drove America," Snyder reflected, but "we took it for granted, didn't change with the times, and let politics get in the way. Not anymore."

In effect, in Michigan, we were told, government would be void of politics, as accounting and technocrats made sure, above all else, that the numbers would add up. While overtures to technocratic principles and austerity may be seen as politically correct, we should remember that this authoritarian populism has deep political roots, pushed for decades and reinforced with millions of dollars by those who regarded the democratic process as too much government for their liking. This postpolitical agenda was years in the making and, in the case of Rick Snyder's government, was supported by dark money interests committed to "mov[ing] their political views from the fringe to the center of American political life."[44]

Writing about American genocide of Native Americans, scholars Dean Neu and Richard Therrien remind us that accounting as a technology of control and a technique of government has remained central to meeting the objectives of American imperialism, both at home and abroad.[45] As it turned out, the residents of Flint had other numbers on their mind, like 15 parts per billion. Or, "How many IQ points did my child lose?" The "delusion that we are going to make these numbers add up," one resident sighed, "makes me bitter." Such a ledger, residents argue, has blood on the pages. "What austerity does," an activist explained to me, "is that it will take from you, and then blames you because they took it from you." It is not simply that the problems that people of color confront today are of their own making—that narrative is long standing—but that the collective crusade of white supremacy to fix "their self-inflicted problems" has become so politically self-serving, not to mention extremely profitable.

In the wake of the Obama presidency, some advocates argue, economic differences between the races and sexes—racial and sexual inequality— must rest with deficient values, beliefs, and behaviors of nonwhite people themselves—that is, with natural or innate differences, inequality that originated outside the economic system, rather than inequality created by that system.[46] Communities of color, then, that are financially bankrupt, that are foreclosing on their homes, or that are having their water shut off for nonpayment have no one else to blame but themselves. Moreover, the more people of color are disadvantaged by this form of white supremacy, the more directed the ideology becomes about the inferiority or superiority between the races. So the inability to pay rapidly rising water bills in Detroit is seen as a pathology of the Black and brown household. Similarly,

municipal bankruptcy stemming from failure to meet bondholder obligations is deemed a pathology of irresponsible Black and brown leadership.
Conversely, lack of student retention and progress in school is seen as a
reason to defund public schooling in Black and brown communities. Why
waste money on students who don't have the capacity to learn? Into this
void step the cities' heroes—the Ilitch family, the Gilberts, the DeVos family, and the Motts to name a few—to restore the ruins and replace the
derelicts. Today, the eugenic conception of "fitness" and colonial tropes of
inferiority and irresponsibility saturate the discourse of urban austerity in
Michigan's Black cities, once again making the errant condition of people
of color ever the excuse for further discrimination and profit making.[47] It
is not simply that poor people and people of color are excluded in this
technocratic image of the midwestern city but that their dispossession and
erasure have become so vital to advancing the city's class interests.

·   ·   ·   ·   ·

This research was produced with and for the citizens of Detroit to help in
their efforts to build a more democratic city and a more inclusive political
economy. They have deployed their efforts on a wide range of fronts, from
community organizing to legal and legislative work. "The research itself is
part of a larger project, led by We the People of Detroit, which also includes
a city-wide community survey, a citizen-science project to test water quality, and individual and collective narratives."[48] From its inception this
truly grassroots environmental justice effort has been "dedicated to community coalition building and to the provision of resources that inform,
train, and mobilize the citizens of Detroit to improve their quality of
life."[49] This research embodies the beloved community envisioned by Dr.
King, a pursuit that requires "a qualitative change in our souls, as well as
a quantitative change in our lives."[50]

Speaking at the Michigan Environmental Justice Coalition Summit
about the Detroit bankruptcy and the city's foreclosures and water shutoff
policies, Monica Lewis-Patrick explained, "we only do research with
researchers that are willing to allow the community to own it and control
it. So all of the work that comes out of We the People of Detroit, we own it,
and we control it, because we hold it in proxy for our community." This

new method of civic and scholarly research has left Lewis Patrick questioning traditional environmental justice expertise and research. "And what I need to tell many of you," she said, "that want to believe that only scholars bring brilliance to the table: it's not true. And I think the scholars would agree with me. Because what we found over and over again in many episodes, they weren't thinking in the ways that everyday people have to think." Frustrated by the inability of academic scientists and researchers to understand and voice their lived experience, Lewis Patrick asserted that "we've got . . . to evidence and expose these criminal activities. . . . There is more expertise in this room that understands what's on the line, and has the solutions to address it, than is out there. You all stop waiting on them to tell us what to do." Her last caveat is telling, as it affirms the legitimacy of academic researchers representing their communities and asserts that academic interests have sidelined community understanding, knowledge, and voice. Knowing fully well, as Audre Lorde and other women of color do, that "without community there is no liberation," Lewis Patrick challenges academics to educate themselves about the ways in which inequality and injustice are experienced by communities of color.

But the water warrior had an equally compelling message for community members, as well: "We better stop acting like we don't know what time it is," she said to participants at the Coalition meeting. "There has been a conspiracy, and just because I'm paranoid don't mean nobody ain't out to get me. This is where we are." For Lewis Patrick, this is that moment when the personal and the political are one in the same: "My grandmother told me—she was born in 1898—she said, 'Every generation has to deal with the tyranny of their day.' This is the tyranny of our day," she declared, reminding those in the auditorium that "freedom is a constant struggle," as Angela Davis put it.[51] Lewis Patrick continued:

> You are the same people that knocked on doors, that tested your water, that proved that this [lead poisoning] was happening to you. You are the same people that went across the state of Michigan and organized and defeated emergency manager [law]. You are the same people that continue to get up every day and haul water from house to house to house to house. So, you mean that we can't overturn this political regime and make it look like what it should look like to people? We better decide. We don't have a lot of time. Because you better believe they are fully prepared to kill us.

For Monica Lewis-Patrick the struggle for environmental justice requires not only a deep understanding of white supremacy but also a passion to overturn its oppressive structures and logic. Anything less is simply academic. *Toxic Water, Toxic System* bears witness to the multiple, intersecting, conflictual, and flexible efforts to disrupt environmental racism and white supremacy. It reveals how two water fountains still exist in contemporary America, one for people of color and the other for white folks. I begin with a chapter that provides some historical context for the ways in which the control of water has been used to further both white supremacy and environmental racism in this country.

1 In the Service of White Privilege

From segregated public beaches and pools to separate drinking fountains and toilets, water has remained a persistent conduit through which white privilege has flowed. Water's symbolic association with purity and its direct link to human health and illness have also made it a powerful biopolitical determinant in delineating the conditions in which people live and die, profit and peril, sink or swim. Federal and state laws and policies have ensured that water infrastructure and access have always remained in the national interest as a project of modern statecraft supposed to benefit the greater good.[1] Water supply, historian Martin Melosi writes, was the first important public utility in the United States and the first municipal service that demonstrated a city's commitment to growth and external investment.[2]

Water is not merely a physical resource, anthropologist Veronica Strang points out.[3] In every culture water is densely encoded with social, spiritual, political, and environmental meanings, and these social constructions deeply shape our relationships to it.[4] For example, the Canadian settler nation prides itself as being composed of "drawers of water" as well as "hewers of wood." And as we drive through California's Imperial Valley—the country's so-called breadbasket—billboards remind us that "food grows where water flows." Everything that renders the modern state possible—electricity, agriculture, industry, public health, and recreation—depends intimately on its ability to access and control its water supply. Water activists in Flint and Detroit know this fact far too well. As do First Nations in Canada, which made water protection and climate change the number one and two priorities of their annual general assembly in the summer of 2019.

As historian Carl Zimring observes, access to water, in addition to sewers, water treatment facilities, and garbage collection, made US cities both clean and white.[5] The notoriously low bridges over the Long Island Parkway built by New York City planner Robert Moses, which kept Black urban folk from traveling by bus to de facto white-only beaches, provide another example of the way in which white supremacy and white privilege delineated water access in American cities. We often talk about the "other side of the tracks," but we rarely acknowledge how access to clean and affordable water divides American society, as well. For instance, Jim Crow segregation in the heart of the South ensured that the everyday and ordinary act of taking a drink of water was a form of racial injustice. Bathrooms also were spaces where the relationship to water for people of different races remained "separate but equal" prior to the Civil Rights Act of 1964.

Public swimming pools too, became racialized places where people of color, seen as impure and dirty, could be excluded. When forced to integrate during the New Deal, white pool operators protested, arguing that pools would have to be emptied, scrubbed clean, and filled with fresh water after Black people swam in them.[6] In fact, since the end of the Civil War, Carl Zimring notes, the history of environmental racism in the United States has worked with an understanding that "white people" are clean, and "nonwhite" people are less than clean.[7] Environmental racism today, as in the past, is premised on the absence and expendability of the Black and brown subject in white spaces. Amy Cooper, the white women who called the police on Christian Cooper (a Black man) while he was bird-watching in New York's Central Park is just another contemporary demonstration, this one caught on video, of this point.

In Michigan, the doctrine of white supremacy was once again invoked as nonwhite people and communities of color were framed as dirty, polluted, and somehow undeserving of access to clean and affordable drinking water. It shouldn't be lost on any of us that the current official state maxim is "Pure Michigan," and travelers to the state are encouraged to pursue their own pure moments. This campaign is supported by the Michigan Economic Development Corporation, and the state motto can be seen on license plates and road signs, on radio announcements and state-supported commercials. Walking through Detroit's McNamara Airport, one cannot help but stare at the beautiful floor-to-ceiling prints of Lake Michigan while filling up one's water bottle with chilled and filtered water from the latest Elkay water fountain. Edward McNamara served as mayor of Livonia from 1970 to 1986, and as the Wayne County executive from 1987 to 2002. During his three-decade tenure as an administrator, McNamara helped organize other white suburban leaders against Detroit's efforts to have the suburbs pay a more equitable share of the region's water infrastructure costs. "This is supposed to be 'Pure Michigan,'" a resident remarked to me. "I don't know who thought about that [slogan] but they obviously don't live in Flint."

The weaponization of water has also protected the interests of state and corporate power, albeit with mixed effects. High-pressure hoses were repeatedly turned on Black activists by the Birmingham Fire Department in what became ground zero for the civil rights struggle in the segregated South. With a force that ripped the bark off trees and the shirt off protest marchers' backs, water would be used to cleanse the white streets and cities of the dirt and filth of brown bodies that refused to go away silently. In the late 1980s New York City's ill-fated Commando Cleaning program used high-pressure water hoses to blast subway stations clean of homeless people in an effort to make these shared environs appear safe and acceptable for mostly white commuters. More recently, law enforcement officers in riot gear used a high-pressure water canon mounted atop an armored vehicle against hundreds of unarmed activists protesting against the Dakota Access Pipeline. In subzero temperatures, frozen water and a barrage of (supposedly) less-than-lethal weapons, including tear gas, rubber bullets, and concussion grenades were fired into the crowd, causing hypothermia, frostbite, and internal injuries among the more than three hundred protesters. Native Americans and other protesters were detained, crowded into vans, and numbered. It is worth noting that these tactics of state terrorism and extermination, including the use of water cannons, were developed in pre-Nazi Germany in the 1930s. In North Dakota, Native women were detained in large cages that one protester described as a "dog kennel." "They treat us like we're not human beings," said Russell Eagle Bear, a member of the Rosebud Sioux Tribe, one of the many people arrested for standing in the way of settler state–backed corporate interests that are endangering their water supply, destroying their sacred lands, and jeopardizing their cultural heritage.[8] Again, it's worth repeating: "Water is the last weapon to move you off your land," a symbol of cleanliness that is increasingly being coupled with state-sanctioned racism.[9]

A similar strident example of white supremacy was on display during the Flint water crisis, when, in the Genessee County jail, the mostly white prison guards were advised to drink bottled water, while, as guards looked on, the mostly Black and brown inmates, some of them pregnant women, drank poisoned water. "We knew something was going on," a Black city worker told me, "as water coolers started showing up everywhere white folks drank." The Flint water crisis is undoubtedly the most recent and certainly the most disturbing case of water inequity to delineate the city's color line, but it was certainly not the first. Members of the city's Board of Education prohibited African American students from using the Central High School swimming pool until 1944. Likewise, park managers at the Berston Field House maintained segregationist water policies until the 1940s, permitting Black swimmers to use the pool only on Wednesdays and promptly draining the pool after their use. To accommodate Black residents on the remaining six days, city officials operated outdoor sprinklers across the street from the Berston Field House.[10] Today that property sits vacant.

In the case of Detroit, water provision was also adjudicated in the service of white supremacy. What was, in part, so successful in the planned collapse and takeover of the city's water department was the overt use of racialized narratives to foreground city corruption, frame infrastructural disrepair, and explain (away) both urban dispossession and the usurpation of the city's most valuable public asset by white suburban interests. This strategy worked seamlessly to sidestep any real discussion or debate about the continuing significance of race and racism in the fight for water access and control. "Racial intervention has been nothing less than definitive for Detroit," wrote Mayor Coleman Alexander Young in his autobiography, "realigning it, undermining it, slicing it up, isolating it, condemning it, abusing it, ditching it, screwing it—and then, after the returns are in, insolently blaming it's black leadership."[11]

In the analysis that follows, I contextualize Coleman Alexander Young's words and advance a critical environmental justice perspective from which to examine the extent to which the war over water and sewage infrastructure in Detroit is engrained in both past and present patterns of racialized disadvantage and white privilege. This perspective directs our gaze to white suburban and state leaders' active, explicit, determined, and continuing role in upholding this uniquely American style of environmental racism. The names of these architects of white supremacy mark our streets, cities, airports, schools, and libraries. In addition to their names, we need to know the parts they played in undoing water justice in Detroit and elsewhere. "Detroit of today," Young claimed in 1994, "has always been your town of tomorrow. . . . Detroit remains a surpassingly purposeful place, as important to the nation right now as it has ever been—maybe more so, because right now it is telling us that the [Black] cities are in trouble. Detroit is the advance warning system—the flashing red light and siren—for what could be a catastrophic urban meltdown, and the country had damn well better pay attention."[12] As I show in this chapter, Young's words have turned out to be prophetic.

THE SANITARY CITY

Cities, writer Gerald Koeppel reminds us, are like all living things: they need water to survive and even more to flourish.[13] This ecological constraint implies that any additional growth of the city organism is inextricably tied to both the quantity and quality of its water supply. Strategies to obtain water, usually devised by city elites in search of economic growth and competitiveness, often take the form of large-scale urban development projects that effectively outsource the city's needs to surrounding areas. For example, the modern city of New York was made possible, in part, through its ability to outsource a clean and inexpensive water supply from the Catskill and Delaware watersheds, over a hundred miles away from New York's City Hall. The city of Detroit has owned and managed its drinking water system since 1836. Yet, unlike New York, Detroit supplied water to both the city and the rapidly expanding suburban municipalities of southeastern Michigan.[14] The extension of water systems to 125 suburbs, and sewer systems to 77 suburban communities, allowed those suburban municipalities to avoid taking on the debt to support their rapidly expanding and exclusively white suburbs, effectively shifting the investment burden of the water delivery system from white suburbia to Metro Detroit.[15]

Conventional wisdom about who is to blame for Detroit's financial woes and its eventual bankruptcy—the largest municipal bankruptcy filing in US history—is often attributed to failures of city management, relentless spending, and corruption on the part of city officials. The corruption claim, a media favorite, was much easier to justify as Blacks and other people of color migrated to cities like Detroit and Flint for work, and as some, albeit very few, were eventually elected to public office. In particular, the election of the city's first African American mayor, Coleman Alexander Young, in 1974 was a watershed moment in the bitter controversy for economic control and political self-determination between a Black city in control of the regions water supply and white suburbs desperate to take it.

As mayor of Motown, Young was repeatedly described by white journalists as "aggressive and assertive." In his autobiography he wrote,

> Nobody else could understand, as I do, how the federal government has toyed wantonly with the fortunes of Detroit over a period of decades; how the suburbs have dissociated themselves from the problems of Detroit even as they have maneuvered to control our assets; how the press has been caught up in a program that indulges the suburban appetites at the expense of the city. For those parties and their influential collaborators, the enemy has consistently and seemingly forever been personified in me.[16]

Activists recalled that Young never walked away from a good fight. He was not about to walk away and give up on his city and its people. Young was one among a rising tide of Black civil servants committed to advancing a distinct political sensibility by raising issues of police brutality, economic inequality, and employment discrimination against Black people in his city and across the county. He pushed against the popular notion that the problems of Black people and of Black Detroit were of their own making. Young told the *Detroit Free Press* in 1987, "It starts with economic pressure, and the first economic pressure was slavery."[17] Many whites, as whites tend to do, resented being lectured by a Black man, choosing rather to portray him as militant, self-aggrandizing, and a racist himself. The prevailing white orthodoxy of the time, underpinned by the 1965 "Moynihan Report," was that the poor Black family and community were dysfunctional and trapped in a "tangle of pathology."[18] Those whites fleeing to the suburbs were reassured by the report, which blamed Black unemployment and poverty on Black families, rather than the economic system that privileged white lives at the expense of others.

Young's tenure as mayor began in the shadows of the 1967–68 race riots that had engulfed many US cities and sent whites fleeing to the suburbs in droves. "In Detroit," Melosi found, "core population dropped by 20 percent, while the immediate suburbs increased by more that 200 percent."[19] The growth patterns of core cities like Detroit and their surrounding suburbs were essentially mirror images between 1940 and 1970.[20] Detroit stands out in this pattern of white flight, as its suburbs quickly became the most segregated in the United States.[21] They also became very powerful. "Oakland County has been the economic center of Southeast Michigan for about 30 years now," a retired Builders Association of Metro Flint employee told me. "Detroit has been irrelevant for a long time. Detroit is starting to show a little bit of progress in the city, in the downtown areas, but I mean, Oakland County has been the commercial, industrial growth [center], the total economic engine of Southeast Michigan since we began to come out of the previous great recession of 1980, '81, '82."

Yet as convincing as this popular memory may be, scholars and journalists have given little attention to the history of suburban hostility and defensive localism, even "white rage,"[22] that structured both Oakland County's emergence as the "economic center" and Detroit's "irrelevance." Also noteworthy is the degree to which this rose-colored memory is completely and conveniently colorblind, ignoring the obvious fact that a prosperous, stable, and secure Oakland County is also completely white, while adjacent Detroit is a largely Black metropolis.

Mayor Coleman Young recognized this system of white supremacy: he told *New York Times* reporter Ze'ev Chafets in 1990 that Detroit had been fleeced and abandoned by its white suburbs. "I don't know of any other city in the nation where there's such a preoccupation in the suburbs for control," he explained. "The same people who left the city for racial reasons still want to control what they've left."[23] Arthur Johnson, former president of the Detroit chapter of the NAACP and former senior vice president for university relations at Wayne State University, concurred with the mayor's interpretation. "Whites don't know a goddamned thing about what's gone wrong here" in Detroit, he told Chafets. "They say, 'Detroit had this, Detroit had that. . .' But economic power is still in the hands of whites. It's apartheid. They rape the city, and then they come and say, 'Look what these n——s did to the city,' as if they were guiltless.'" It has now been two decades since Coleman Young's passing, and still many Blacks in the city "look beyond the Eight Mile Road border and see an undifferentiated, uncaring world of suburban affluence where they are neither liked nor wanted."[24]

Urban historians and sociologists have highlighted the role of structural racism has played in Detroit's demise, including the various ways in which federal housing policies, zoning, taxation, and urban renewal orchestrated white flight and urban abandonment. Other explanations stress discrimination in the real estate market and lending institutions. The point to be stressed here is, as sociologist James Loewen's careful research makes obvious, that "sundown suburbs" like Livonia, Oakland, and Warren, Michigan, were all-white *on purpose*.[25] The harmful effects of this racial segregation in terms of household income, wealth, home values, educational attainment, and life expectancy have also been well documented. Yet, with few exceptions, little attention has been paid to how larger technical systems such as water and sewage infrastructure, which lie beneath the cities' surface, have also systematically channeled assets to suburban whites while denying them to Blacks and other "undesirables."

·   ·   ·   ·   ·

Federal backing of mortgages, which Congress authorized in the 1930s to energize a stagnant housing market, made the possibility of homeownership, amortized over 15 years with mortgage insurance, a possibility for many middle-class Americans. Between 1933 and 1935, the Home

Owners Loan Corporation (HOLC), made slightly more than one million loans. As part of federal New Deal efforts to encourage residential and commercial real estate investment, the HOLC standardized lending practices. Using data and evaluations that local lenders, real estate developers, and appraisers gathered on the housing stock in each city, and questionnaires about the occupation, income, and ethnicity of potential buyers, HOLC agents assigned grades to residential neighborhoods that would measure their "mortgage security" for banks and other mortgage lenders.[26] "Mortgage security" was visualized on color-coded maps. Neighborhoods scored as minimal risks for banks and other mortgage lenders received the highest grade, "A," and were colored green on the maps. Such neighborhoods had to be exclusively "white" and non-Jewish at the time of the maps' creation.[27] Jews were eligible for mortgage-backed loans in neighborhoods that were scored "B" and colored blue on the maps. A "C" grade was assigned to neighborhoods described as "definitely declining," which were shaded yellow. Those receiving the lowest grade, "D," colored red, were characterized as "undesirable," "inharmonious," or "lower grade" populations. This "colored infiltration" was considered to have an adverse influence on neighborhood desirability, and prudent lenders were recommended to refuse to make loans in these neighborhoods.[28]

The "Area Descriptions" of mortgage risks, written by government agents in Detroit and its surrounding suburbs, are certainly telling. Section D38 (fig. 2)—the neighborhoods of Lafayette Park, Eastern Market, and the southern part of Forest Park—was scored red for posing a hazardous risk.[29] "Class and Occupation" was judged "labor," and the agent estimated the district's population as 95% "Negro." HOLC described Section D38's housing stock as "many untenable, boarded up houses. Area of high foreclosure. Unreliable tenants. Slums and fire hazards. Vandalism. Negro low cost housing project from Mack to Browster between Beaubien and Hastings of 949 units" (fig. 3).[30]

Section C119, located in the northeast corner of Dearborn, Michigan, was characterized as "middle class—skilled mechanics—clerks," with a population consisting of 35% foreign families, "Shifting or Infiltration: Polish," and 0% Negros (fig. 4). The HOLC agent described the area as "a fairly desirable neighborhood convenient to Ford Motor Co. Housing is not very uniform and some houses are in poor condition. Development

Figure 2. The Detroit neighborhoods of Lafayette Park, Eastern Market, and the southern part of Forest Park. The darker-shaded areas are red in the original map. From Nelson et al. 2015.

continues with modest homes which are affecting prices on older units. The population is largely Polsih [*sic*], but of substantial character. . . . Although this section is being rapidly built up, contruction [*sic*] is not the best and general appeal of the neighborhood is only fair" (fig. 5) On the map C119 was shaded yellow.

Section A9, which covered most of Grosse Pointe Park, was shaded green (fig. 6). Its class and occupation were marked "upper class—business and professional men." The proportion of "foreign families" was estimated to be 0%, and the "nationalities" and "Negro" blanks were left empty. This "high class residential section, now about 80% built up," the agent wrote, "is one of the most desirable areas in and around Detroit. Hosues [*sic*] are substantial and of homogeneous character, although there is wide variation in prices. Deed restrictions are protective and the area is zoned for residential purposes only" (fig. 7).

AREA DESCRIPTION

Security Map of Detroit, Michigan

1. **POPULATION:** a. Increasing............ Decreasing............... Static Yes

   b. Class and Occupation........ Labor $600-1500

   c. Foreign Families____%   Nationalities.............................   d. Negro 95 %

   e. Shifting or Infiltration..........................

2. **BUILDINGS:**

	PREDOMINATING 50 %	OTHER TYPE 50 %
a. Type and Size	2 & 4-flats	Singles
b. Construction	Frame	Frame
c. Average Age	35 - 50 yrs.	35 - 50 yrs.
d. Repair	Poor	Poor
e. Occupancy	80%	80%
f. Owner-occupied	10%	20%
g. 1935 Price Bracket	$ 900-3300 %change	$ 500-2500 %change
h. 1937 Price Bracket	$1200-4400 +25 %	$ 700-3300 +25 %
i. March 1, 1939 Price Bracket	$1100-4000 -10 %	$ 600-3000 -10 %
j. Sales Demand	$1000-3500	$600-2000
k. Predicted Price Trend (next 6-12 months)	Downward	Weak
l. 1935 Rent Bracket	$ 8 - 17 %change	$ 8 - 20 %change
m. 1937 Rent Bracket	$ 11 - 22 +25 %	$11 - 27.50 +25 %
n. March 1, 1939 Rent Bracket	$ 10 - 20 -10 %	$10 - 25 -10 %
o. Rental Demand	$10 - 20	$10 - 20
p. Predicted Rent Trend (next 6-12 months)	Firm	Firm

3. NEW CONSTRUCTION (past yr.) No. 0 Type & Price___-___ How Selling___-___

4. OVERHANG OF HOME PROPERTIES: a. HOLC 4*   b. Institution 166 2 & 4-flat / 119 singles

5. SALE OF HOME PROPERTIES (2 yr.)   a. HOLC 6   b. Institutions 193 2 & 4-flat / 83 singles

   HOLC Loans: Outstanding - 173; paid off 4

6. MORTGAGE FUNDS: Very limited 7. TOTAL TAX RATE PER $1000 (1938⌐) $ 32.71 / 1939 Assess. fair

8. DESCRIPTION AND CHARACTERISTICS OF AREA:

   Area of stores and business. Many untenable, boarded up houses. Area of high foreclosure. Unreliable tenants. Slums and fire hazards. Vandalism. Negro low cost housing project from Mack to Browster between Beaubien and Hastings of 949 units.

   *See explanation sheet for Area Descriptions.

9. LOCATION Detroit, Mich.   SECURITY GRADE 4th AREA NO. D-38 DATE 3-1-39

Figure 3. HOLC agent's "Area Description" of Section D38. From Nelson et al. 2015.

Figure 4. Section C119, in the northeast corner of Dearborn, Michigan. From Nelson et al. 2015.

These three neighborhood assessments, D38, D119, and A9, are among thousands in more than two hundred cities in the country completed by HOLC housing appraisers between 1935 and 1940. They were used to refinance tens of thousands of mortgages, and in two years (from June 1933 to June 1935) injected more than $3 billion into the exclusively white and mostly suburban US housing market.

.   .   .   .   .

A year after Congress created the HOLC as part of the New Deal, it passed the National Housing Act (1934), which created the Federal Housing Administration (FHA). The FHA provided insurance for long-term

AREA DESCRIPTION

Security Map of __Detroit, Michigan__

1. POPULATION: a. Increasing __Steadily__ Decreasing _____ Static _____

   b. Class and Occupation __Middle class – Skilled mechanics – Clerks__

   c. Foreign Families __35__ % Nationalities __Polish__ d. Negro __0__ %

   e. Shifting or Infiltration __Polish__

2. BUILDINGS:

	PREDOMINATING 85 %		OTHER TYPE 15 %	
a. Type and Size	One-family 5-7 rooms		Two-family	
b. Construction	Frame – Brick veneer		Frame	
c. Average Age	15-18 years		15 years	
d. Repair	Fairly good		Fairly good	
e. Occupancy	99-100%		99-100%	
f. Owner-occupied	65%		70%	
g. 1935 Price Bracket	$4000-6000	% change	$5000-7000	% change
h. 1937 Price Bracket	$4800-7500	+ 23 %	$5800-8500	+ 20 %
i. March 1, 1939 Price Bracket	$4500-7000	-7 %	$5500-8000	-6 %
j. Sales Demand	Up to $6000			
k. Predicted Price Trend (next 6-12 months)	Firm		Firm	
l. 1935 Rent Bracket	$25-40	% change	$25-40	% change
m. 1937 Rent Bracket	$30-50	+23 %	$30-50	+23 %
n. March 1, 1939 Rent Bracket	$25-50	-6 %	$25-45	-12 %
o. Rental Demand	Up to $50			
p. Predicted Rent Trend (next 6-12 months)	Firm		Firm	

3. NEW CONSTRUCTION (past yr.) No. __150__ Type & Price One-family __$4000-6000__ How Selling __Fairly well__

4. OVERHANG OF HOME PROPERTIES: a. HOLC __7__ $4200-6500 b. Institutions _____
   1-2 fam.

5. SALE OF HOME PROPERTIES (2 yr.) a. HOLC __3__ 1-F $4000 b. Institutions _____
   Somewhat $6500

6. MORTGAGE FUNDS: __limited__ 7. TOTAL TAX RATE PER $1000 (1938.) $ __30.49__

8. DESCRIPTION AND CHARACTERISTICS OF AREA:

A fairly desirable neighborhood convenient to Ford Motor Co. Housing is not very
uniform and some houses are in poor condition. Development continues with
modest homes which are affecting prices on older units. The population is largely
Polish, but of substantial character. Rentals on one-family houses are more or
less limited to a $50 top and these better units were, therefore, not reduced
in rent during the past year. Although this section is being rapidly built up,
construction is not the best and general appeal of the neighborhood is only fair.

9. LOCATION __Dearborn__ SECURITY GRADE __3rd__ AREA NO. __C-119__ DATE __3/1/39__

Figure 5. HOLC agent's written assessment of Section C119. From
Nelson et al. 2015.

Figure 6. The Grosse Pointe Park neighborhood. From Nelson et al. 2015.

mortgage loans made by banks and other private lenders for home construction and sales, effectively providing federal loan guarantees to financial institutions and shifting the risk of mortgage default to the federal government. The FHA's mortgage insurance program adopted existing assumptions and appraisal methods from the HOLC and used some of the data it had collected. The consequences were devasting for people of color. Between 1934 and 1962, George Lipsitz found, the FHA and later the Veterans Administration financed more than $120 billion worth of new housing. Almost all of this investment went to new-home construction in the suburbs. Less than 2% of this real estate was available to African Americans and other nonwhites, with the rest going to whites. FHA appraisers flatly denied federally supported loans to the majority–African American population (Negro: 95%) in the so-called "slums and fire hazards" neighborhoods of Lafayette Park, Eastern Market, and Forest Park.

AREA DESCRIPTION

Security Map of __Detroit, Michigan__

1. POPULATION: a. *Increasing*__Steadily__ *Decreasing*_____ *Static*_____

    b. *Class and Occupation*__Upper class - business and professional men__

    c. *Foreign Families*__0__% *Nationalities*_____ d. *Negro*_____%

    e. *Shifting or Infiltration*_____

2. BUILDINGS:

	PREDOMINATING 100 %	OTHER TYPE %
a. *Type and Size*	One-family 7-10 rooms	
b. *Construction*	Masonry - Frame	
c. *Average Age*	1-15 years	
d. *Repair*	Good	
e. *Occupancy*	99%	
f. *Owner-occupied*	75%	
g. 1935 *Price Bracket*	$ 8500-22,500 %change	$ %change
h. 1937 *Price Bracket*	$ 11,000-27,500 +24 %	$ %
i. March 1939 *Price Bracket*	$ 10,000-25,000 -9 %	$ %
j. *Sales Demand*	Up to $12,000	
k. *Predicted Price Trend* (next 6-12 months)	Firm	
l. 1935 *Rent Bracket*	$ 80 - 135 %change	$ %change
m. 1937 *Rent Bracket*	$ 100 - 175 +28 %	$ %
n. March 1, 1939 *Rent Bracket*	$ 90 - 150 -13 %	$ %
o. *Rental Demand*		
p. *Predicted Rent Trend* (next 6-12 months)	Firm	

3. NEW CONSTRUCTION (past yr.) No.____ *Type & Price*_____ *How Selling*_____

4. OVERHANG OF HOME PROPERTIES: a. HOLC_____ b. *Institutions* 50

5. SALE OF HOME PROPERTIES (2 yr.) a. HOLC_____ b. *Institutions* 10

6. MORTGAGE FUNDS: Ample **7. TOTAL TAX RATE PER $1000** (193 8) $ 9.18

8. DESCRIPTION AND CHARACTERISTICS OF AREA:

This high class residential section, now about 80% built up, is one of the most desirable areas in and around Detroit. Houses are substantial and of homogeneous character, although there is wide variation in prices. Deed restrictions are protective and the area is zoned for residential purposes only. There are a number of large estates South of Jefferson valued well over $100,000, but the average home is valued at about $12,000. Sales during 1937 were very slow, but during 1938 activity increased somewhat, although there is still considerable overhang on the market.

9. LOCATION Grosse Pointe Park **SECURITY GRADE** 1st **AREA NO.** A-9 **DATE** 3-1-39

Figure 7. The HOLC agent's assessment of Section A9. From Nelson et al. 2015.

Prospective buyers in the racially mixed neighborhoods of Detroit were also denied mortgage insurance. But seven miles away in the 100% white, deed-restricted, residential-zoned neighborhood of Grosse Pointe Park, federal loans would be guaranteed in spades.[31]

At the time, the FHA required that all of its new mortgage-backed developments included federal and state assistance for sidewalks, paved roads, highway projects, water and sewer lines, and other utilities. So, while white families were being heavily subsidized by FHA housing development, and white suburbs were enjoying massive public and private investment, majority-Black and mixed neighborhoods in cities like Detroit were being systematically abandoned. In addition to increased real estate values, subsidized white homeowners enjoyed neighborhood stability, a better quality of life, superior public schools, and growing employment opportunities—safe white spaces for capital to invest in.[32]

In addition to contributing to the soaring rates of white suburban homeownership, the FHA mortgage housing program also created a rapid decline in vacancy rates for renters of color in the form of a rash of evictions by landlords eager to profit from a vibrant real estate market. [33] Black and brown families migrating to the region for work were forced into highly segregated and crowded urban neighborhoods. Those Black professionals who wanted to leave the rapidly forming urban ghettos and take their own advantage of Michigan's possessive investment in white suburbs, quickly found out the degree to which white supremacy would be defended, as banks, insurance companies, field surveyors, and real estate agencies implemented a "system of popular, legal, and administrative Jim Crow."[34] The combination of rising population, massive evictions, soaring real estate prices, and a rigid residential color line, historian Andrew Highsmith argues, helped make Flint and Detroit among the most segregated cities in the country.[35] But structures of Jim Crow segregation in southeastern Michigan were not only a matter of New Deal housing policies; first and foremost they were a function of how water was paid for and subsidized.

·   ·   ·   ·   ·

Since 1950, Detroit's white suburbs have almost doubled in size, to around 3 million people in 2020. This rapid exodus from the urban core forced the

city's water infrastructure to expand at an unpreceded pace, largely by taking on more debt to facilitate the growth of services to the suburbs.[36]
Moreover, the cost of this extension to the suburbs was disproportionately
higher than that of maintaining city infrastructure because of the larger lot
and house sizes combined with the low population density of higher-income
and wealthier households.[37] Research has linked the Michigan Subdivision
Control Act (SDA) of 1967 to accelerating rates of land fragmentation and
farmland loss and to urban sprawl in southeastern Michigan.[38] The SDA
allowed landowners to divide their land into parcels of 10 acres or more
without a formal permitting process. The long-term result was the creation
of an abundance of lots under 20 acres in size, increasing the overall costs
of water and sewer service lines to the city of Detroit.[39] Data suggest that
the cost of distribution to the suburbs represented as much as two-thirds of
the total investment in utilities since 1950.[40]

In other parts of the country, many central cities extended water lines
to the suburbs because water service was commensurate with the city's
future annexation ambitions and would qualify for federal subsides. In
fact, some cities, such as Los Angeles and Milwaukee, used water service
as leverage to annex adjacent suburbs.[41] This was not the case in Detroit,
as a 1926 state law prevented the annexation of suburban municipalities.
Beginning in 1955, Lawrence G. Lenhardt, the Detroit water department
director, began calling on suburbs to annex *themselves* to the city in order
to get Detroit water; thereafter, Lenhardt threatened, Detroit's system
would be capped at forty-two cities and no new suburbs could access its
water. For the previous three summers drought had greatly reduced the
cheap water supply to the surrounding counties. Some suburbs had
banned new housing, and industry was unable to locate in the region due
to the chronic water shortages. During prolonged droughts trucks delivered water to residents (something Flint residents repeatedly asked for
but were denied during their lead-contaminated water crisis.)

Despite pressure, Lenhardt wouldn't budge.[42] He correctly predicted
the department's looming crisis: as the region continued to expand, the
department would be forced to take on significant new debt to meet growing suburban water needs as whites exited the city, eroding Detroit's
tax base further and its ability to afford, much less control, its own infrastructure. During this phase of the water war between Detroit and its

increasingly white and powerful suburbs, the city was under the leadership of Republican mayor Albert E. Cobo, a self-proclaimed champion of white homeowners. Under pressure from the combined force of business and civic suburban leaders, Mayor Cobo eased Lenhardt out and installed Gerald J. Remus, who built the county's regional system to the leaders' specifications. During his eighteen years as director, Remus added fifty-one new suburban municipalities to the Detroit-run system, making it the third largest water and sewer utility in the United States.[43]

One of these suburbs was Warren City. Located just 20 miles north of Detroit, it was one of the fastest-growing municipalities in the country between 1940 and 1970. Warren City was what James W. Loewen has called a "sundown suburb," where people of color were not welcomed after sunset. In 1970 it had 179,260 residents, only 132 of whom were Black; many of the blue-collar white residents had moved there to get away from Detroit's "racial problems."[44]

Most of these residents opposed government programs that encouraged racial economic integration in Southeast Michigan. One such program was the Department of Housing and Urban Development's (HUD) Open Communities program between the summer of 1969 and early 1970. Recognizing racial tensions, evidenced in the Kerner Commission report and the assassination of Martin Luther King, Jr., the policy offered urban renewal funds for water and sewers, open space, mass transportation, and urban beautification contingent on the construction of low-income housing.[45] Opposition in Warren City to public housing drew national attention as the mayor, Ted Bates, and other city officials claimed that their town was being used as a prime target of an aggressive federal housing policy. And Warren City was not alone in its opposition: other majority-white suburbs of Detroit, including Dearborn, Dearborn Heights, Ferndale, Hazel Park, and Royal Oak Township, were also determined to protect the racial discrimination ingrained in their city plans. Warren City residents doggedly pushed back against HUD pressure to prohibit discrimination in housing, and its voters rejected the federal housing program altogether, which included $10 million in federal assistance, making Warren City, Michigan, the first town in the nation ever to rebuff an urban renewal program through a local election.[46]

The message was clear: Warren City, like its surrounding powerful and white suburbs, would get by without federal subsidies and forgo HUD's assistance if accepting such aid meant it had to comply with sweeping social changes. In response to urban race riots, the civil rights movement, or even legislation prohibiting race-based lending, substantial suburban opposition to integration kept the Housing and Urban Development Act of 1970 from being implemented and prevented HUD from withholding funds for water and sewer infrastructure from suburbs that refused to provide low- and moderate-income housing to their residents.[47] Richard Sabaugh, a county commissioner and public relations executive who, as a Warren City council member, helped lead the fight against HUD integration efforts, said at the time, "The attitude isn't as much racist as one of fear."[48] That racist fear, however, motivated increasingly powerful suburbs to lobby for and accept other sources of federal welfare to construct the water and sewer infrastructure needed to support new single-family white neighborhoods—subsidies, however, that did not require them to provide low- and moderate-income housing to people of color.

At the same time, as federal investment was being exclusively directed toward suburban infrastructure, recipient neighborhoods like Grosse Pointe Park were also introducing point systems that ranked potential homeowners by such discriminatory measures as skin color, spoken accent, religion, and whether they lived a "typically American way of life" (fig. 8)[49] This grassroots redlining effort blanketed the existing racialized schema of the HOLC and FHA. Voters in Dearborn, the seat of the Ford empire, elected an openly segregationist mayor, Orville L. Hubbard, in 1941 and kept him in office for thirty-six years. "I just don't believe in integration," he said in 1967. "When that happens, along comes socializing with the whites, intermarriage and then mongrelization."[50] Both federal and state laws prohibited discrimination in housing, yet federal agencies and programs continued to fund white suburban development to openly anti-Black racist mayors and their constituents and, as a result, not only maintained but forcefully advanced a uniquely US system of racial oppression and white supremacy.

Martin Luther King Jr. had earlier recognized this tried-and-true tactic of white supremacy while a sophomore at Morehouse College. In a letter titled "Kick Up Dust," he likened the strategy of white racist leaders like

```
*(1) What descent.  Mr? _____ Mrs? _____
*(2) American born.  Mr? _____ Mrs? _____
   *If not, how long in U.S.A.?  Mr.? _____ Mrs? _____
 (3) Is way of living typically American?
     *(a) What is his occupation? _____
     *(b) His immediate business associates?
          Typical? _____
     *(c) His church? _____
          No church? _____
     *(d) Clubs? _____
          No Clubs? _____
     *(e) Are his friends predominantly typical? _____
          _____
 (4) Appearance:
     *Mr. Swarthy Very _____ Medium _____ Slightly _____ Not at all _____
     *Mrs. Swarthy Very _____ Medium _____ Slightly _____ Not at all _____
 (5) Accent:
     *Mr. Pronounced _____ Medium _____ Slightly _____ None _____
     *Mrs. Pronounced _____ Medium _____ Slightly _____ None _____
 (6) A. Names typically American?  Mr. _____ Mrs. _____
```

Figure 8. An excerpt from the questionnaire used from 1945 to 1960 to exclude minorities from author's hometown of Grosse Pointe Park. From Wu 2017.

Hubbard, Sabaugh, Bates, and McNamara to "obscure the real question of rights and opportunities" to kicking up dust.[51] "I often find," King wrote, "when decent treatment for the Negro is urged, a certain class of people hurry to raise the scarecrow of social mingling and intermarriage." This dust screen, King suggested, worked to obscure the real social problem: access to the basic rights and opportunities afforded white American citizens, including "the right to earn a living; . . . equal opportunities in education, health, recreation and similar public services; the right to vote; equality before the law"; common decency, and, I would add, fair and equitable access to water and sanitation.[52]

THE RACIALIZED CITY

The 1975 rate hike by the Detroit Water and Sewerage Department (DWSD) marked a watershed moment in the racialization of water politics in southeastern Michigan.[53] One year into Coleman Alexander Young's mayoral tenure, white suburban leaders did not take kindly to the fact that a Black administration would be raising their rates by almost 40%, even if it was the first water rate increase since 1972. The DWSD budget proposed for the 1975–76 fiscal year was $94.7 million, up from US $73.8 million the year before. Archival research by sociologist Dana Kornberg reveals that Detroit then had the lowest wholesale water rate among the nation's large urban areas. But that did not prevent the suburban leaders from mounting a concerted effort against the newly elected Black mayor, accusing him and his water department of corruption, graft, and ineptitude.[54] An alliance of ninety-six white suburban municipalities, which called itself the Suburban Association of Detroit Water Customers, quickly went on the attack, launching a class action lawsuit against the city and demanding a state audit of DWSD finances.[55] Although the lawsuit was eventually dismissed, the case was tried and took nine years to reach the Michigan Supreme Court on appeal. During the same decade, the Suburban Association filed two additional lawsuits, along with two federal cases. Suburban white leaders used these prolonged court cases to prove that the water department and the city were greedy, mismanaged, and corrupt. Combined with years of favorable media coverage, the racialized narratives cultivated by suburban white leaders became a totalizing force de jure. And for more than three decades, Mayor Young and Black urban leadership became a convenient racial handle to convince white suburban rate payers that Detroit was benefiting from a scheme of unfair water rates.

Two political cartoons by the *Detroit News* cartoonist Draper Hill symbolize white suburbanites' paranoia about the root problem of the water department—Black leadership. The first cartoon depicts a menacing Coleman Young in total control of the water department, threatening to shut off the water supply to the surrounding suburbs (fig. 9). It tugs on white fears of Black power. Recall the Warren City council members comment "The attitude isn't as much racist as one of fear." "People don't see every Black as bad," this longtime champion of white flight reminisced. "We just want to live in peace." And for many white suburbanites, nothing good was going to come from Detroit's first African American mayor. The second cartoon, sketched almost three years later, seems clearly meant to escalate white anxiety about Black leadership into full-blown panic.[56] Here, the Black mayor is holding a shotgun instead of a wrench and is sitting watchfully in the shadows of the city border, Eight Mile Road, making sure, the caption reads, "that no

Figure 9. Cartoon from the *Detroit News*, June 4, 1981, A18. Reproduced in Kornberg 2016, 274.

wily suburbanite steals his metropolitan jewels" (fig. 10) This sort of blatant race-baiting stood in stark contrast to the ghastly uneven socioeconomic and political power relations that had helped bring about Detroit's exclusively white and privileged suburbs. "White people," observed Young, "find it extremely hard to live in an environment they don't control."[57]

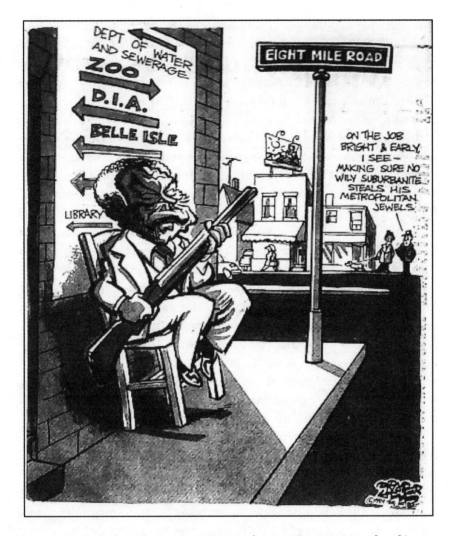

Figure 10. Cartoon from the *Detroit News*, March 14, 1984, A10. Reproduced in Kornberg 2016, 274.

Legal counsel representing suburban counties put forth a racialized hypothesis similar to that of the mainstream media and suburban political leadership, arguing that the suburban water users were providing water welfare to their urban counterparts. This narrative claimed that suburban customers pay more than their fair share in water rates but have no voice in its decision making—a form of taxation without representation. They misleadingly argued that suburban customers paid about 80% of DWSD's water revenue and about 50% of its sewerage revenue, implying that Black folks in the city were not paying their fair share of the regional water burden. It was true that suburban customers had experienced rate hikes, but the majority of that increase came from their own suburban water authorities, which added county rate and fee structures to Detroit's wholesale prices. Each suburb set its own markup and kept its own revenue. For example, in 1979 the DWSD sold water for $3.11 per cubic foot to Avon Township, but the township charged its residents US $11.43 per unit.[58] All suburban townships charged their customers retail rates, some as high as 1000% of the wholesale rate.[59] Even today, most cities that buy Detroit water double, triple, and even quadruple the water charges to their residents. At the turn of the twentieth century, former Detroit water plant operator Russ Bellant acknowledged, the average markup was 146 percent on water rates and 168 percent on sewer rates.[60] In effect, local communities had turned Detroit's subsidized water pricing into a moneymaking machine for suburban counties. Despite these realities, the legal establishment, political leaders, and major media outlets continued to accuse the city of Detroit of overcharging its suburban customers for water, leaning heavily on convenient racialized tropes of inner-city mismanagement, urban welfare, and wrongdoing.[61]

A Detroit City Council investigation into the 1975 rate hike found that the 39% increase could have been reduced to 20% if the department had opted to fund the rest of the needed money by issuing bonds in the municipal market. The director of DWSD at the time argued that it was less expensive in the long run to draw on revenues to pay for upgrades than to resort to debt financing.[62] Suburban leaders were outraged, describing the director's decision not to engage in deficit spending as irresponsible and incompetent. White suburban leaders were not about to tolerate being inconvenienced, even if going into debt worsened the economic climate of the city that continued to subsidize their water and sewerage infrastructure, and even if it jeopardized the economic benefits they increasingly took for granted. In the following decades, suburban leaders sought court and legislative action to wrestle control of the water board away from the city. At the time, the water department's board of directors included four city and three suburban members appointed by the mayor, an institutional arrangement that obstructed suburban seizure. State representatives now joined county drain commissioners, mayors, and other county executives in a concerted and "colorblind" effort that faulted the city's mismanagement for the proposed suburban rate increases.[63]

Richard Sabaugh balked at the idea of raising taxes to help Detroit, no matter what the reason. "There is no feeling of pity for Detroit in the suburbs," he told the *New York Times*.[64] The collective refusal of Detroit's white suburbs to pay for their water and sewerage infrastructure forced the DWSD to cover an increasing part of its expenditure with borrowed funds rather than tax revenues or infrastructure charges. A mountain of debt accumulated over time, and the interest on it increased as well. No one gave the critical questions of costs and resources much thought until the city became poorer and its residents darker in skin color. Current expansion had made Detroit's wastewater treatment plant among the top ten in the world as measured by average daily flow. But as its overbuilt infrastructure began to age and deteriorate, and cost more, cracks both in the pipes and funding structure started to show.[65] Moreover, new permitting regulations implemented in 1972 under the Clean Water Act placed increasing cost burdens on local utilities. Yet these new regulatory demands came with no offsetting federal investment. In Michigan, suburban public officials pushed bills through the legislature that restricted the rate increases that Detroit could pass on to suburban customers, ensuring that the brunt of the cost of any improvements to water infrastructure would be borne, once again, by the city in the form of additional debt.[66]. In 1977 the DWSD was cited for violating the Clean Water Act because its wastewater treatment plant exceeded new effluent discharge standards.[67] The US Environmental Protection Agency sued the city to stop pollution of the Detroit River, and the parties moved to resolve the conflict through a consent decree under the oversight of federal judge John Feikens.

THE PRIVATIZED CITY

Over the following thirty-five years—one of the longest durations for a US environmental legal case—Judge Feikens's oversight grew from limited technical compliance with federal environmental laws on wastewater treatment and water quality to prescribing specific enhancements to DWSD management, financing, and suburban control.[68] Some Detroiters familiar with the judge's leadership over the three decades characterized him as Detroit's first true emergency manager. In response to ongoing tensions over rate increases and DWSD management between the city of Detroit and its suburban water and wastewater customers, Judge Feikens moved the DWSD toward regional reform, something white suburban leaders had aggressively pursued for decades (fig. 11). In 2001 Feikens helped organize the Southeast Michigan Consortium for Water Quality, thereby empowering suburban voices in debates over water quality in the region.[69] Feikens's regionalism expanded the scope of both public and private actors involved in discussions about water provision and wastewater disposal in southeastern Michigan. He circumvented democratic decision-making processes and transformed the court into a roving power broker, effectively undermining the city's sovereignty over its water resources in favor of the white suburban coalition.

In 1979 Judge Feikens appointed Detroit mayor Coleman Young as administrator of the DWSD. Yet efforts by his administration to raise water rates to help the agency comply with federal regulations and maintain its one thousand–plus square miles of service area were repeatedly thwarted by the 125 majority-white suburbs. This organized refusal to endorse reasonable rate increases turned out to be an effective strategy to further defund the public organization and undermine its existence. In fact, on several occasions (1993, 1995, 1997, 1999, and 2001–2) the suburban counties of Oakland, Wayne, and Macomb, separately and together, introduced bills in the Michigan Senate to create an elaborate, suburban-controlled regional water authority, consistent with Feikens's approach, which would effectively have wrestled the control of water away from Detroit. Then Warren City sued the DSWD, claiming the department was overcharging for water. Yet, according to a 2003 DWSD report, it was Warren City that was marking up the water charges by 125%, from $5.86 per thousand cubic feet to $13.14.[70] Most suburban cities that bought Detroit water continued to inflate the water charges to their residents. That meant that most of the money collected in the region for water bills stayed in the local suburban communities that billed their residents.

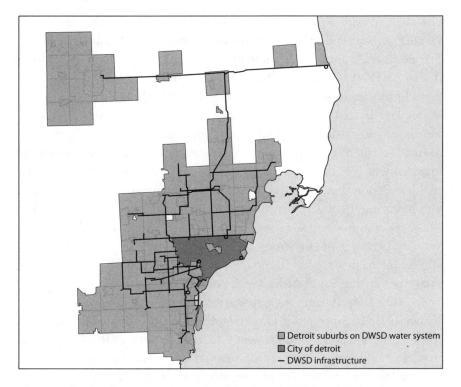

Figure 11. Regional water supply system of the Detroit Water and Sewerage Department (DWSD) as of 2015. We the People of Detroit Community Research Collective 2016.

It did not go to Detroit.[71] Despite the racialized rhetoric of suburban officials that claimed Detroit was somehow ripping off the suburbs, the opposite was true. Detroit continued to subsidize suburban water infrastructure and the suburbs continued to profit from it. In fact, of the twenty largest US cities, Detroit's rates were the fifth lowest in 2002.[72] Despite these realities, the racialized rhetoric of the fleeced white suburban water user proved to be a useful strategy for political elites to deploy in maintaining access to cheap city water.

Judge Feikens, described as an "arrogant racist and longtime opponent of school desegregation," followed his own doggedly colorblind agenda in moving the DWSD toward privatization.[73] He ignored Article VII, Section 25, of the Michigan Constitution and Sec. 7-1504 of the Detroit city charter, which prohibited both regionalization and the sale of the DWSD without consent of three-fifths of city voters.[74] Lobbied hard by private water management companies, Feikens hired Victor Mercado to direct the DWSD in 2002. Mercado, who worked for two (of the three) giant European-based water multinationals—British-based RWE Thames Water and United Water, a subsidiary of Suez—immediately adopted a hardline, pro-business approach to water governance in the region. Mercado's management approach exacerbated an already-uneven arrangement between city and suburb. Running the DWSD like a profit-making corporation, he began to cut costs by laying off unionized workers and replacing them with private contractors. He also eliminated services to the poor; even going so far as to cement areas around the valves to prevent desperate residents from turning the water back on, mimicking similar forms of state-sanctioned terrorism used by multinational water purveyors during South Africa's and Bolivia's water wars.

In 2003 Detroit water rates rose 9 percent and the following year they increased by 16.9 percent.[75] Concurrently, Mercado initiated the debt collection program and shut off water to 40,752 households in Detroit in his first year as director. During this time corporations together had three hundred unpaid water bills, amounting to millions of dollars in arrears. Yet none of these corporate accounts were shut off on the basis of nonpayment. Michigan water rights activists estimated that businesses and government-owned properties owed nearly twice as much as residences. In 2015 businesses owed the DWSD $41 million compared with $26 million from homeowners. Some of the biggest debts were on government-owned properties, such as the Detroit Housing Commission, the Detroit Reentry Center prison, Belle Isle, and the city's golf courses, according to city records. "They don't get threats. They don't get shutoff notices. They get to dispute their bills," said Maureen Taylor, state chair of the Michigan Welfare Rights Organization.[76] These dirty water schemes routinely transgress both ethical and legal boundaries. And for his role in awarding the rigged bid to Bobby Ferguson, a private contractor, between 2002 and 2008, Victor Mercado pleaded guilty to conspiracy in November 2012.

In addition to building a massive regional water supply system to serve white suburban communities, the city of Detroit also built a massive wastewater treatment system to serve the region and a treatment plant off

Lake Huron to supply drinking water to the growing northern suburbs of Oakland and Macomb counties, as well as the greater Flint area (fig. 12).[77] In 1999 Judge Feikens signed and implemented a rate settlement agreement in an effort to bring the utility into compliance with regulatory standards. The agreement required that 83% of the new construction costs for any combined sewer outflow (CSO) control system must be covered by Detroit residents and the remaining 17 percent covered by suburban wholesale customers.[78] The 83-17 split decision meant that Detroit residents were responsible for the lion's share of the cost of building CSO systems that serve only suburban customers. In addition, Detroiters would also be responsible for 100% of the cost of CSO control systems that served only Detroit customers.[79] In a combined sewer system, sewage, gray water, and stormwater are all diverted and processed by the same central wastewater treatment plant. This type of sewerage system is no longer built, in part because the process of separating sewer from stormwater and grey water is an expensive and lengthy process.[80] During wet periods combined sewer systems can present a major environmental risk as the combined volume from sewer and storm is often too much for the treatment plant to handle. During these events, sewers can overflow and the effluent containing sewage and industrial waste is discharged directly into freshwater, a violation of the Clean Water Act.

The logic behind the 83-17 split was likely rooted in the fact that most of the combined sewage systems are located in Detroit.[81] However, such a truncated perspective ignores the historical conditions with which the city was effectively forced to subsidize the construction and investment of both water and sewer infrastructure for the suburbs. DWSD's decades-long suburban infrastructure construction project has left the city with an antiquated combined sewer system. Moreover, many of the city's businesses, employment, and service amenities, including its universities, hospitals, entertainment venues, and government buildings are used by people throughout southeastern Michigan and beyond who travel to the city on a daily basis. These interlocutors with the city share the infrastructure with Detroit residents but not the responsibility of maintaining the city's aging water services system.[82] In other words, the most disadvantaged customers of the DWSD, the primarily African American residents of Detroit, contribute the most financial support to the regional CSO system,

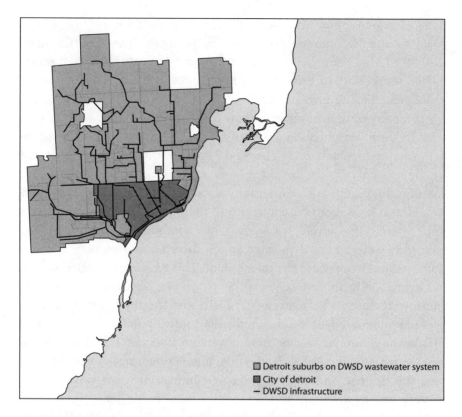

Figure 12. Regional wastewater system of the DWSD in 2015. We the People of Detroit Community Research Collective 2016.

and the most advantaged customers of the DWSD, the primarily white residents of suburban municipalities, contribute the least. This has led to hugely inflated sewerage costs for Detroit customers. And, as with the water rate structure, most of the financing for the sewerage expansion came from debt financing, not rate increases.

·   ·   ·   ·   ·

In addition to infusing a pro-business culture into the DWSD and defunding its ability to provide potable water and wastewater treatment, Judge Feikens fanned the flames of privatization and white hostility in the suburbs with his derogatory remarks about the city's Black leadership and administration. When asked in an interview to discuss what he had learned while he and Mayor Young were administering the sewage treatment plant, Feikens replied:

> One of the things we have to give Black people the time to learn to do is to learn how to run city governments, to run projects like the water and sewer plant. . . . Unfortunately, they're still in an era of development, many of them, in which they think all you have to do is talk about this thing. So, you hear a lot of rhetoric. Talking is important; words are important. But you have to do more than talk about it. And I think that as the Black people come into political power in all the big cities of the United States, they have to learn how to climb hills.

Feikens also called Mayor Young "a very poor administrator." Describing the mayor as someone who "just doesn't have a grasp" of some city issues, Feikens also portrayed Young's Black staff as "lousy"; such remarks fueled nascent white anxiety and racial animus in the region.[83] For Feikens, Black leaders could never match the administrative skills of their white European counterparts. The extraordinary length of Feikens's thirty-five-year tenure no doubt reflected the fact that he and other whites who kept him in his position thought Black folk were neither smart nor capable enough to run their own water department, let alone city. Feikens shared the popular belief regarding Detroit's decline. As Mayor Young described it: "Detroit has nothing but problems since the white people got the hell out, which goes to show that black people can't run anything by themselves, much less a major city, especially when it's in the hands of a hatemongering mayor like the one who's been entrenched there for twenty goddam years."[84]

Under Feikens and Mercado's control, DWSD rates steadily increased, employee layoffs continued, and new private contracts proliferated. In 2002 Feikens allowed newly elected mayor Kwame Kilpatrick to approve certain "red-tag" (i.e., big-ticket) construction contracts without the consent of the city council, a practice that once again circumvented the authority of locally elected city officials, accelerated the privatization of public infrastructure, and facilitated graft. The corrupt practice later landed the former mayor in jail after he was convicted of extortion, bribery, fraud, and conspiracy.[85]

To keep DWSD in compliance with federal standards, Feikens ordered the department to hire Detroit Wastewater Partners (DWP) as a consultant at a projected cost of $550 to $700 million over five to eleven years. His assumption, once again, was that current staff and administration were unable to keep the department in compliance by themselves. In 2003 Feikens and Mercado also brought in Infrastructure Management Group, Inc. (IMG), based in Washington, DC, to help manage new, large private contracts. IMG had been founded by Steve Steckler, a key architect of President Ronald Reagan's Commission on Privatization in the 1980s. IMG had previously arranged the privatization of the Milwaukee Wastewater System and the outsourcing of the water and wastewater system in Lee County, Florida. For many working in Detroit's water department, the writing was on the wall. By 2004, reporter Diane Bukowski found, IMG and its employees had been paid at least $3.3 million from DWSD funds. Mercado and one of IMG's top officers were colleagues at United Water Resources, the global water privatizer and subsidiary of Suez.

In 2003, John Joyner and Steve Steckler coauthored a 2003 Reason Foundation study advocating for the privatization of public resources like water, street lighting, jails, airports, roads, and bridges. Joyner had previously worked with Mercado at United Water Resources, a global water privatizer now owned by the German-based Suez Company.[86] The Reason Foundation is an American libertarian think tank committed to advancing the values of individual freedom and choice, limited government, and market-friendly policies. Among its largest donors are the David H. Koch Charitable Foundation and the Sarah Scaife Foundation. The latter two organizations, as journalist Jane Mayer has documented in her *New York Times* bestseller *Dark Money*, are among a "small, rarefied group of hugely wealthy, archconservative families that for decades poured money, often with little public disclosure, into influencing how Americans thought and voted."[87] These American oligarchs, like their followers, have a pattern of lawbreaking, political manipulation, and obfuscation. Some families, like the DeVos' have clearly committed tax crimes, and other forms of manipulation and deceit to realize their neoliberal agenda. But unlike Kwame Kilpatrick, these white elites were never convicted or charged for their crimes.[88] The brother of Trump-appointed Secretary of Education Betsy

DeVos, Erik Prince, the founder of Blackwater Worldwide, has received more than $1 billion worth of government contracts. In September 2007, Blackwater employees opened fire in Nisour Square in Baghdad, killing fourteen unarmed civilians and prompting a debate about the accountability of private contractors in war zones. The private mercenary firm tried to escape the fallout of the Nisour Square massacre and other scandals by changing its name first to Xe and then to Academi. Prince was back in the news recently for his connections to the Trump administration and back-channel communications with high-ranking Russian officials.

The entire DeVos clan has worked tirelessly to make the state of Michigan its free enterprise bastion, going so far as to structure its company, Amway, so as to avoid federal taxes. Over time, its pyramid scheme company has grown into a marketing behemoth, generating annual revenues of nearly $11 billion by 2011.[89] The family's political influence, informed by a unique conjunction of extreme free market idealism and Calvinist tradition, is unprecedented, even in Michigan. Richard DeVos Jr. was the finance chair of the Republican National Committee (RNC) during the Reagan presidency. He was criminally charged, along with his business partner Jay Van Andel, in 1982 for tax fraud by the Canadian government, which dropped the charges when the two agreed to pay a $20 million fine.[90] Unphased, in 2006 DeVos ran for governor of Michigan but lost to the incumbent Democrat, Jennifer Granholm.

"All of this comes out of the CATO Institute funded by the Koch Brothers," Debra Taylor from We the People of Detroit explained to me. "It comes under the generic name of 'state intervention law,'" an ideology that views any state intervention as a hinderance to economic growth. "Detroit was actually targeted," explained Monica Lewis-Patrick. "The city's assets," the water department being among the most valuable, "were seized and parceled out to friends and family and relations of many of the elected officials." And they are "benefiting right now from either being in power or using it to get access to contracts," she emphasized. For Lewis Patrick and Tayor, Detroit has become the testing ground for maintaining urban austerity and using critical public resources for private gain. Judge Feikens, like many of the suburban white leaders, claimed that the city's Black leadership and administration were responsible for what ailed the water and sewerage department. Yet a water department worker commented to a journalist, "Mercado and Kilpatrick claimed lots of capital expenditure was needed, money for pipes, CSO basins, failure of mains, et cetera. They claimed increasing demand for water demanded more building and investment. This was a scam." Department workers and activists alike claimed that the money from annual rate increases went instead to private contracts with friends and family members, who raked in millions on the premise of capital expenditure.

To persuade Detroit to voluntarily cede control of DWSD, John Feikens created the Business Leadership Group (BLG), which further cultivated privatization and regionalism.[91] In the wake of the Kilpatrick corruption scandal, David Bing was elected mayor. A professional basketball Hall of Famer, Bing owned the Bing Group, an automotive parts manufacturer, and Bing Steel. In 2008, the year prior to his election, the Bing Group grossed $130 million in revenues. David Bing was a member of BLG, along with his close ally Anthony Earley, who at the time was board chair and CEO of DTE Energy. DWSD contractor James Nicholson of PVS Chemicals, a major contributor to both Bing's and Kilpatrick's campaign, was also a member of Feikens's BLG. In 2008, PVS Technologies received a sole-bid contract for $31,050 for an emergency procurement of sulfur dioxide to the city. The city also paid PVS $300,000 for an emergency procurement of ferric chloride. PVS Technologies also received a lowest-bid contract for $5 million to supply the city with ferric chloride from June 1, 2008, through August 31, 2011, with the option to renew for three additional one-year periods. PVS-Nolwood Chemicals received two additional contracts. The first was for $78,000 for caustic liquid soda, and the second was a lowest-bid contract of $4.4 million to provide the city with hydrofluorosilicic acid from January 1, 2008, through December 31, 2009, with the option to renew for two additional one-year periods.[92]

Other beneficiaries of Feikens's BLG included Detroit Meter Partners (DMP), a joint venture among the construction firms Weiss, Hale, and Walbridge Aldinger, which received a $154 million contract to install and retrofit some 278,000 water meters with electronic data-gathering capability to more accurately track water and sewer use in the city. At the time executives of Weiss and Walbridge Aldinger were regular contributors to mayoral and city council campaigns. Walbridge Aldinger CEO John Rakolta Jr. was a top campaign supporter of Governor John Engler, for whom his daughter worked. City residents were required to have the automatic meters installed in their plumbing at a cost of anywhere from $150 to $350 per household. Owners or occupants refusing to give DMP employees access to their basements, crawl spaces, or furnace rooms to install new meters or retrofit their existing meters had their water shut off, even if they had paid their previous water bill. Up to 45,000 Detroit households had their water shut off for having delinquent bills or for not paying the fees charged for the meter installation.[93] Surveillance is a key component of any system of control, and the installation or retrofitting of 278,000 water meters ensured that water usage in this majority-Black city would conform to an audit culture in which the private management of public utilities could be fully realized. The consequences for some were dire. "Unknown numbers of families have lost their children after state social services discovered they were without water," Diane Bukowski reported in the *Voice of Detroit* in 2011, and "thousands more have lost their homes after exorbitant unpaid water bills were attached to their property taxes."[94]

A year later, in 2008, the city awarded several major contracts to the Walbridge Aldinger Corporation, including $3.8 million to improve the chemical storage and feed systems and enhance the chemical mixing at the Springwells Water Treatment Plant. Another contract was awarded for $45 million to restore existing secondary tanks. Another, $36 million contract was awarded to Walbridge Aldinger for further rehabilitation of the Springwells plant. City council records also reveal that Walbridge Aldinger received two additional contracts in 2008, one for $73 million and the other for $87 million. All of these contracts to the same company were 100% city funded, even though suburban residents and users also benefited from these investments in the regional system. In addition to its water meter contract, Weiss Construction also received a $17.9 million contract to rehabilitate the Woodmere Sewage Pumping Station.[95]

When Detroit Public Schools was placed under state control in 1999, Rakolta's Walbridge Aldinger was awarded a $4 million contract by Wayne County deputy executive Mike Duggan to refurbish twenty schools over the summer. Controversy still swirls around the lack of a formal bidding process or advertisements for this and other city contracts pertaining to the $1.4 billion bond issue for this school renovation. Later that summer, John Rakolta Jr. hosted a $1,000-a-plate fundraising dinner for Mike

Duggan, who was running for Wayne County prosecutor. More notably, the *Detroit Metro Times* reported, many of the schools that were worked on that summer were closed within a few years. Unsurprisingly, Walbridge Aldinger was also the program manager in the demolition of Mackenzie High School project in 2012.[96] More than half of the contracts awarded by the former school board went to contractors who contributed to board members' political campaigns, the *Detroit News and Free Press* reported. The newspaper also found that the district paid for work that was never performed, hired inexperienced companies to manage the construction work, and awarded contracts without competitive bids.[97] The Walbridge Aldinger company was also embroiled in cost escalations over a Wayne County jail project, and concerns were raised over its demolition contracts with the Detroit Land Bank Authority.

Walbridge Aldinger CEO Rakolta Jr. served as finance chairman in Utah senator Mitt Romney's two presidential campaigns, in 2008 and 2012. Rakolta is also related by marriage to Ronna Romney McDaniel, who chaired the Republican National Committee and the Michigan GOP at the time Trump was elected. Rakolta also contributed the maximum amount to Rick Snyder's gubernatorial campaign. His daughter Lauren Rakolta, also a Walbridge Aldinger executive, worked for Snyder on the campaign. In 2017, Walbridge Aldinger reported $1.5 billion in revenue. Rakolta's family members contributed over $275,000, combined, to Trump's 2016 campaign fund, and Rakolta was a top donor to Trump's 2017 inauguration, giving $250,000. And, in September 2019, the US Senate confirmed Trump's nomination of the company's CEO as ambassador to the United Arab Emirates, where his engineering company has completed major projects.

The largest private equity firm in the world, the Carlyle Group, was not going to sit idly by amid all this opportunity for contractor abuse and government malfeasance. In 2007, in anticipation of millions of dollars in profits from the ongoing privatization of the city's resources, the Carlyle Group bought Synagro Technologies in a $772 million deal. Detroit was to be Synagro's largest municipal sludge disposal contract, bigger even than New York City. The company expected profits of up to $5 million a year for twenty-five years from annual revenues of $47 million, and, like the DeVos clan, it would let nothing get in its way. That fall the $1.2 billion blockbuster sludge-hauling contract was coming to a vote in the city council. To seal the deal, Synagro vice president James Rosendahl and consultant Rayford Jackson delivered secret payments and perks to Mayor Kwame Kilpatrick; his father, Bernard Kilpatrick; council member Monica Conyers, and others.[98] Rosendahl later pleaded guilty to bribery and was fired from Synagro. Neither the corporation nor its owner, the Carlyle Group, however, were criminally charged in the scandal even in the face of evidence that Carlyle and Synagro's top executives likely approved or at least knew about the illicit efforts to land the sludge contract.[99]

The continued outsourcing of infrastructure construction, maintenance, and repairs—outsourcing with a pattern of lawbreaking, political manipulation, and obfuscation—to the private sector displaced thousands of residents from their homes and city workers from their jobs, particularly those in the skilled trades. Moreover, journalist Diane Bukowski reminds us, "public jobs have frequently been the only avenue for women and workers of color in the trades to get employment."[100] This was particularly true in Detroit's Black administration, where for the first time in the city's history nonwhites and women were given access to the city's unionized job market. This form of racialized and gendered job loss underscores the ways in which racialized environmental injustices that begin in one place—work—often affect another—the home. Equally striking is how these intense efforts to profit from the privatization of public infrastructure, replete with both corruption and nepotism, were neither foregrounded nor condemned in explanations for what drove this iconic city to bankrupty.

THE BANKRUPTED CITY

The subprime housing crisis that began in 2008 was not the first financial shock to drive the city of Detroit to the brink of financial ruin. The twelve years of the Reagan and Bush I presidencies subjected Detroit and other American cities to federal disinvestment and neglect. For twelve years, Mayor Coleman Young wrote, "the nation completely kissed off such basic civil concepts as entitlements, governmental responsibility, and social sensitivity."[101] The rich prospered from massive tax cuts as white middle-class Americans became increasingly comfortable with their own racial prejudice, experiencing marginal gains as Black cities like Detroit were clipped at their knees. The drain of resources in the wake of white flight continued to cripple the city as the suburbs continued to take more out of the city than they put in. No other city in the country in the early 1980s had such a disparity between resident and nonresident income tax burdens.[102] Even as the buzzards circled overhead, the city and its mayor were able to do little things at least, such as streamlining garbage collection, to ease Detroit's monstrous economic liabilities. Mayor Young also negotiated wage concessions from state and city employees, and somehow persuaded an already-overtaxed majority-poor and -Black population to raise the city income tax at a time when no other city or state in the country did so. So extraordinary was his and fellow Detroiters' commitment to save their city. "There isn't an urban area in the county—the world—that has had to deal with the commercial, industrial, governmental, and social abandonment that has been tearing at Detroit's flesh since the end of World War II," Young observed, describing the systematized social machinery of white supremacy. "Yet, by the resilience of our people, we have managed to survive where others have failed. Two years after the fiscal crisis of 1981, Detroit was actually showing a surplus. At the end of the decade, we balanced five consecutive budgets."[103] Those wanting a second chance to take down this resilient Black stronghold would do well to learn from Detroit's history. It was urban poor Black and brown folks who were willing to make personal economic sacrifices to keep their city afloat, while whites fled to the suburbs and resisted every effort to pay their fair share. This reality stands in stark contrast to the dominant narrative, with its supporting Moynihan Report, that continued to blame Black leadership and its majority-Black residents for this city's problems.

Notwithstanding their efforts, Detroit's elected officials could do nothing to reduce Judge Feikens's discretionary power. Under his long "managerial" tenure, the DWSD entered into such an indebted state that the department would pay more to service its debts than to repair and maintain its infrastructure. As detailed earlier, massive contracts overseen by Feikens assisted in privatizing and downsizing Detroit's public services and workforce. Monies that should have been allocated to improving infrastructure and employing city residents went to the banks and white-owned corporations instead.

And as the water department and city got more in debt, Feikens, Mercado, and Kilpatrick became even more brazen. It was Feikens who suggested that the water department enter into interest rate swap agreements. However, instead of being protected from rising interest rates, the city fell victim to the LIBOR-rigging scandal, perpetrated by global and US banks. The London Interbank Offered Rate, or LIBOR, is the average interest rate at which leading banks borrow funds from other banks in the London market. It is the most widely used global benchmark, or reference, rate for short-term loans. The LIBOR is also among the interest rate indexes most commonly used to make adjustments to adjustable-rate mortgages. It is also used in derivative pricing and setting interest rates for student loans.

The LIBOR scandal, which went undetected for years, involved collusion among many major financial institutions to report false interest rates in order to manipulate the markets and boost their own profits. Ratings agencies, such as Standard and Poor's, conspired with banks to, among other alleged crimes, steal billions of dollars from cash-strapped cities like Detroit, and their homeowners. The US government has accused the rating agencies and banks of fraud in a $5 billion lawsuit. Regulators in both the United States and the United Kingdom levied some $9 billion in fines on banks involved in the scandal. Swiss banking giant UBS, a key architect in the LIBOR scandal, foisted a pension obligation certificate loan of $1.5 billion on Detroit in 2004, which became a major source of the city's debt crisis. This global financial scandal, combined with the subprime mortgage crisis, was enough to push the city off its financial moorings forever.

In March 2013 the city of Detroit was placed under the control of Kevyn Orr, the state-appointed emergency manager. In July Orr declared bankruptcy on behalf of the city, giving the banks direct control to the city's finances. The total DWSD debt at that time was $6.4 billion, but none of it was reduced in the bankruptcy. Instead, billions in pensions were forfeited, schools were closed, and city assets were sold off on the cheap. In total 150,000 families—one in three—lost their homes to foreclosure between 2005 and 2010. Documents reveal that during the pendency of the Detroit bankruptcy, the city, DWSD and the counties of Macomb, Oakland, and Wayne engaged in extensive negotiations regarding the potential formation of a regional water authority to assume control of the

DWSD.[104] Hanging over the choice between this and an alternative approach was Orr's threat to fully privatize water and wastewater provision in the region. On October 10, 2014, the city and the counties formally approved the formation of the Great Lakes Water Authority (GLWA) as part of the bankruptcy proceedings. The new regional water authority would lease the water and wastewater infrastructure for the city, operate the entire system, and set all water rates. Under the new agreement, Detroit would be one of the lessees to its own system. In an effort to appease suburban concerns about unpaid bills, the DWSD began shutting off water to households with delinquent water bills. Thirty thousand households had their water shut off in the summer of 2014.[105]

.   .   .   .   .

It took some time, but what Lawrence G. Lenhardt, the water department's director in the mid-1950s, had warned of had come to pass: actions of tax-opposed white suburbanites had necessitated debt financing, the welfare policies of government housing and "public" infrastructure had, again, privileged whites, and government functions had grown increasingly privatized. All of these developments eroded not only Detroit's tax base but also its ability to afford and control its own infrastructure. Water-subsidized white flight both reinforced intermunicipal racial segregation and led to the organized abandonment of the city and its water department as people and capital took flight, leaving the city owning capital-intensive infrastructure without the means to pay for it. As costs got out of hand, the city continued to provide favored treatment and full municipal services to the white neighborhoods, cities, and counties of southeastern Michigan, all the while denying them to the residents of Detroit, most of them people of color. With few exceptions, little attention has been paid to the making of this epic municipal abandonment and its devasting racialized injustices.

Detroit's eventual bankruptcy and the regional takeover of its water and sewerage department were not simply the inevitable consequence of deindustrialization and disinvestment, for every US city in the country experienced the social impacts of those global processes. Moreover, relying on global processes produces too passive an explanation, as it erases the people who made decisions to further their own financial and political interests. Many of the suburban politicians, some of them openly racist, who collaborated in undermining the department and its Black leadership went on to enjoy successful political careers lasting decades. Their racist actions were widely endorsed by white voters who kept them elected, some for decades. Many still hold their elected office. The suburban white households that voted them in also benefited from their discriminatory strategies, and many of them cast their votes for that specific purpose. They benefited by having access to affordable housing, well-paying, steady employment, and high-performing public schools. White-owned businesses got major government contracts, many of them via the old-boy network, and white elites turned their gains into political favors. In all of these transgressions, the companies themselves were never sued or criminally charged. In fact, they were rewarded with more contracts, larger campaign contributions, reelection to public office, and in John Rakolta Jr.'s case, appointed as a US ambassador. Moreover, decades of racialized media coverage, long-running court cases, and white intimidation tactics together provided a powerful discursive veil to cloud the efforts of federal, state, and suburban governments to take possession of Detroit's water and wastewater systems and disgrace its leadership. The levels of profiteering were unprecedented. Uncovering the true extent of the program of extraction is limited only by one's archival research and analysis. The archive echoes what many activists in Detroit have been saying for decades: their city was the beta test for how to strip a well-functioning city of its public goods for personal gain, and private go-getters stopped at nothing to get their way. The same could be said of Flint, Michigan.

2 Flint

THE ANVIL OF DEMOCRACY

The tragedy that occurred in Flint is a complicated story. Its magnitude alone, namely the poisoning of more than 100,000 residents, has led many to ask: How did so many people miss this? Were there no checks and balances? How did so many people not see this coming? It's worth repeating the sentiment of then Michigan attorney general Bill Schuette, who was initially reluctant to investigate the Flint water crisis. Once he did, however, even he proclaimed, "Words can barely describe this tragedy." Much of the analysis and debate surrounding the breakdown of Flint's water system has been focused on state agency and official neglect. "They missed the part when kids went back to school in September, and they were drinking poisoned water in the schools," a public school administrator told me. "It's Michigan, it's the water state, you can't let this happen [here]." But it did. Some in government say, "They just missed this," while others in the community say, "They didn't care." The most recent report by the Environmental Protection Agency (EPA) inspector general seems to echo the community's assessment, citing an utter lack of urgency on the part of state and federal authorities in the delayed response and prolonged crisis for nearly 100,000 residents.[1] In this chapter I explain how the Flint Water Crisis was no accident and not the result of an absence of checks and balances afforded by government agencies, but rather the result of enacting differing laws and practices affecting the region's urban Blacks. Moreover, as I explain, the environmental racism that culminated in Flint came about through the active participation of particular actors, groups, and networks eager to exploit the racialization of austerity politics in the state.

In some ways, I find the usefulness of structural racism to describe what happened in Flint and Detroit to be lacking. I am uncomfortable with the passiveness the concept implies. The harms imposed on the people of Flint and Detroit are not due to the functioning of some old recalcitrant system but rather the result of new technologies of race and racism imposed on an already-racialized superstructure with specific ends in mind—in this case, to exert economic and social control over majority-Black cities in Michigan. "To the cities of Flint and Detroit, we can add Benton Harbor, Highland Park, and Pontiac," a longtime city council member said to me. In every case, he believed, the state placed cities of color under its emergency manager law, not for financial reasons but to "shrink government, sell off assets to their private sector buddies, [and] frame government, [in an effort to] take over control of [Black] cities."

As in the case of the Detroit bankruptcy and water shutoffs, conservative explanations of the Flint water crisis have discounted the central role of powerful families and business elites in scaffolding and then deploying the state's technologies of racial capitalism and financial fascism. Simply stated, the Flint crisis resulted from a poorly thought-out strategy to remove Flint from Detroit water, with the explicit intention of transferring management of Flint's water system to its county, Genesee. Flint's participation was a necessary condition for the state's abandonment of Detroit and the takeover of the region's water infrastructure. "So my theory is this," explained longtime city council member Tim Jones:[2]

> Flint and in Detroit . . . controlled the water from here to Detroit. . . . [It] was controlled by Black people in Black cities. The real purpose of the emergency managers [was to] go [in and] dilute the control of the water [supply in the region]. . . . So, they came up with the Great Lakes Water Authority [to appropriate control from] the Detroit Water and Sewer, and they came up with the KWA—the Karegnondi Water Authority—to usurp control of the water that feeds Genesee and two neighboring counties (Lapeer and

Sanilac) from [the city of] Flint ... and they started making decisions through the emergency manager [authority] to break up the [water infra-structure] relationship between Flint and Detroit.

"Detroit, for them," Jones emphasized, "is Black. And the city, the munici-pality, ... Detroit Water and Sewer [were] Black. Flint, [too,] predomi-nantly Black. The election process, the mayor, who they appointed in these positions over the authority, the elected officials, the city council, we were in control of the water from here to Detroit. We decided whether we renegotiated contracts with Detroit, and when Detroit supplied Flint [with water], Flint supplied Genesee County, and they had to pay us."

The underlying strategy, as this council person made clear to me, was to strip the control of the third largest public water and sewerage utility in the United States from its two Black cities by any means necessary, even if that meant poisoning the residents of one of them.

RACIALIZATION AS TECHNOLOGY

Racialization is a *technology* of racial capitalism. White elites and white publics employ it to rationalize how the racial character of a group is somehow responsible for what ails it, all the while ignoring their own investment in white privilege.[3] When prudently inserted into debates about racialized environmental inequality, racialization works to uncou-ple race-based exploitation from capital accumulation. When the news first broke that Flint residents' water was contaminated, the Michigan Department of Environmental Quality (MDEQ) at first questioned the residents' health concerns. In a radio interview, MDEQ spokesman Brad Wurfel said, "Let me start here—anyone who is concerned about lead in the drinking water in Flint can relax." And, while the racial identity of Flint residents was never mentioned, Wurfel's candid response signaled a complete disregard not only for local concerns but for their lives as well.

Equally revealing, in terms of marginalizing Flint residents' claims, was how quickly the MDEQ labeled EPA whistle-blower Miguel Del Toral, who leaked a memo documenting high lead levels in the city's water, a "rogue employee." At the same time, the department removed two high-lead-level samples from its initial report, a step that put the drinking water system within federally mandated levels.[4] These actions, too, reveal the degree to which the health risks of this population were not a concern the government took seriously. Later, as the Flint water crisis garnered public attention, residents were depicted as bill dodgers, corrupt and generally ignorant of their water problems. These forms of racialization proved effective in hiding the state's racist agenda and its indifference regarding the multiple harms inflicted on Flint residents. "What is so special about Flint?" a US Customs and Border Protection officer asked me as I crossed the border into Michigan. "They're just trying to make this political." Trying to make something out of nothing, he and others thought.

Others in Flint were called liars. "I'm getting emails from people out of town through the [our] magazine," recalled Jan Worth Nelson, former editor of *Eastside Magazine*. After the lead crisis came to public attention, Jan recalled, the magazine started getting emails "offering us contradictory data." Many suburban onlookers depicted Flint residents to be untrustworthy. Other residents said "that this is not a real problem. This is made up. Saying this is going to turn out to be the biggest hoax." "It's a plot by Hillary," one person joked. But the racialization of the Flint water crisis did two things: first, it reduced the harms of austerity to local incompetence; and, second, it served to justify both state polices and state's timid response to the human suffering of people living in this majority-Black city. In effect, racialization functioned to rationalize austerity in Black Michigan.

.   .   .   .   .

How did those most harmed by the Flint water crisis understand what happened in their city? First, many believe that all the checks and balances were removed once Flint was placed under state-imposed emergency management. "You had the city of Flint under the control of the state through an appointed state emergency manager making the decision to use the river, and then the Department of Environmental Quality under the control of a director appointed by the governor, overseeing it," recalled Curt Guyette, a reporter with the Michigan ACLU. "So there was no independence." Second, Guyette explained, "everything could essentially be traced back to the state, and so they were covering for each other. It was the state that made the decision—the fateful decision—not to use corrosion control. It was the state that made the decision to rush into using the Flint water treatment plant when it was clearly not ready or prepared to begin the . . . complicated job of treating the Flint River water." In fact, the person running the water treatment plant vociferously objected to switching to the Flint River. The simple truth is that the city's plant "did not have the equipment in place to add the corrosion control chemicals—the orthophosphates"—to make the water safe to drink.

A CAROUSEL OF EMERGENCY MANAGERS

Flint had a total of four emergency managers between 2011 and 2017: Ed Kurtz, Mike Brown, Darnell Earley, and Gerald Ambrose. Kurtz served twice, first when appointed by Governor John Engler, from July 2002 to June 2004, and again when appointed in 2012 by Governor Rick Snyder. All four emergency managers made decisions that advanced state and suburban interests, including the construction of a new pipeline from Lake Huron as part of Flint's financial restructuring. Many in Flint were outraged at county drain commissioner Jeff Wright and the emergency managers for saddling the city with a staggering $600 million more in debt to undertake this project. But as I detail below, the roles of the city elite, the Land Bank, and the Charles Stewart Mott Foundation—the collective "city fathers"—also contributed to the city's financial crisis. Their combined influence helped bring about a massive segregationist effort to seize critical water infrastructure—Black infrastructure—in southeastern Michigan.

"I will tell you this much," a former city administrator told me over lunch at a Coney Island restaurant: "Mike Brown was the first [real] emergency manager we had." In his role as temporary mayor of Flint, from February 2009 to August 2009, Brown was supposed to get "some specific things done for the state . . . in terms of contract negotiation." But he wasn't able to do so. "After he left there [the mayor's office], he went to work for the Mott Foundation. He was on their payroll for two years. Then, what happened there is, a deal got cut" with the Mott Foundation, and Mike Brown "became the CEO of Prima Civitas [a think tank based in East Lansing, Michigan]. And then the Mott Foundation sent Mike Brown a $3 million investment with Prima Civitas." There was a meeting at Genesee Regional Chamber of Commerce, the ex–city administrator recalled, between Mike Brown and Ridgway White, CEO and president of the Mott Foundation; Tim Herman, CEO of the Chamber of Commerce; Fred Shaltz from the Uptown Redevelopment Group; and state treasurer Andy Dillon. (Dillon would soon step down.)

The parties met to discuss who was going to be the next emergency manager in Flint. These "city fathers" decided that it would again be Mike Brown. "I had breakfast with Rich Baird," the right-hand man to the governor, a former administrator explained to me. "and I asked him, 'So how did you arrive at making Mike Brown emergency manager? He has no fiscal background, he has never managed a municipality, he really don't understand that.' He said, 'Well, the Mott Foundation and the Chamber of Commerce wanted him.' So we said, 'If you want him, you can have him.'" The governor didn't even meet with Brown before he became emergency manager. Brown was hired to complete some projects the governor wanted the Mott Foundation to fund. "So the deal that Mike cut was that economic and development funds [from the state would] go from the city to the Chamber [of Commerce]." The same way that the Mott Foundation cut the deal that "avoid[ed] having emergency managers being put into Flint school systems," as had happened in Detroit. Duane Miller, who served as interim city administrator under Michael Brown, was later named executive vice president of core initiatives at the Genesee Regional Chamber of Commerce, from which position he made sure everything ran according to the Mott's plan.

However, Brown's appointment as Flint's emergency manager was cut short due to a technicality in state law.[5] The Emergency Financial Assistance Loan Board now appointed Ed Kurtz to be the new emergency manager. The city council protested, with council president Scott Kincaid arguing that the city's financial condition had improved and it no longer met the criteria spelled out in the law. But Kincaid's position fell on deaf ears. Kurtz had served as the city's emergency manager under Governor John Engler from July 2002 to June 2004. During that first stint, Kurtz raised water bills 11 percent in order to pay off the city's debts. During his sequel performance, Kurtz appointed Mike Brown as the city administrator. "So, yes, Ed Kurtz is just a shell," explained a previous city employee, "because, what it did [Kurtz's appointment] is it enabled Mike Brown, as the city administrator, to implement everything that he was doing" with the folks who were in control of the city. Committed to submitting a balanced budget, Kurtz fired 20 percent of the city's workforce, doubled its water rates, and outsourced its garbage collection services.

Ed Kurtz left in October 2013, and Darnell Earley was appointed as the city's third emergency manager. Mike Brown also resigned as city administraor that same month. When I asked why, the former city employee replied, "Well, word has it, the governor wasn't pleased with his performance as the city administrator and as the emergency manager. . . . The governor didn't really want him. But, because the Mott Foundation was involved, he kept it [his position]. But his performance got so bad" that he had to be recalled. Particularly alarming to the governor was Brown's hiring of Barnett Jones as Flint's public safety administrator. The *Detroit Free Press* soon discovered that Jones was already employed as the chief security and integrity officer for the Detroit Water and Sewerage Department (DWSD), in which position he earned an annual salary of $138,750. As Flint's public safety administrator, he had wide authority over all the city's public safety operations, including police, firefighting, communications, and related services. For this, Jones made an *additional* $135,000 and received a city vehicle and laptop, a cell phone stipend, an allowance for uniform and equipment, and other benefits. Officials said his salary was paid with grant money from the Mott Foundation. When questioned about this gross misuse of city funds, Brown candidly replied, "I guess you could say Jones was burning the candle at both ends."[6]

When appointed Flint emergency manager, Darnell Earley was about to be fired from his position as city manager by the Saginaw City Council, the former city administrator told me. So becoming emergency manager was a windfall for him. "And there was a feeling that the governor realized the optics of imposing white managers on Black people," the administrator went on. "So the story goes that one of the governor's lynch men, Harvey Holland, contacted Earley with this new opportunity. At first, it was rumored that Earley complained about emergency management to the governor, saying 'the way you are approaching this, you are devastating cities.' So, I was surprised that he took the job, but I guess he's going to pay into him," then that might "change my mind." Earley was paid enough to take the job despite his concerns about emergency management.

Darnell Earley was appointed Flint's third emergency manager in October 2013 and served until January 2015, when the water crisis was brought to national attention. Earley's budget for fiscal year 2015 cut thirty-six police officer positions and nineteen firefighter jobs, in addition to raising water and sewer rates by 6.5 percent. Although previous emergency managers had all but solidified the master plan to disconnect from Detroit's water system and move to the Karegnondi Water Authority, it was Darnell Earley who oversaw the switch to the Flint River for its interim water supply. At a city council meeting, Earley confidently claimed that much work had gone into preparing the city of Flint to eliminate its dependence on the Detroit Water and Sewage Department. This strategy was a "huge step in the right direction," he claimed, because it gave the city "the choice to better control the cost" of its water. Yet, contrary to this pronouncement, Flint residents continued to pay the highest price for water in Genesee County. It was Earley who turned down the offer to continue to purchase water from DWSD after the previous contract termed out. Yet, contrary to written evidence, Earley and spokespersons for the governor's office continued to claim that it was the DWSD that cut Flint off from its water supply.[7] After his appointment in Flint ended, Earley was assigned to the position of emergency manager of Detroit Public Schools.

"In early 2015, a church ministers' group in Detroit working with ministers up in Flint told my supervisor about water problems in Flint," recalled Curt Guyette, with the ACLU of Michigan. "I think the first meeting I went to involving an emergency manager was in March of 2015." Gerald Ambrose, former city financial officer under Michael Brown and Ed Kurtz, was now Flint's fourth emergency manager, and it was his signed order that cleared the way for the switch to the Flint River.[8] As soon as the switch occurred in April 2014, complaints started. The water coming from residents' taps "looked bad, smelled bad, [and] tasted bad." Then there were the series of boil-water notices because of *E. coli* in the drinking water. "They just didn't know how to treat the water," explained Guyette. "They [had] never[had] to treat the water [before]. They got the water pretreated from Detroit, and they would add some chlorine to it and send it on its way. They went from that to the very complicated job of treating the river water, which changes all the time." The chemistry of the water "changes based on the amount of rainfall." In the spring, snow melt enters the river, along with salt from road residue. The temperature also fluctuates. "All of those things affect how the water gets treated and they just didn't know how to do it. . . . To deal with the *E. coli* problem," Guyette said, "they upped the amount of chlorine," but that created high levels of a carcinogenic by-product of chlorine called trihalomethanes (TTHMs) in the drinking water for months. Yet the emergency manager and state officials said nothing. In fact, the Michigan Department of Environmental Quality let two six-month monitoring periods pass before advising the public about the TTHMs. Some say the MDEQ staff misinterpreted the Lead and Copper Rule (LCR) of the federal Safe Drinking Water Act (1974); others say they were hoping the high concentrations of TTHMs would dissipate with time. One thing was certain, their inaction subordinated the well-being and basic needs of this majority-Black city to the state's fiscal agenda. "So it wasn't until, I think, January of 2015," Guyette continued,

> that they disclosed the fact that there were high levels of this carcinogen in the water and that was really on top of all the other problems. . . . People were complaining [that] their hair was falling out in clumps, and they were getting these strange rashes. . . . Animals were dying, which now in retrospect could be attributed to the lead contamination because one of the things [with] lead, among other things, it causes miscarriages.

A City Hall meeting in March revealed the degree to which Black lives mattered in an era of austerity politics. At the meeting, people in the audience asked Emergency Manager Ambrose, "Why didn't you tell us about the TTHMs?" Ambrose replied, "As soon as we found out about it, we started to address the issue." And people in the audience responded, "Yeah, but that is not telling us about it. Why didn't you tell us about it?" And again Ambrose repeated, "As soon as we found out about it, we started to address the issue." "But that is not telling us about it!" Flint residents insisted. "Why didn't you tell us about it!" they repeated. To which Ambrose eventually replied, "Well, I'm telling you now." "That was kind of a crystallizing moment for me," a member in the audience that night later told me. "No elected official would ever talk to their constituents in such a cold and callus, disrespectful way."

Residents at the meeting repeatedly pleaded with the emergency manager to return their water supply to the DWSD. To which he replied that the water in Flint was "safe by all standards." But records obtained through the Freedom of Information Act revealed that Ambrose made these statements two weeks after he had been told by health officials that an outbreak of Legionnaires' disease in Flint was suspected to have been caused by Flint River water. In other words, what Emergency Manager Ambrose really meant was that *the water in Flint was good enough for Black people to drink*. When Flint city council members voted in another meeting in March to move the city back to Detroit water, Ambrose called the move "incomprehensible," again reflecting the extent to which he devalued the well-being and basic needs of nonwhites. When Al Mooney, interim city treasurer asked at the meeting, "Can we hook up again to Detroit water?" Ambrose answered, "We can if we have a money tree . . . so that is the answer to that question."

PREDATORY AUSTERITY

The pricing of water is a central story line linking the city's emergency management measures and water crisis, though, for the most part, it has remained in the background. In an attempt to reduce labor costs associated with the manual measuring of residents' water meters, the city in the early 2000 purchased an automated meter-reading system. Transponders on the city's waste management trucks would read the meters automatically, providing accurate and current water usage data without having to pay human readers. When the first emergency manager came into power, however, one of his first directives was to sell off all the waste management trucks to a third-party company. Shortly after that sale, the waste management company went bankrupt, and the city was no longer able to measure residents' water consumption. "Most of the water bills . . . are [now] estimated, because most the water meters don't work," explained a city employee. "I was in the process of trying to negotiate with a new company to replace all of the meters" when the emergency manager put an end to that strategy. "What the emergency manager did is he increased the water and sewer rates. That's when the water bills, like in my case, for me and my wife, went from what is normally $80 or $90 a month, to $250 a month."

The emergency manager also imposed a one-time $400 fee to turn city water on or off. In January 2011, Flint residents saw their water and sewer rates increase by 25 percent and 22 percent, respectively. The following September, the emergency manager again raised the city's water and sewer rates, this time by 35 percent. In total, water and sewer rates were raised by 57 percent in 2011 alone. "So, you as a consumer, you say, f– you, I am not going to pay it [because it is inaccurate and unfair]," the former city employee recalled thinking. Flint residents were being charged the highest water and sewer fees of any city or town in the country. In response to this escalation, Flint city council president Scott Kincaid filed suit against the emergency manager–controlled city seeking to repeal the rate increases and claiming that the city had violated the Michigan constitution by raising its water rates twice without the council's authorization. In addition to raising water and sewer rates illegally, the suit alleged, the city transferred the money raised from the water and sewer fund—in excess of $15 million—into the city of Flint's general fund and used them to pay for its "general obligations," including operating expenses and bond obligations.[9] Again, the emergency manager deemed affordability of water for Flint residents secondary to repaying bondholders. "We have to do what we have to do to balance the budget," explained Mike Brown in response to outrage against his 57 percent rate increase.

"All of the problem that a lot of the people in the city have," the city employee told me, "is that the water rates that the emergency manager were charging people in the city wasn't the same water rates they were charging people in the county." For most white people in Genesee County, he said, water bills were $40 to $45 per month.

> But people in the city are getting charged $200 in water bills and that was a major problem. But how do you voice that when you have no voice? How can [the] city council voice that when they have no power? People who could leave, left. You have around about 12% of them have moved just across the street, to Beecher. Because the difference in living in Beecher is ... $50 a month for water instead of ... $150.

Those remaining—those who couldn't afford to pick up and move—were forced to shoulder the increased financial burden that came with urban austerity. The situation amounted to redlining all over again. In 2009, the US Census Bureau estimated the proportion of people in Flint living below the poverty line in Flint to be 34.9%. By 2016, it was over 40 percent, constituting the second-highest rate in the country.[10] By that time, Flint residents also had the most expensive water in the country, with an average annual water bill of $864.32.[11]

Inability to pay these high rate resulted in household water shutoffs and liens for past-due bills. More than 2,000 water and sewer customers were scheduled to have their services terminated as of May 2, 2011.[12] As a result of the liens, many households fell into delinquency on their property taxes. Increases in the pricing of water were a major factor in contributing to mortgage foreclosures as unpaid utility liens were added to the property taxes. This was another way emergency managers targeted low-income Black homeowners in order to balance their annual budgets. In April 2015, months after a state of emergency was declared, the city mailed out 5,503 letters to residents for water and sewer charges in arrears. Two years later, that number had grown to 8,002 for a total of $5,806,448.62 of delinquent water and sewer charges.[13] These lost revenues, however, were advanced by the Genesee County treasurer in the form of delinquent tax anticipation notes for unpaid taxes.[14] Each year the Genesee County treasurer advanced funds to the city based on the number of foreclosures the city had on its books, and that number grew steadily as unpaid–utility bill liens were added to households' property taxes. In effect, the county incentivized the city to foreclose on residents' homes, having particularly devastating consequences for Black homeownership. In 2008, Flint resident Teddy Robertson wrote, 53 percent of the homes in Flint were owned by investment companies, 29 percent by real estate companies, and 16 percent by private individuals.[15]

Moreover, the growing arrears in household water and sewer charges added to property taxes meant that each year's charge-backs from the county for monies advanced to the city would be greater than the previous year's. "I think the county was worried now," a city administrator observed, "because in attaching the water and sewer bills to property taxes, it was going to cause a major problem." However, "if the emergency manager had been doing their job, they would have noticed these things," he explained. *"They created this problem."*

"If you had an emergency manager that had a background in fiscal management, they would have questioned the advances" from the county, the administrator asserted. The manager would have seen that the gap in the advances could pose a problem for balancing the deficit, "especially because they knew there was a [legal] case against the city for the excessive charging of water bills to the constituents." But, instead of helping to balance the city's annual budget, the county advances functioned as a form of predatory lending, which the emergency managers facilitated.

Realizing that the "books aren't balancing," the emergency managers now took a different route, the administrator explained. "They . . . came up with this brilliant idea of maxing out the amount of mills [millage] that the city had to pay." A millage is the rate (mills per dollar) used to calculate local property taxes. Millages are usually expressed mathematically; for example, one mill is equal to one one-thousandth of a dollar—or $1 for every $1,000—of property value. Historically, the city of Flint had always kept its mill rate at around 16, or $16 for every $1,000 of property value. "What the emergency manager saw was an opportunity to increase revenues by maxing out the mills, charging 21 mills," or $21 per $1,000 of property value. This new "public safety millage" would generate $5.3 million per year for five years. The emergency manager at the time, Ed Kurtz, told constituents that revenue from this increase would be used to stabilize police and fire staffing. "And he pitched this [idea] to get support [from] the Black community because that is where you had the highest crime rate" in the city. "So it was overwhelmingly supported, and Black people did it on the basis that they were told they would get more police officers. . . . But they never did. So they [city administrators] take the $5.3 million, and it goes . . . to balancing off the operating budget."

"So even though you may balance the budget," another city officer said, "it has nothing to do with you coming into deficit. [The] deficit is still there. . . . And the purpose of having an emergency manager is to eliminate the deficit. . . . And you need to verify this," he insisted. "When I left, there was an $8.5 million deficit. Five years after I left, it is somewhere between $8 to $9 million deficit."

"The reality is," he continued,

you can't do it, because when you move from 200,000 [in population] down to 102,000, you lost 98,000 jobs, the income tax revenues and the property tax revenues—it's 50 percent of your population. Property tax revenue, business tax revenue, income tax revenue—you cannot make up for that. So the problems that most municipalities have is not because they have had corrupted management . . . it is a result of our economy . . . that devastated these cities.

And all the emergency manager law did in Flint, my interlocutor believed, was to make matters worse. For example, the managers sold off assets to balance the annual budget. As he explained: "A building is an asset. So, when you sell off the assets, then how does he balance the budget? When you sell off an asset and get money less than what the asset is worth, what you end up doing as part of balancing the budget is having [fewer] assets. When you sell off those assets—and there are major assets in some cases—you give them away [and get practically nothing in return]." For example, the Uptown Reinvestment Corporation, a 501(c) (3) organization, bought downtown Flint's nineteen-story Genesee Towers (after its condemnation) from the city for $1 (with a plan at the time to use Neighborhood Stabilization Program funds). Another resident commented, "I remember, we were joking that we were going to open a dollar real estate store downtown. Buy a building for a buck. Because they were selling so many of those buildings for a buck."

Genesee Towers was Flint's tallest building, and some say its ugliest, so many were happy to see it demolished in 2013. The city condemned the nineteen-story vacant building in 2004, as it was not only ugly but dangerous as well. Mayor Donald J. "the Don" Williamson and the building's owner, V. Kumar Vemulapalli, agreed to enter arbitration in 2006 to determine the value of the property. "So, long story short," explained a longtime city resident, "it went to court, the judge ruled in favor of the owner, and we had to cough up $8 million."

"And we got a special tax assessment on our tax bill for that," another resident explained. "Fast forward to the emergency manager, Mike Brown," she continued. "He sold that building to Uptown Reinvestment Corporation for a dollar" after the residents of Flint were forced to pay $8 million for it. To pay for the building's demolition, the emergency manager appropriated federal money from the Neighborhood Stabilization

Program of the Department of Housing and Urban Development. The federal program provided emergency assistance to local governments to "purchase foreclosed or abandoned homes and to rehabilitate, resell, or redevelop these homes in order to stabilize neighborhoods and stem the decline of house values of neighboring homes."[16] In total, the city of Flint received $4,224,621 in emergency assistance from the Neighborhood Stabilization Program. "That's right," adds the lifelong resident, "they took federal dollars that were supposed to go to the neighborhoods" and used it "to tear that building down." "We paid for it," commented another resident. "Somebody said, that is the most expensive park bench in the country," to which other residents I was interviewing in the room laughed. And that was just "one of the many assets that were given away," another resident commented.

"This revolving door of people" serving as emergency manager, yet another resident said, meant "you didn't even know who was running the show at any given time." "When Ed Kurtz kept reappearing, it kept reminding me of *Apocalypse Now*," a women joked. To which another person responded, "I love the smell of Flint in the morning." The sobering point here is the extent to which unfettered austerity facilitates the unequal exchange of both resources and debt along racial lines. And when the reality is too hard to stomach, many residents turn to comedy to cope with a system that renders their lives cheap and expendable.

Other deals were also cut by emergency managers for the benefit of the city's elite, which continued to shift the city's increasing tax burden to its residents. For example, the city asked the Mott Foundation "for three or four million dollars to bring it [the water treatment plant] up to snuff," a city administrator recalled. But the "Mott Foundation wouldn't give them the money," so "the emergency manager, Mike Brown, . . . sells off the assets [in this case Atwood Stadium] to Kettering, and then the Mott Foundation gives Kettering $8 million to do what they need to do at the state. That is the kind of stuff that goes on around here." "So the city of Flint, for all intents and purposes," the Flint administrator told me, "should have never went into emergency management. . . . If you look at the books, they should have never gone into emergency management. And I fought this." But his and others' concerns were discounted. Emergency managers told them, "[W]e don't have to listen to you." Other managers candidly stated, "I don't care where you go" because "the governor controls every court all the way down to the State Supreme Court." In other words, emergency managers were not appointed by the state to balance the books but rather to leverage the city's financial crisis by raising water rates, increasing mill rates, and auctioning off derelect buildings. And this strategy was premised on explicitly subordinating the lives and livelihoods of Flint residents to the extractive objectives of city fathers in liquidating the city's assets.

3 Defending the Karegnondi

If the real reason the state appointed four successive emergency managers in Flint wasn't to reduce the city's debt, what was it? Many believe their mission was never about saving money but about removing the region's water supply from the control of two majority-Black cities. First, emergency managers would break a thirty-year water delivery contract with the Detroit Water and Sewer Department, effectively depriving the struggling city of its largest water customer. Second, despite conflicting data about the merits of switching, Flint's emergency managers remained adamant in their promotion of the Karegnondi Water Authority (KWA), requiring a massive investment in the construction of eighty miles of pipeline and pumping stations to transport water directly from Lake Huron to Genesee, Lapeer, and Sanilac counties, including the city of Flint.[1] By contract, the city of Flint purchased water directly from the DWSD for more than thirty years. Flint then resold the water to the Genesee County Drain Commissioner, who then sold it to municipalities in the county. The county wanted water independence for decades and has repeatedly cited the high cost of Detroit water, a complaint that engendered much public anger toward the majority-Black city and its water department. It was true that Flint's water rates had doubled in recent years, but that was because emergency managers had raised the rates far above wholesale prices paid to DWSD in order to balance the Flint municipal budget. Yet the rhetoric of "greedy Detroit" worked in gaining support for the KWA, particularly among white suburbanites in Genesee County.

"Back in the 1940s," a local historian told me, "the county wanted to originally have the KWA because they didn't want any water from Detroit. There has always been a racial divide. They wanted their own water. And the county resented having to get their water from the city [of Detroit]." So local politicians came up with the idea of building a pipeline directly from Lake Huron. Several attempts failed, the most notorious one occurring in 1963 when a couple of county commissioners were indicted for profiteering. The plan was then shelved for a long time, in part due to its ugly past in the county. In the late 1980s, backers in the county approached Woodrow Stanley, the mayor of Flint with the idea, but he felt it wasn't in the City's best interest. Then in 2007, Genessee County Drain Commissioner Jeff Wright hired political consultant Sam Riddle in a $2,000-a-month contract to help convince Detroit to back the planned pipeline. After Riddle was convicted of conspiring to bribe Detroit city officials on another matter, Detroit turned down Wright's proposal and renewed its contractual agreement with Flint, noting that the county had, by seeking its own independent contract, always tried to take away DWSD'S largest water customer. Moreover, Detroit was not about to aid in the county's racist politics, knowing all too well that the city would suffer dearly from the county's water independence.

A retired member of the Metropolitan Home Builders Association (MHBA) explained why access to water became such a central economic and political issue in the outlying counties. "Genesee County was growing in all directions up until the 1980 recession," he told me. Thereafter, "all the growth started going to the south [of the county], as southern Genesee County was becoming more of a suburb of metro Detroit." So almost all the housing development in the county was occurring in the townships of Grand Blanc, Goodridge, and Davidson. "Even Fenton, Argentine, and Mundy townships," located further east of Interstate 75, "were booming," he said. "Then it really began to pick up in the nineties . . . [as] it just all of a sudden became very, very convenient for people to live in the southern part of Genesee County." Land was much cheaper than in Oakland County, "so it was really good for development" in Genessee County. Infrastructure, particularly roads and water, were key to building these suburban havens. A short drive south from Flint down US Highway 23 is Ann Arbor, home to the University of Michigan. A slightly longer drive down the newly reconstructed Interstate 75 brings one into Oakland County and then downtown Detroit. And while everyone in Michigan likes to complain about the state of the roads and the price of water,[2] these two conduits of public infrastructure changed the course of suburban development in the region while denying equal investment to neighboring majority-Black cities like Flint and Detroit.

"Listen to this one," the former development director told me:

> When I was development director for the county, we had on average 175 housing starts per month, 2,000 annually. I also remember one data point, when you had that many housing starts, you have another $16 million in furnishings that people built. And I think places like Las Vegas were like maybe 500 housing starts per month; 575 comes to mind. But, nonetheless, what we had was impressive. We became a bedroom community to southeast Michigan in a matter of years. Even as General Motors was closing, the housing [market] . . . kept us afloat and said that we were stable, even with the announcement of the Buick City closing. We had Moody's [Investor Services] officials riding with us. We gave them a tour [showing them] where all of these beautiful subdivisions were being built.

"What was Moody's interest in it?" I asked.

"Well, because they had to do the credit rating for the county," he responded. "Yes sir. We had to do our general obligation kind of bonds, both Standard and Poor's and Moody's." The bond-rating agencies were also shown "the best housing in Flint—East Court Street area, near Mott Community College. We took them through there" as well, the former director remembered. And, as long as the roads were paved and water remained cheap, the exclusively white housing market in suburban Genesee County would remain promising as a tax base, and Moody's and other bond rating agencies would continue to rate the county's loan portfolio composition and credit quality favorably, even as the housing markets and credit values of the majority-Black neighborhoods were eroded in the process. For those investors looking to the future, wresting direct control of the county's water supply was imperative, even if doing so necessitated a new phase of redlining.

"It was a good system," explained the former MHBA member about the KWA. "Let me tell you a great story about that. Way back around the turn of the century, . . . Genesee County's drain commissioner at the time, Ken Hardin (before Jeff Wright), . . . wanted our own water system." Hardin served as the Genesee County Drain Commissioner from 1997 to 2000 and campaigned for the county's own pipeline from Lake Huron. "And the Detroit Water and Sewerage Department," the former MHBA member went on, "they wanted us to stay with them" and started reaching out to members in the county, even the Builders Association. At the time, "Oakland County wanted to join with Genesee County in the Lake Huron pipeline that they were developing." And then Detroit cut a deal with Oakland County whereby it would stay with Detroit. "Then Detroit went to work on trying to keep Genesee County as a customer."

"What did they do?" I asked.

"They made a lot of promises that I really didn't want them to keep," he replied. "Anyway, Genesee County really wanted its own water supply and I think in the long run, it's probably a good thing it did."

"Why didn't you want Oakland County to join the KWA?" I asked.

"Why didn't I like it?" he echoed. "Because I liked the fact that there was no water line in northern Oakland County. For example, we had a couple of developments in Genesee County that fall over into the crossline [the county line] into Holly Township. Well, those are on the Genesee County water system. I would much rather keep them all there. It's basically, . . . more than anything else, [about] who is going to control growth and development [in the area]."

Having access to water meant that Genesee County could control growth and development not only within its boundaries but in other counties too. The fact that Oakland was unable to build housing in between Clarkston and the county line meant that Genesee County could corner the suburban housing market along the I-75 and I-69 corridors. Both the county development Officer and the building association representative I talked to insisted that water-driven housing starts kept the county afloat. The County Drain Commissioner then, Jeff Wright, wholly agreed. It was Genesee County that would clearly gain the most from the pipeline construction. Lapeer and Sanilac counties mostly used well water and didn't need to purchase water from the KWA. Ken Hardin, who had championed

the KWA before losing the commissioner job to Jeff Wright, later decided
that the economic forces at work in Flint and Genesee County, including
the decline in population and industry, had doomed the project forever.[3]
The new water pipeline from Lake Huron ultimately cost a staggering
$600 million, a debt Hardin said the county was in no position to
shoulder.[4]

WATER GRABBING

In addition to cutting its ties to Detroit, the county knew it stood to make
hundreds of millions of dollars by having its own water supply. The county
now ramped up its efforts to end its decades-old relationship with the
iconic city. The influence of Jeff Wright is undeniable. In his dual role as
county drain commissioner and KWA CEO, it seemed as if he would stop
at nothing to build the eighty-mile pipeline to link Flint and the county
directly to Lake Huron.

"So, fast forward, it's 2010," a Flint city employee told me. "Jeff Wright
... approaches Flint mayor Dayne Walling about the Karegnondi pipeline." For his support, Wright offered Walling the position of chair of the
KWA Board of Trustees. "Dayne lit up like a Christmas tree," the employee
said, and immediately took the offer and agreed to support the pipeline
project.

"The emergency manager and interim mayor of the city, Mike Brown,
had been behind the KWA project from the very beginning. . . . [He was]
the one who actually cut the deal with the county." Brown held a public
hearing, recalled a Flint resident, but it was just for show, "trying to justify
to the community why Karegnondi made sense. . . . So most of us said, no,
that doesn't make any sense. It doesn't add up costwise and from a logical
standpoint, it doesn't make any sense," either. The KWA project was con-
servatively estimated to cost $285 million dollars, and Flint was respon-
sible for 30% of the expected costs, or $85 million. In addition, the KWA
commitment obligated the city to a multimillion dollar upgrade of its old
water treatment plant (WTP). So people wanted to know how the city,
which was under emergency management because of its financial woes,
could afford this costly project.

Moreover, at the request of State Treasurer Andy Dillon, the engineering firm of Tucker, Young, Jackson & Tull, Inc. (TYJT), performed an analysis of the water supply options the city was considering. The firm's final report raised concerns about KWA cost estimates and system governance, predicting $25 million in additional costs to Flint.[5] The first of the two water purveying options the consultants evaluated was the KWA system, and the second was continued supply from DWSD. TYJT's analysis indicated that the DWSD option would cost less for Flint. As for the other option, the report noted that, in addition to costing more, KWA would require Flint and the Genesee County Drain Commissioner to make large capital investments for the system's construction. The report also noted that the KWA supply system offered less redundancy to Flint than the current DWSD system, and warned of additional costs and risk considerations given that the final costs and time needed to complete the KWA were unknown. The report also drew attention to the challenges for smaller systems like the KWA, versus larger systems (DWSD), to pay for future unfunded mandates and regulations.

In addition to all of these financial red flags, the consultants made two additional points. First, the KWA supply option ran counter to the state treasury's Competitive Grant Assistance Program, which was established to help communities consolidate their services and save money. In removing Flint and Genesee County, along with other potential customers, from the DWSD to create another water system, the KWA option contradicted the program's guidelines.[6] Second, and more important for Flint's autonomy, was the fact that in joining the KWA, Flint would effectively turn over the control of its water supply to the surrounding white-majority counties. For while the city would be responsible for 30 percent of the project's construction costs, it would hold only a minority vote on the KWA board, which included trustees representing Lapeer County, the city of Lapeer, and Sanilac County.[7]

Perhaps to get a more favorable evaluation of the KWA plan, Emergency Manager Ed Kurtz sought a second report. He commissioned Rowe Engineering, a subcontractor of Lockwood, Andrews & Newnam (LAN), which had already written previous reports—by both single and multiple authors—in favor of the KWA, to write another one. Not surprisingly, Rowe's less detailed analysis recommended the KWA proposal, and it alone became the basis for Kurtz's adamant support of the KWA pipeline. Kurtz also approved a sole-source contract with LAN to prepare the Flint WTP to handle full-time treatment of Flint River water until the pipeline was fully operational. On March 25, 2013, Emergency Manager Kurtz conveniently gave powers back to the mayor and city council to vote on the resolution to buy water from KWA and contract with the authority to build a pipeline from Lake Huron to Genesee County. And with the limited information provided to them, the council voted 7–1 to leave DWSD and go to KWA for their the city's supply. The vote was largely ceremonial, as the emergency manager had already decided the city's fate many years prior. The city council, however, amended the resolution from the 18 millions of gallons per day (MGD), proposed by the emergency manager, to 16 MGD, saving the city $2 million. Kurtz, however, contracted the original proposal for 18 MGD, ensuring higher costs for the city of Flint, both in the short and in the long run.[8] On April 16, Flint emergency manager Ed Kurtz signed the agreement with KWA and informed the state treasurer of his action. The decision was officially announced on May 1, 2013.[9]

A SWEETHEART DEAL

"Actually," Flint resident Dean Jones[10] explained to me, "all of this was [a grand scheme] to be able to get a certain amount of water to the middle of the state." And KWA CEO Jeff Wright, for many the man behind the curtain, knew that if he based the move only on the population of the three counties—Genesee, Lapeer, and Sanilac—"they would have had to make the pipes smaller in diameter," in which case his dream to have Genesee County not only water independent but water rich could not have been justified financially. "So they had to get Flint to buy in, to join in, so that they could add that population, so they could make the pipe diameter that you wanted." Without Flint's commitment the pipeline was not financially viable, either. But "Flint couldn't afford it," Jones added, because it "had a crappy credit rating, and so they did this deal where Flint says, 'We promise we'll use that water to clean up a solid waste dump,' and in exchange we were allowed to borrow that money that we didn't have the credit to be able to borrow. So it's predatory lending from the state to the city. Huge!"

The deal, which has been referred to as sweetheart, was concocted Miller Canfield, the law firm advising KWA on its bond issue; its attorneys worked with officials in the state treasury and the Michigan Department of Environmental Quality (MDEQ). Because Flint was in receivership, it was subject to the Home Rule City Act, which limited the city's ability to borrow funds. However, the act contained an exception, or "loophole," according to Miller Canfield attorney Dan Massaron, in the form of an administrative consent order (ACO). ACOs are issued by state agencies to force local governments to fix urgent environmental problems, such as those caused by fire, flood, or some other calamity. ACOs also permitted the legislative body to borrow for relief, even if that meant exceeding existing debt limits, to alleviate the threat to the city's inhabitants and property.[11] In an email to Gerald Ambrose on which Emergency Manager Darnell Earley and others were copied, Massaron wrote, "If the KWA project is done to comply with an ACO, the debt associated with the project would not 'count' toward the City's debt limit." The contrived ACO called for a relatively inexpensive restoration of wastewater lagoons outside the city's treatment plant, and by linking the lagoon restoration to the KWA pipeline project as a whole, Flint was able to secure its portion of the financing for the pipeline construction. The bond attorneys were integral not only in crafting the justification for the use of an ACO to circumvent Flint's state-imposed debt limit but also in drafting the language of the order itself. In so doing, they committed the broke city to making additional and costly improvements to its water treatment plant and, more important, to using the Flint River as a temporary source until the KWA water was available.

Many people point the finger at Jeff Wright, for obvious reasons. Some argue that without the Karegnondi Water Authority there would have been no Flint water crisis. In 2016, the Flint Water Advisory Task Force (FWATF), which was commissioned by the governor, recommended a "complete and thorough review of the development and approval of KWA and of the City of Flint's commitments to KWA water purchases."[12] Genesee County drain commissioner and KWA CEO Wright admitted to the FWATF that he had known few details about the negotiations that preceded the bond issue. But that is really difficult to believe. Wright was no stranger to controversy. In an article outlining some of his business dealings, *West Michigan Politics* reported that Wright had been the target of an FBI public corruption investigation in 2004. Instead of facing charges, however, he became an informant in the FBI's investigation of political consultant Sam Riddle, the man whom he hired to help drum up support in Detroit for his planned new pipeline. Later, in 2005, federal agents confiscated Wright's campaign finance contribution documents from the county clerk's office as part of a public corruption investigation of Burton city officials. Wright had been accused of money laundering by Burton developer Blake Rizzo, who later pleaded guilty to bribery and misdemeanor insurance fraud charges.[13] *West Michigan Politics* and other news sources reported that whether Wright was a target of the federal investigation was unclear, and he was never charged in the case. Former Genesee County prosecutor Arthur Busch told the *Detroit Free Press* in 2016 that "he wanted to charge Wright with money laundering [related to campaign contributions] in 2005 but was unable to do so because of legal issues involving the statute of limitations."[14] What many people, including Busch, find so surprising is that Wright has avoided any prose-cutorial scrutiny given his influence in getting the pipeline project completed.

SHOW ME THE MONEY

Jeff Wright's campaign contribution records reveal a who's who of poten-tial benefactors of the pipeline project, including L. D'Agostini & Sons, Inc., LAN, and Rowe. L. D'Agostini & Sons was named in a federal lawsuit with Detroit mayor Kwame Kilpatrick for overcharging on a sewer repair project in Sterling Heights. And for their involvement in the Flint water crisis, both LAN and Rowe are facing criminal charges and civil lawsuits. Another donor worth noting is James Rosendahl, a former Synagro execu-tive who served jail time and a fine of $200,000 for bribing public officials in Detroit to sign a $1.1 billion sludge removal contract.[15] As campaign contributions to Jeff Wright from potential KWA beneficiaries poured in, his support for the project remained steadfast, and, like the state-appointed emergency managers, he would stop at nothing to see its completion. A *West Michigan Politics* investigation of Wright's campaign finance records revealed that as CEO of KWA he wrote himself "loan repayment" checks and provided corresponding donations to the campaigns of "local and state officials like Dayne Walling, chairman of the KWA board, and [Flint mayor] Sheldon Neely in order to get their support for KWA."[16]

Wright has always vowed that the KWA was never about politics but about economics. Speaking at the Flint city council meeting on March 25, 2013, Wright insisted "that there will be several million-dollar cost reductions to all the communities involved."[17] However, research by Dan Casey-Dunn at Michigan State University's Institute of Public Policy and Social Research indicates that "the cost savings offered by such a switch were questionable."[18] In addition, recall that Tucker, Young, Jackson & Tull (TYJT), in its report commissioned by the state to compare the two water options, found the KWA plan would cost Flint $25 million more.[19] Both studies pose a serious challenge to the recommendation that Flint leave the DWSD because it would save the city money in the future. Flint residents too were asking questions. A member of the Flint Democracy Defense League told me that when Dayne Walling became mayor, "we were trying to get him to explain what the Karegnondi Water Authority was, and he wouldn't. He just said he was for it and he was really trying to push it through."

"But that was one of the first things we were really suspicious and fighting about," she explained. "Now we had no idea that it would be connected to the privatization of water and to the eventual poisoning of water and lead and Legionnaires. But . . . we were trying to get answers. Who is it for? Who are the bondholders? Whose interest is it serving? Because we really didn't trust that it was going to serve the citizens' interests."

"And as we found out" more about the project, she continued, she and other League members started to become convinced that "there actually is a master plan; we are just not privy to it. And it's kind of pieced out to us strategically, so that you're constantly playing catch-up." For League members and other citizens of Flint, the KWA was simply "a corporate bid to privatize the Great Lakes."

Yet Wright's defense of the KWA was steadfast, and his rebuttals to anyone daring enough to raise questions or contradict his narrative were scathing. In his written testimony to the Michigan Civil Rights Commission's Flint water crisis hearings, Wright wrote that the only reason the TYJT report commissioned by the state was not in favor of the KWA was "the substantial amount of work it does for DWSD," which, in his opinion, constituted an "obvious bias." "Tucker Young's independent study was not independent, and it was flat out wrong," Wright wrote in his testimony. He enlisted two engineering reports in his economic defense of the KWA. The first report, "Lake Huron Water Supply Study: Karegnondi Water Authority Preliminary Engineering Report," was prepared by AECOM, Jones & Henry Engineering, LAN, O'Malia Consulting, Rowe Engineering, and Wade Trim. The second report, on the feasibility of using the Flint WTP and Flint River as primary sources of water was completed by ROWE and LAN.[20] Wright neglected to mention that all of the authors except one— Jones & Henry Engineering—had been major contributors to his political campaigns in recent years: LAN with $15,000 since 2010, ROWE with $31,000 since 2006, Wade Trim with $34,700 since 2006, and the list went on (see table 1). Two of the lead authors—AECOM and Wade Trim— were employed as program managers for the KWA project. "An ACLU of Michigan analysis of contributions to Wright's 2016 campaign," investigative reporter Curt Guyette wrote, "reveals that, of the nearly $270,000 he raised during that election cycle, at least $188,000—roughly 70 percent— came from political action committees and employees of companies doing business directly with the KWA or working on the pipeline in some capacity."[21]

.   .   .   .   .

Wright held nothing back in his disdain for the testimony of Peter Hammer, director of the Damon J. Keith Center for Civil Rights and A. Alfred Taubman Endowed Chair at Wayne State University Law School. First, Wright took exception to Hammer's claim that the TYJT report was "rejected by Flint because it was 'apparently not the answer that the Emergency Manager and other KWA backers in Flint wanted to hear.'"[22] In his testimony, Professor Hammer wrote that the Flint water crisis was the result of strategic and structural racism. Hammer defines structural racism as the inter-institutional dynamics that produce and reproduce racially disparate outcomes over time. "These racially disparate outcomes," he wrote, "occur in the areas of health, education, income, transportation,

Table 1 Contributors to Jeff Wright's campaign for Genesee County Drain Commissioner

	Type of business	Amount donated	Comment
L. D'Agostini & Sons, Inc.[a]	Construction	$27,900 since 2007	Submitted low bid of $24.6 million for Lake Huron water pipeline intake Named in a federal lawsuit with Detroit mayor Kwame Kilpatrick for overcharging on a sewer repair project in Sterling He
Lockwood, Andrews & Newmann (LAN)[b]	Engineering	$15,000 since 2010	Charged with professional negligence and public nuisance for its involvement in the Flint water crisis (FWC). "They violated their legal duties and caused the Flint Water crisis to occur, continue and worsen."[c]
Rowe Professional Services Company (a LAN subcontractor)[d]	Engineering	$31,000 since 2006	Commissioned by Emergency Manager Ed Kurtz to write a report in support of the KWA pipeline over buying water from Detroit
Spicer Group[e]	Engineering	$18,000 since 2006	Convinced regulators that open cutting was less disruptive to endangered-species habitat, saving both time and money for pipeline construction[f]
Zito Construction4	Construction	$13,000 since 2007	Made the winning bid of $7,221,285.16 to install an iron transmission main along part of the pipeline route
E+L Construction	Construction	$6,400 since 2014	Was awarded the contract to build the intermediate pump station on the Karegnondi
American Cast Iron Pipe Company	Building materials	$24,000 since 2006	Provided much of the piping for KWA
Wade Trim	Engineering	$34,700 since 2006	Program manager for KWA project

(continued)

Table 1   Continued

	Type of business	Amount donated	Comment
AECOM John O'Malia	engineering	$18,000 $1,500 since 2006	Program manager for KWA project
James Rosendahl	Engineering consultant	$2,500 from 2006 to 2009	

[a]Fonger 2013.

[b]https://www.michigan.gov/documents/ag/Veolia_LAN_Complaint_539723_7.pdf.

People of the state of Michigan v. VEOLIA NORTH AMERICA, INC., a Delaware Corporation, VEOLIA NORTH AMERICA, LLC, a Delaware Limited Liability Company, VEOLIA WATER NORTH AMERICA OPERATING SERVICES, LLC, a Delaware Limited Liability Company, VEOLIA ENVIRONNEMENT, S.A., a French transnational corporation, LOCKWOOD, ANDREWS & NEWNAM, P.C., a Michigan Corporation, LOCKWOOD, ANDREWS & NEWNAM, INC., a Texas Corporation, and LEO A. DALY COMPANY, a Nebraska Corporation (Circuit Court, County of Genesee, 2016). https://www.michigan.gov/-/media/Project/Websites/AG/releases/2016/october/Veolia_LAN_Complaint.pdf?rev=16820a1d1e1f48d0922bce55c1cd4078

[c]Ridley 2016.

[d]Ridley 2016.

[e]Gregerson 2014.

[f]With open cutting, pipeline is laid a section at a time by temporarily diverting water; the alternative is to tunnel beneath the river, adding complexity to the project.

[g]Cooper 2014.

housing and the environment."[23] Flint's participation in KWA, Hammer concluded, was the result of strategic racism on the part of the KWA, the state treasury, MDEQ, and the succession of emergency managers.[24] Jeff Wright, however, insisted that all Hammer did was give a dishonest critique of the KWA born of "an ideologically driven agenda":

> Professor Hammer says KWA and its people are strategic racists. . . . Professor Hammer's [*sic*] provides no such proof. The Professor cites no statement I made or any other person associated with KWA made, which even hints at racial animus. He cites nothing, no statement, no action, no fact, that even suggests I or anyone else at KWA are racists. Instead of providing facts, Professor Hammer's testimony piles innuendos, upon speculation, upon suspicion. Professor Hammer defames people he doesn't know and has not even met. Instead of presenting facts, Professor Hammer provides a narrative to a world that exists only in his mind.[25]

Wright's defense is predicated on the simple yet widely shared belief that, since he has never said, at least in public, anything derogatory against Black or other people of color, he is obviously not a racist. The same applies to others associated with the KWA project. This simple sentiment, widely shared among whites, conveniently distinguishes them and their actions from members of white supremacist organizations whose violent manifestations of identity politics is deeply rooted in their race. This narrow conceptual focus on racism as individual prejudice and hostile action, however, not only assuages white guilt and growing white fragility in this post–George Floyd era but also reduces the sources of widespread racial inequality in the United States to the actions of a few bigots. Equally telling in this conceptual framing is the assumption that we would recognize racism when we saw it. That somehow, Jeff Wright, I, and indeed others, if necessary, would recognize it and agree that this action or that behavior is racism, as opposed to, say, some other form of discrimination. The disagreement outlined above between Hammer and Wright obviously contradicts this belief. Also noteworthy is Wright's indignation at being singled out or implicated in the Flint water crisis. Racism, Wright argued, "is also one of the most severe and insulting accusations one person can make against another in this society."[26] Here Wright claims to be the victim, falsely accused by his irresponsible aggressor.

As sociologist Eduardo Bonilla-Silva has observed, "Whites have developed powerful explanations—which have ultimately become justifications—for contemporary racial inequality that exculpate them from any responsibility for the status of people of color."[27] Wright, like most Americans, largely conceptualized racism as individual prejudice and discrimination. In so doing, such thinking easily downplays the myriad racial projects, deeply embedded in major US institutions, that have redistributed power and resources along racial lines. Yet, by his actions, in collaboration with the state emergency managers and the city's mayors, Wright exacerbated racial inequality in Flint, a majority-Black city, by undermining both its control of water services and future land development in the county. It is also fair to say that he has benefited dearly—personally, economically, and politically—from the KWA project and the consequent poisoning of Flint residents.

Moreover, Wright positioned the KWA against supposed corrupt water provisioning in southeastern Michigan. The KWA, he implied, would end years of localized water politics between Flint and Detroit, cities that had clearly demonstrated their incapacity to effectively manage the region's water resources. "Racially neutral decisions," Wright wrote, were "taken to provide Flint and Genesee County residents with high quality Lake Huron water at guaranteed reasonable prices from an *honest and reliable source*" (emphasis added).[28] Wright positions himself above the fray of local politics in these majority-Black cities, which simply can't get their act together to manage their finances, let alone their drinking water. Wright doesn't use race in his colorblind narrative. He doesn't have to. Instead, he advances two colorblind stereotypes—(dis)honesty and (un)reliability—to invoke and rationalize his civilizing mission. The message is loud and clear.

Every white male implicated in the Flint water crisis has responded in the same aggressive manner—Coming out with guns blazing against their questioners to attack their expertise, motivation, and actions. It is not so much white fragility on display at this moment as a hypermasculine form of white privilege. Historian Carol Anderson characterizes this white male rage as a direct response to Black advancement. In the case of Michigan's water wars, it is not the mere presence of Black leadership in Flint and Detroit that is the problem; rather it is that these cities have resisted decades of attempts by white suburban leaders to wrest their city's water systems and other resources away from them. And in Detroit's case, city leaders like Coleman Alexander Young flaunted a *Blackness with ambition*, actively recruiting people of color to leadership positions in the city, which infuriated white male suburban leaders. White rage, Anderson explained, is not about visible violence; rather, it works its way through the courts, the legislatures, and a range of government agencies.[29] In Flint it took the form of engineering reports downplaying the health risks of switching Flint's water supply, lobbying and campaign contributions to Jeff Wright, and emergency management laws that denied these two African American cities, and others, the right to local government. This unspoken truth, Anderson explains, plays beautifully into the colorblind language of substituting economics for race.[30] In this way, the Jeff Wrights of this world can enunciate positions that safeguard their racial interests without sounding "racist." Instead, Wright promulgated a racialized narrative around the declining morality of Black leadership, which proved politically useful to fan white suburban fears and pent-up resentment.

Wright advanced three colorblind reasons to explain why the KWA was the only reasonable course of action: cost, corruption, and unreliability. "The price of water more than doubled for Flint and Genesee County from 2002 to 2013," Wright reported. "After 2013, Genesee County's rates increased by an additional 50%. From 2012 to date, the rates quadrupled." To which he added, "These rate increases are simply unsustainable." It was true, water rates had increased, to the point that many in the county struggled to pay their water bills. But the rate increases in Flint and Genesee County had very little to do with Detroit's water pricing.[31] Emergency Manager Mike Brown increased Flint's water and sewer rates by 57 percent in 2011 alone. In fact, during the revolving door of four state-appointed emergency managers, Flint residents saw their water and sewer bills soar from around $80 a month to $250 a month. Wright's colorblind narrative also ignored the fact, as I discuss earlier, that municipalities purchased water from DWSD at wholesale prices. The water authorities of these municipalities then sold the water to residential and commercial customers at retail rates. All suburbs receiving water from Detroit marked up their water rates, some charging as much as 1,000% of the wholesale rate.[32] Wright also stepped around the fact that DWSD is a public utility and is required by state law to charge municipalities only wholesale

prices—that is, what it cost the utility to treat and deliver water to its customers. And, like most public utilities, DWSD was both highly regulated
and forbidden to earn a profit.[33] The unsustainable price increases had
very little to do with local—read Black—politics or incompetence.

Also absent from Wright's colorblind narrative about rising water
prices in the region is the growing corporate influence in public water
delivery services. The multinational corporation Nestle, which seems to
have its straw in everyone's well, pays just $200 a year to the state of
Michigan to use 1.1 million gallons every day of water provided by Osceola
County. Other multinationals, including Coca-Cola and PepsiCo, have
made similar arrangements for taking public water in return for nothing
or very little. In contrast, Wright and other leaders have shown no concern
about companies such as Veolia, the world's largest water privatization
corporation, even though these corporations have lobbied governments
incessantly over the last decades to loosen regulations and relax impedi-
ments to corporate control of public water sources and municipal water
utilities. And they have been very successful.

Federal funding of drinking-water services has declined by 82% since
1977, when it peaked. That year the federal government spent $76.27 per
person (in 2014 dollars) on water services, but by 2014, as Flint residents
drank poisoned water, that support had fallen to $13.68 per person.[34]
Wright says little about the fact that the Republican-controlled Michigan
legislature cut its revenue-sharing program during this time, which disproportionately harmed major majority-Black urban centers in the state.
The program had distributed a portion of sales tax collected by the state
to the municipalities. Between 2002 and 2012, the same time period in
which Wright wrote that "rates [began] to soar," Flint lost $54.9 million
from the state's cuts.[35] Yet neither the massive federal cuts to drinking-
water services, nor the raid on revenue-sharing dollars by the state, forcing the city into insolvency, nor the subsequent raising of water rates by
state-appointed emergency managers seemed to be of interest to Wright
and others who articulated the prevailing narrative about what ailed water
provision in southeastern Michigan.

Second, Wright also highlighted the role of Victor Mercado, DWSD
director from 2002 to 2008, who was convicted of corruption. Mercado
pleaded guilty to charges of conspiring with then Detroit mayor Kwame

Kilpatrick "to illegally rig nearly $72 million in contracts."[36] For Wright and others, the Black former mayor Kwame Kilpatrick was the poster child for troubled Detroit. And portraying Kilpatrick's behavior as synonymous with *all* Black leadership became a useful colorblind handle for those seeking to reshape water ownership, control, and access in the region. Wright makes no mention of Kilpatrick's race. He doesn't have to. Yet his testimony omits the fact that the DWSD was under the control of federal judge Feikens's oversight when its rates steadily increased. In fact, in 2002, Feikens directed Mayor Kilpatrick to approve certain major "red tag" contracts without the city council's consent. Feikens's directive was intended to circumvent the authority of locally elected city officials, and ultimately created the setting in which extortion, bribery, and fraud could thrive.

Conversely, those parties most likely to benefit from privatizing water services in the region seemed to garner little attention in Wright's commonsense narrative. For example, Wright spares Veolia from contempt, even though it was later charged with unjust enrichment and fraud for withholding information from city officials and the public about the risk of lead contamination. "I know that Veolia was really interested in some kind of a deal to own the water that was coming into Flint," a water consultant told me. "To privatize it." There had been a number of layoffs at the water treatment plant, so it was understaffed, a city employee explained, and instead of hiring and training local expertise, the city brought in Veolia as consultants. Faced with the decision whether to secure $15 million to $30 million annually in future contracts or share what it knew about the potential risk of lead contamination, Veolia choose to bite its corporate lip. "I don't think they [Veolia managers] were even aware of the corrosivity of the water," a local water expert said. "And I think there was a general sentiment amongst city EMs [emergency managers], Mayor Whaling, and their consultants that the switch to the Flint River was temporary, and any water problems would simply dissolve away once connected to the KWA." LAN, too, is conspicuously absent in Wright's depiction of corruption in the region's water services. Yet LAN, like Veolia, was also later charged for providing professional advice that compounded the city's corrosion problems. Wright also left out the James Rosendahl–Synagro bribery scheme from his assessment of what and who had corrupted water services in the region. LAN and James Rosendahl have also been regular political contributors to Wright's campaign offices leading some to believe that Wright's ambitions had little to do with lowering costs for the residents of Flint and surrounding communities.[37] Others were more direct, accusing him of being the man that poisoned Flint.[38]

Wright pointed to DWSD's unreliability as a third and final colorblind justification for the KWA. During the blackouts of 2003, Wright noted, Flint and Genesee County were cut off from DWSD water delivery for four days. "Hospitals, city residents, and businesses were without water: the public health and safety were placed in peril."[39] But the only example Wright cites of DWSD's unreliability was a result of the largest blackout in American history, covering eight states in the US Northeast and Midwest and the province of Ontario, Canada.[40] And that such a widespread and unprecedented power failure would also have shut down the KWA goes unnoted, as well, in Wright's testimony.

"What we find so laughable now," Monica Lewis-Patrick, coleader of We the People of Detroit, told me, "as people are ridiculed in Detroit about our dysfunctions and malfeasance," is that "we never poisoned anybody. Never did. So, evidently, we knew how to do something well." Detroit was providing water to almost half the state of Michigan, Lewis Patrick pointed out, about 4.3 million Michigan residents. It was an award-winning system that was run predominately by persons of color. Race may not have been an explicit motivation in the justification to build the KWA pipeline or to use the state's hastily cobbled together emergency powers, but one thing is for certain: both were substantiated by the targeted use of a colorblind narrative that manipulated popular racial stereotypes. Race was never mentioned. It didn't have to be, so institutionalized is the power of colorblind racism and white supremacy.

Wright, Dayne Walling, and the emergency managers repeatedly asserted that the KWA would not only provide Flint with cheaper water but also eliminate the city's dependency on the DWSD. "This is a huge step in the right direction," avowed Emergency Manager Darnell Earley in a presentation to City Hall in March 2014, because it would enable the "city to better control the cost" of its water supply. "It's a historic moment for the City of Flint to return to its roots and use our own river as our drinking water supply," echoed Flint mayor Dayne Walling. Ironically, it was Mayor Walling, who also sat on the KWA board, who raised the city's water rates by 35 percent in 2011 to ensure the city complied with its water bond agreement with the state to maintain a certain level of revenue.[41] In fact, all of the recent rate increases came at the discretion of the Flint mayor and state-appointed emergency managers, the very people now proclaiming the city should switch to a cheaper and more reliable water system because of a crisis they had manufactured.

If we are searching for real answers, we would have to admit that this water war between city and suburb was never really about water rates, corruption—because there is plenty to share—or even reliability, but rather about the Black control of white water, and Jeff Wright and others were tired of it. And during the whole saga—the suspension of local democracy, the lead poisoning of thousands, and the resulting intersecting forms of racial violence it advanced—Jeff Wright and other white "city fathers" were able to maintain both the moral high ground—insisting they knew what was best—and, apparently, the upper hand as well, profiting dearly from the decades-long dream of stealing Detroit's crown jewel and owning it themselves. The $285 million needed to construct the KWA pipeline, of which the indebted city of Flint was responsible for $85 million, was a substantial amount of money to control and hand out, as Peter Hammer perceived.[42] And most of the contractors who had contributed to Wright's sixteen-year political career were about to be substantially rewarded for their patronage. Flint is a complicated story, but it is not a story about Black people not paying their bills or about Black leaders' corrupt tendencies. Rather, the Flint water crisis can provide a perspective on how the ostensibly colorblind, mundane, and taken-for-granted workings of austerity have devalued Black assets and democratic autonomy for the benefit of white political and economic elites, and that is why the KWA is not only a racial but also a racist project.

.   .   .   .   .

As it turned out, Flint never joined the KWA, even though it raised its portion of funds for the water megaproject. In November 2015, city residents elected their first female Black mayor, Karen Weaver, who beat the incumbent, Dayne Walling, by 1,764 votes.[43] Weaver vowed to take a closer look at the KWA contract, which the previous mayor had signed. After months of research and collaboration, in spite of much political pressure to approve the KWA agreement, including an attempted recall, Weaver announced that "staying with GLWA [Great Lakes Water Authority] as the city's primary water source is the best option when you consider factors related to public health and when it comes to being fiscally responsible."[44] In November 2019 the city council voted 5–4 in favor of a thirty-year water contract with the GLWA, a restructured version of the DWSD.

The new water deal for Flint took the form of a three-way partnership between the city, the Genesee County Drain Commissioner, and the GLWA. First, Flint would be provided with treated water, priced at wholesale rates commensurate with what other GLWA customers paid. Flint would also have access to Water Residential Assistance Program funds to help low-income customers. The city would have a representative added to the six-member GLWA Board of Directors, which was responsible for determining rates and recommending and approving other major changes in the water new authority.[45] In effect, Flint would still get its water as it always had, from Detroit, but future delivery and pricing would now be at the discretion of white suburban counties that controlled the new water board. Second, GLWA would take over control of Flint's water rights in the KWA. In return, GLWA would pay Flint's future bond obligations of approximately $7 million annually to cover the cost of Flint's borrowing to build the KWA pipeline.[46] Third, per a state-mandated accord, GLWA and the Genesee County Drain Commissioner would provide each other with reciprocal backup water services. MDEQ provided a grant of $7.5 million to the Drain Commissioner to provide water from its new water treatment plant to its customers. In return, Flint would get back a section of the water transmission line that connected "GLWA's pipeline to Lake Huron—the same section former emergency manager Darnell Earley sold to Drain Commissioner Jeff Wright for $3.9 million."[47] Under this deal, Flint no longer provided Genesee County and its outlying townships with water; that service now belonged to the KWA's oversized capacities. However, Flint's thirty-year contract with the GLWA also rendered its water interests subservient to those of the suburban, white, and largely affluent counties of Wayne, Oakland, and Macomb, which in addition to the city of Detroit, had representation on the six-member GLWA board.

To sum up, the Flint water crisis can be understood as a significant outlier among water justice struggles. The city water's lead contamination was the result not of a lack of regulation or government oversight but of a lack of democratic accountability, whereby people's right to water was suspended by government-sanctioned economic austerity. The end of revenue-sharing programs by the state of Michigan, on the heels of the Great Recession, provided the economic mechanism to catapult many, mostly Black cities into deep financial stress. Then, a hastily cobbled emergency manager law provided the structure for unchecked anti-democratic "reform." In Flint, four state-appointed emergency managers systematically increased the city's water rates while misdirecting blame and public anger at the DWSD and city corruption. The use of colorblind racism—specifically the racialization of austerity—provided legitimacy to this form of financial fascism. In Flint, emergency manager law became a formidable political tool and all but guaranteed racially discriminatory outcomes, and the lead poisoning of 100,000 citizens was the most infamous manifestation of this racist project. As regional politics around water played out, racialization became the *x factor*, or determining variable, that balanced the math equation of white elite's austerity tactics. And the more obscure the math, the more the derivative of racialization was advanced. Advocates emphasized mismanagement, corruption, and debt in Flint and Detroit, playing on the region's long-held racialized tropes. This widely used strategy also drew attention away from decades of economic policies that had "redirected jobs, taxes, and capital from cities to suburbs."[48] In this way, racialized austerity shifted the regional debt burden to the increasingly Black and poor cities while subsidizing suburban white flight and investment. "These suburban migrants," historian Andrew Highsmith writes, "were part of one of the largest and most significant population shifts in American history."[49] In Michigan today, as during the postwar era, "tens of thousands of white taxpayers" continue to move "away from the city in search of newer and better housing, schools, and jobs in the segregated suburbs of Genesee County."[50] And now that suburban, white, and affluent counties have successfully wrested away the control of water, we should expect a new iteration of racial and economic inequality in the region.

4 Foundation Colonialism

No story or book about Flint's recent bankruptcy and water crisis would be complete without including its "great-grandfather," the Charles Stewart Mott Foundation. "We're talking about a big, powerful" global institution, with assets of more than $3 billion, explained a longtime Flint resident, "who doesn't really want you to know anything." "The very first truth-and-reconciliation process after Apartheid was funded by the C.S. Mott Foundation in South Africa. I didn't know it either," he told me, "and it was to protect mining interests. There isn't a hospital that would survive in Flint without them. There isn't a school that would survive without them. Every single nonprofit ... in Flint survives only because of the money they get from the Mott Foundation. Every nonprofit that makes grants gets that money to make grants from the C.S. Mott Foundation. So it's colonialism. Totally."

As the Flint resident succinctly noted, the Charles Stewart Mott Foundation's involvement in the Flint water crisis and related developments has attracted a great deal of debate and scrutiny. Many, like this resident, firmly believe that the charity's aim was not relief but reform. And the austerity measures introduced by the state and resulting crises have presented the giant nonprofit with yet another opportunity to exercise its "civilizing" mission. Officially, the Mott Foundation gave a $4 million grant to help the city reconnect Flint to the Detroit water system shortly after state officials conceded that Flint had a water problem. Together with other organizations, including the W. K. Kellogg Foundation and the Carnegie Corporation of New York, this charitable-industrial complex committed $125 million to help Flint recover.[1] And, while its philanthropic efforts might be well-intentioned, history has taught us that how charity gets distributed and spent is never clear.[2] Yet, despite its central role in city affairs, particularly in the African American community, critical consideration of the actions of this charitable-industrial complex and their consequences is an area of much-needed scholarship; hence the second part of this chapter.

Longtime residents point out that most of the charity bestowed in response to the water crisis has not gone to the people who needed it and has been directed not toward relief efforts but rather toward renewal of the city's downtown core. In addition, another resident observed, "we have got emergency managers giving property to friends or Uptown Development." The latter recipient, Uptown Reinvestment Corporation, was formed in 2002 specifically to acquire and renovate real estate in downtown Flint. Its website publicizes the corporation's investment of nearly $30 million dollars in downtown Flint for seven different building projects,[3] including a luxury loft apartment complex with commercial space, which includes the headquarters of Rowe Engineering, the firm that wrote several reports in favor of the KWA (see chapter 3).

Reports indicate that the Ruth Mott Foundation and the Community Foundation of Greater Flint have donated a combined $33,480,494 to various programs aiding both children and adults affected by Flint's lead-in-water crisis.[4] But that charity came with a price. In Flint, the Charles Stewart Mott Foundation seems to wield exceptional political and economic power. Its influence extends everywhere, from education, health care, and housing to political reform and investment. Even the *East Village Magazine*, an influential monthly that focuses on community life, needs a grant from the C. S. Mott Foundation to remain in the black. "We are finishing our second year of a three-year grant," the editor told me. Acknowledging the tension between free speech and who pays for it, she explained, "It's kind of weird as a journalist to know that we are getting

money from our 'big daddy' there downtown." Her candid remark underscores the extent to which this civil society organization has become truly
governmental in Flint. "In hindsight," another resident explained, "Flint
was built by the Motts, the Ballingers. You go through the list of a half a
dozen or dozen big names—they were the clique back in the 1920s who
built this town, and in some ways it's just a reoccurrence of the same thing,
I suppose." Wealthy individuals have always used their status to promote
a vision for humanity's future consistent with their views, and in Flint it is
deceptively unclear where the Motts' vision begins and ends.[5]

The driving forces in Flint, both past and present, historian Andrew
Highsmith writes, "have always been renewal and reinvention more than
decline and abandonment."[6] And "reform," in its most recent rendition,
has slowly and systematically stripped local governments—Flint, Benton
Harbor, and Detroit being the exemplar cases—of their ability to raise
local revenue through taxes and fees. The state of Michigan took local fiscal autonomy from these majority-Black cities with a one-two punch of
gutting the state's revenue-sharing program and imposing tax and expenditure limits (TELs) on local city government through constitutional
amendments or legislative enactments.[7] The first punch cut a total of $54
million from the city of Flint's budget between 2003 and 2014.[8] In the
second punch, the Headlee Amendment in 1978 limited increases in local
property tax millage rates to the rate of inflation, and Proposal A in 1994
capped individual property tax values.[9]

The second strategy also involved the enactment of Public Act 436 (PA
436), the "Local Financial Stability and Choice Act," which, as shown in
previous chapters, permitted the state to disempower local governing bodies in majority-Black cities and replace them with state-appointed emergency managers. The governor didn't select these political appointees to
balance municipal revenue and expenditure flows. Most of them didn't
have a clue where to start. Moreover, it was their employer, the state of
Michigan, that had passed the laws and policies responsible for local financial distress. These policies and laws denied mostly Black cities the capacity to generate revenues critical to paying for municipal police and fire
departments, as well as schools, libraries, parks, roads, and water and sanitation. The notion that the state was now going to send in managers to fix
the financial crises in these predominantly Black cities speaks to the power

of racialization, whereby people were willing to blame local Black city government for something they literally had no hand in causing. On the heels of the Great Recession of 2009, this one-two punch not only forced this majority-Black city into bankruptcy but poisoned its people too.

Into this deeply racialized space stepped key players of the philanthropic economy, ready not just to help but also to reinvent its chosen city. Their vision to "rebuild Flint the right way," was carefully and completely outlined in the "Imagine Flint Master Plan for a Sustainable Flint."[10] Besides the Office of Sustainable Communities of the US Department of Housing and Urban Development, major project funders of the master plan included familiar "city fathers": the C. S. Mott Foundation, the Ruth Mott Foundation, and the Community Foundation of Greater Flint. In addition, in-kind contributors included both the Flint and Genesee Chamber of Commerce, the Genesee County Land Bank Authority, and the Center for Community Progress.[11] The master plan included building new infrastructure, including water and sewer lines, roads, and streetlights. Greenbelts and bike lanes were also proposed, these latter often antecedents to gentrification, attracting new wealth and lifestyles to urban communities and transforming both their economies and demographics.

"So, for the last six years, I have been working with a combination of governmental agencies, including the Genesee County Land Bank, . . . the Community Foundation of Greater Flint, the Center for Community Progress, the Ruth Mott Foundation . . . on a variety of projects that are around planning, research, and design" of the city's infrastructure, explains a local planning consultant. "I have worked most extensively with the Genesee County Land Bank." The Land Bank formed in response to what has been described as a lengthy tax foreclosure process that kept affected properties off the tax rolls and out of circulation, a removal that contributed to the city's decline. In 1999 the Michigan legislature created a new, streamlined system for returning tax-reverted properties to productive use. The Genesee County Land Bank is the state-appointed authority charged with acquiring, maintaining, and selling vacant and blighted properties in Genesee County. All tax-foreclosed properties that go unsold at public auction and are not accepted by the state or local unit of government are transferred from the county treasurer to the Land Bank at the end of each calendar year.[12] Once properties are under the Land Bank's ownership, they can be sold on a case-by-case basis; they can be demolished; or they can be held by the Land Bank for potential future redevelopment commensurate with the city's long-term rebuilding plans. The Land Bank is now the largest landlord in Flint, having acquired roughly 15,000 properties since its inception in 2004. Currently, a Land Bank employee informed me, "we own 22% of all properties in the city of Flint." The role of land banks is unprecedented in urban gentrification in the United States, and in the wake of the subprime mortgage debacle, urban development cannot be fully understood without a deeper dive into its affairs.

"It was an alternative to selling them to speculators and investors," the planning consultant explained to me. "We work really hard to raise grant funding and other means to facilitate long-term reuse of the properties. Demolition is one of the biggest things that it [the Land Bank] does. It is really very popular among residents. Very popular." There are exceptions, of course. The historic neighborhood of Carriage Town, just northwest of downtown, is one. "They don't really like demolition and so it doesn't really happen there, which is fine. You know, it's their neighborhood. The Land Bank does really work hard to engage with community-based organizations. It has staff committed to doing that," the consultant told me. "I could talk about the Land Bank for hours," she admitted proudly. The Land Bank has been involved in a lot of commercial redevelopment. "Something like $55 million has been invested in large-scale commercial redevelopment in properties received by the Land Bank," she said. However, while this vision of complete urban renewal and gentrification may be in step with the vision and priorities of the "city fathers," it stands in stark contrast to others' perspectives.

"A group of people were involved" in the city's masterplan, "like Tim Herman and Bill White," an east-side Flint resident told me. "I know some of these guys." "The Whitey camp," he likes to call them. "The Motts' fingerprints are all over everything. . . . They are funded off of each other. They are backing each other up." Another resident agreed. Folks with intimate knowledge of Flint's political landscape told me that the Genesee County Land Bank, the Chamber of Commerce, the Community Foundation, and other similar institutions are vehicles the C. S. Mott Foundation uses to implement *its* masterplan in the city.

"The Mott Foundation is behind the KWA," explained another resident. "I know that Ridgway White [then the foundation's president and CEO] has had investors in with discussions about building an all-new water distribution system, coming from Great Lakes Water Authority." This resident also believed that the new system would be exclusive in distributing water. "Kind of like a toll road, right? This happened in Benton Harbor . . . it is sort of referred to as 'Black people water' and 'white people water.'"

"There have been a number of different contractors and investors who've been [brought] in to talk about that possibility," this resident continued. And pollsters were "going to certain neighborhoods and saying, 'You know, we know the water is super expensive, but if it was 10% more, and you didn't have to worry about any contaminants, would you pay for it?' These are wealthy people—of course they would pay it. [Its] charter schools all over again," he surmised.

In the past, historian Andrew Highsmith explained, the Mott Foundation infused Flint's public schools with millions of dollars in corporate philanthropy to institutionalize "patterns of administrative racial segregation, educational disadvantage, and economic inequality."[13] The notion that it might do the same to the city's water infrastructure seems highly probable to some longtime Flint residents.

Residents and pundits alike continue to speculate about the role of the Mott Foundation in and leading up to the Flint water crisis. "We know that they are one of the driving forces," a former city administrator told me, in determining who was appointed emergency manager in Flint. The Foundation supported the selection of the first two emergency managers, he believes. Together,

Ed Kurtz and Mike Brown made the decision for the third one, who was Darnell Earley. And in every case, there were a series of meetings that every one of those emergency managers had at the Mott Foundation. . . . There were [also] numerous meetings that those emergency managers had with the Chamber of Commerce and C. S. Mott Foundation. The C. S. Mott Foundation was one of the major funders of the Chamber of Commerce. This is what I mean [about] how Mott operates. If the C. S. Mott Foundation decided to go to sleep tomorrow and never wake up, the Chamber is going to die. Literally. . . . So the Chamber has become a vehicle for the Mott Foundation.

Later, Tim Herman, president and CEO of the Chamber of Commerce, hired Duane Miller to be vice president of core initiatives. "He is known as being a racist," a former city staffer told me. "So Tim Herman hired Duane Miller as his vice president to get the Black people off of his ass." Miller was employed from October 2009 to October 2017, and then became a consultant to the Chamber. Many in Flint also believe that the Mott Foundation was influential in the Chamber of Commerce securing contracts to run some of the adult education and after-school youth programs, previously run by Flint Public Schools. "I'm trying to tell you," a former city employee patiently explained: "Mott hides in the back. But every decision [concerning] the Flint schools is made by the Mott Foundation." The Foundation has to be careful, he explained, to make sure it complies with federal regulations and is not seen as politically involved. "So what they do," he said, "is they find fiscal agents that they can work through," like Prima Civitas (a nonprofit economic and community development organization based in Lansing), the Chamber of Commerce, and the Genesee County Land Bank.

THE LAND GRAB

Understanding the Genessee Land Bank and its impact on the city requires going back to the mayorship of Don Williamson. "It was a deal done between Williamson and Dan Kildee, funded by a $20 million grant from the C. S. Mott Foundation," a former city employee explained. "There are many of us who had real questions about the purpose of a land bank and [were] not very clear about how they were going to be a benefit to the community of Flint, more specifically the people of color. Because a higher percentage of these abandoned houses were in the Black community, and in the poor, white community, which is the east side."

To many in Flint, the Land Bank has a reputation for having been the biggest slum lord in the city. Some say it charged the city an exorbitant amount of money to provide general maintenance for some properties. "The city was spending over a million dollars a year," a former city employee reported to me, "just to do grass cutting." Many thought these costs should have been passed on to the speculators and owners who purchased Land Bank properties. "When I hear 'grants,' when I hear '501(c)

(3)s,' when I freaking hear [about] 'churches getting tax exemptions,' and in the meantime we're losing [our homes and our neighborhoods]. . . I get a little sick."

"I'm losing my stuff to back taxes," yet the Land Bank turned around and sold abandoned properties to churches, he explained to me, "who don't pay taxes. That was the city's revenue . . . [and] they gave it all away." This resident and others believed that churches were given Land Bank properties in an effort to buy off Black pastors. It has long been recognized that the church is the center of the African American community. And many in that community were skeptical of the Land Bank's motives. Our church "bought about thirty-three houses around the church," a resident told me. "I was against it, my wife was against it, about half of the church was against it," because they had no resources or capacity to maintain the run-down houses let alone do community development. Many churches therefore applied for and received federal community development block grants (CDBGs) to help maintain the properties they purchased. Economically, such actions made little sense. But, politically, the strategy of discount peddling Land Bank houses to Black pastors served to enlist the Black church in the city's general segregationist efforts. "They knew the pastors didn't have the capacity," the resident said. "They know they are not going to do a damn thing with it [vacant property]. And they know eventually at some point in time, possibly, it [the vacant property] will come back to them. They know that. So, to me, that was crazy. That to me is just as racist as not giving them the property."

Scholarly explanations of neighborhood segregation have commonly emphasized the role of structural or systemic racism in housing and community development.[14] In Flint, however, elite actors have actively recruited the participation of influential members in the Black community to advance their segregationist efforts, knowing all too well that when push comes to shove, it will be the Black community that will take the fall for the city's blight and neglect. The efficacy of this colorblind effort has been extraordinary, creating racial animus in certain neighborhoods, fracturing community, and ultimately pitting neighbors against one another. But perhaps even more underhandedly, the strategy of the Land Bank vis-à-vis Black churches has enrolled some Black leaders into larger racial segregationist efforts in the city.

In other neighborhoods a different land use plan seemed to be in play. The "Mott Foundation [is] trying to just clear out areas of north Flint for investment purposes," a resident told me. "What they are trying to do is take over this whole neighborhood, because they want the houses, they want the properties," she explained. "This house right here," she told me as we walked through her neighborhood, "that went to a landlord who bought it from the Land Bank." At the time, the house sat vacant, and it was obvious to me that the absentee landlord was paying very little attention to the property. "Now I can show you the properties that they own," she told me as we continued to walk, "and ones they kept. Beautiful. And the houses that aren't worth saving, the ones they don't want, destroyed. They come in and tear them down." And "we've been breathing this now for 10 years or more."

"What do you think is going to happen to these vacant properties?" I asked her.

"Well, you know, if you're along the river, you won't be able to buy it from the Land Bank, because they won't let you. There is a big master plan going on. It is something I have been fighting from day one," she told me. "People don't understand." She explained that there is a new zoning board that seeks to implement the city's masterplan. "You can only plant yellow flowers. You can't put a fascia like that. Oh, you like green? Too bad," she sarcastically remarked. "I'm not saying it's all bad. I want to rebuild. I do. But on the same note, I'm not going to concede" to being told how to rebuild.

The real frustration for residents whom I spoke with is that they have witnessed their neighborhoods be systematically dismantled by the very agencies that claim to be saving it, and these same agencies place zoning restrictions in their neighborhoods, limiting what can be done and who is eligible to own homes, even which houses will stay or be demolished. And the fact that these limitations and restrictions are most evident in African American neighborhoods has made many folks wary about the Land Bank's true motives.

"This was Dan Kildee's baby," reflected Tony Palladeno Jr., a notable Flint activist and water warrior, as we walked around the Kearsley Park neighborhood, inspecting the vacant Land Bank properties. "You've got to understand our roots here. We grew up on the east side of Flint. I owned these," he said, pointing to two houses on Washington Avenue, "before the Land Bank came in." In 2004, when the Genesee County Land Bank, the first of its kind in the United States, formally began operating, Dan Kildee was the county treasurer. Today he is a US representative in Congress. "But he gets to say, Well, I step back after three years," Tony inferred. "Bullshit, dude, your hand is still in that kitty, you're running some shit behind them curtains, you've got your boy Phil Stair, which I can't get much information on. He's been there forever, and it isn't good. Check out Phil Stair; he got busted doing shit down in Grand Blanc too."[15]

Philip Stair was the land bank's transaction supervisor from 2002 to 2016. He established the sales price of each property and oversaw all reviews and approval offers from potential buyers. Speaking bluntly to Chelsea Lyons, an environmental activist and independent journalist, Stair, was recorded saying, "Flint has the same problems as Detroit—f——ing ni——s don't pay their bills. Believe me, I deal with them." Later in the conversation Stair also described tenants in Flint houses as "derelict mother f——ers" and "f——ing deadbeats." Stair played to the stereotypes that Black and brown people don't care, particularly about their neighborhoods. "They f—— the houses up and then leave, and we tear them down," Stair declared, revealing whom he blamed for the mounting foreclosures in Flint.[16] Phil Stair is no longer with the Genesee County Land Bank, but for about 14 years an openly bigoted white male controlled who got which properties and for how much in Flint. Stair's shameless diatribe may be particularly jarring, yet his view of African American renters and homeowners was, except for the slurs, nothing but consistent with the federally endorsed Moynihan Report of 1965, which rooted Black poverty in "the deterioration of the Negro family."[17] In many ways, Stair was also repeating the segregationist practices of the FHA, which repeatedly advised that "neighborhoods that contained Black people were 'unquestionable slums.'"[18]

In many ways the Genesee County Land Bank has picked up where the Home Owners Loan Corporation and FHA left off, drawing new redlines in the this iconic postindustrial city. A Land Bank assessment, writes Flint resident Teddy Robertson, ranked the housing stock as either good (rose), fair (pink), poor (violet), or structurally deficient (red), mirroring the 1930s maps.[19] Concurrently, Flint's comprehensive master plan, known as Imagine Flint (2013), divided the city into twelve unique place types,

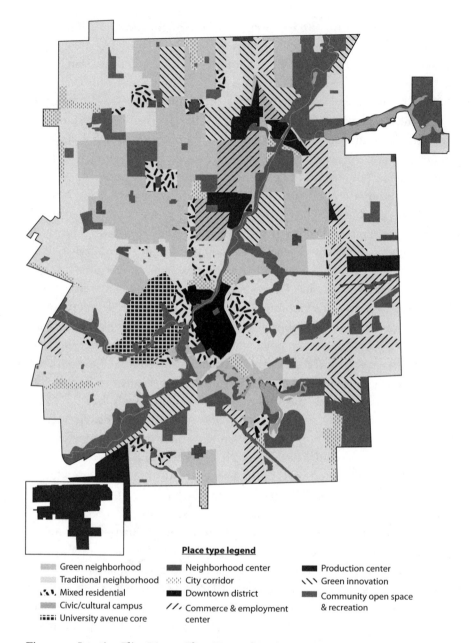

Place type legend

Green neighborhood	Neighborhood center	Production center
Traditional neighborhood	City corridor	Green innovation
Mixed residential	Downtown district	Community open space
Civic/cultural campus	Commerce & employment	& recreation
University avenue core	center	

Figure 13. Imagine Flint Master Plan. Houseal Lavigne Associates 2013b.

characterized by appearance, potential uses, and land-use density (fig. 13). Light blue denoted civic or cultural campus land use, purple denoted "University Avenue Core," yellow indicated mixed residential, and green denoted "Green Innovation." The Genesee County Land Bank used this master plan to align its decisions about which properties to sell, renovate, or demolish within this reimagined city.

The Genesee County Land Bank assessment map has since been removed from the internet and, as mentioned earlier, Phil Stair is no longer with the Genesee County Land Bank, but both are consistent with a long history of purposive racial gerrymandering in Flint, and elsewhere, that has restricted housing opportunities for people of color to the city's worst neighborhoods in an effort to support white property values and improve the city for the right people. "When you look at the redistricting maps, the gerrymandering maps, you can kind of see a pattern," a resident explained to me. "And that pattern is one of racial segregation. There is just story after story, after story about wonderful grassroots—not just organizations, but businesses [too]—grown community ventures that were thriving, that were successful, that were values based." But these predominantly Black businesses were either underfunded or actively undermined, this Flint resident told me, because they did not fit with "the *real* master plan."

Today, the city of Flint is home to seven postsecondary educational institutions.[20] The local economic impact of "eds and meds"—higher education and health care services—has been well documented. Eds and meds spur economic development, increase revenues of local businesses, provide fiscal benefits to government, boost local property values, and contribute to labor market gains.[21] With the declining importance of manufacturing as a source of jobs and economic development, Flint's economy is well primed for rebuilding. The city is easily accessible by major highways, has a surplus of affordable housing stock, and because of the water crisis, new water infrastructure. "It is clear they want to rebuild the city," a resident observed; "they just don't want to rebuild [it] for the people that live there now."

But not everyone is on board with the C. S. Mott Foundation's master plan to rebuild Flint. Two comments made to me indicate other sentiments among longtime Flintstones:

The Mott community is not doing a f——ing thing here, and it's a shame that here you are one of the top fifty foundations in the world, located right downtown, less than two miles from where all this blight is, and you are not doing nothing.

You committed over 350 million dollars to Kettering, you committed over half a million dollars to the University of Michigan, you commit all these millions of dollars to the culture center. But here you are, right down the street—how could this be?

In this way, many residents questioned the motives behind this plan for a new economy. "I'm not saying that that's not a good strategy," a resident clarified. "I'm just simply saying that when you have a community that is faced with these kinds of infrastructure problems, you can graduate a whole lot of people out of these colleges, but that doesn't help Flint."

WHITE PRIVILEGE

"You know, you just get people who kind of just make decisions without any sort of accountability at all," a resident asserted. "And they don't even expect to be accountable [because] they've never had to be," she added. "And when they get caught stealing money, you know, they are like, what?" She explained to me how the Land Bank enabled Hurley Medical Center to own properties adjacent to the hospital. "There's a lot of beautiful, beautiful old homes . . . that were supposed to be used for patient housing and offices." But "they let it deteriorate," she said, and then the Land Bank demolished the homes. "So now it's just a complete meadow, and they lied about it. And that's just one example of how the Land Bank really plays a part in the redevelopment": effectively policing "what and who is allowed to live where, what houses are allowed to remain, what houses are going to go. They are all . . . in their own little clique," she concluded, referring to "Uptown Redevelopment, the Chamber of Commerce, and, of course, all roads lead back to Mott. And Mott's fingerprints are all over everything."

"None of them pay taxes. They all get tax breaks," which further restricts the city's capacity to raise local revenue, making city residents increasingly dependent on the well-intentioned decisions of an all-encompassing charitable-industrial complex.

"You must know that we have a very vibrant cultural center," another resident told me: "the Flint Institute of Arts. My brother and sister are both exhibit designers in New York, and they come back and they applaud the quality of the Flint Institute of Arts." Its website claims: "The Flint Institute of Arts is the second largest art museum in Michigan, and one of the largest museum-connected community art schools in the United States."[22] The institute is also a nonprofit and relies heavily on the support of the Charles Stewart Mott Foundation. Yet another resident mentioned that Flint had one of the "premier farmer's market[s] in the country." But, as with so much else in the new economy of Flint, the costs are rarely shared equitably, and the decision-making processes are often hidden from those who are most impacted. Many were confused about the new arts millage, a longtime Flint resident explained. "It's going to be voted on next Tuesday." It would be the "third biggest millage for Genesee County," amounting to "about $45 to $50 a year per family on a $100,000 house. The 0.96 arts millage will generate $8.7 million a year for the Cultural Center," underwriting the public funding of twelve private arts organizations in Flint. "This is Flint for you," she said sarcastically. The money would go to the county Board of Commissioners, which would serve as a pass-through to the Flint Cultural Center Foundation, she explained. The latter would then dole out $8 million a year to various arts and cultural organizations (table 2). "They are not elected bodies, right? So it's public money going to private nonprofit institutions."

"You know, there used to be rich people here that supported the arts," another resident said. "And so they all have this legacy, and a lot of them have endowments and everything." This gentry class comprise the real creditors of the city, constantly trying to rebuild it "in order to save the ones who live there from themselves and their lives."[23] "I remember when he was alive," explained a lifelong resident, "he [Mott] would walk around the streets and impose himself on residents. And come up to young people and kind of do that 'Pull yourself up by your bootstraps, and get resilience' type of crap, [or] 'You know, you can make something of yourself like I did.' And he was excused for that behavior because he was Charles Stewart Mott."

At the front of the C.S. Mott Foundation's 2016 annual report is a full-length picture of one such encounter (fig. 14), in which Mott is seen literally talking down to a Flint student. The front cover also depicts Mott, stoic,

Table 2   How millage funds were to be divided among private arts nonprofits in Flint, 2018

Organization	Amount
Flint Institute of Arts	$1,792,413.11
Flint Institute of Music	$1,792,413.10
Sloan Longway	$1,792,413.10
The Whiting	$1,792,413.10
Floyd J. Mcree Theatre	$412,246.63
Friends of Berston Fieldhouse	$412,246.63
Greater Flint Arts Council	$87,756.54*

SOURCE: Jackson 2018.
*Administrative fee

wearing a hat and wool suit in front of a GM vehicle parked outside the GM Building in Detroit (fig. 15).[24] "People still talk about him as if he were alive," another resident admitted. "It's like the ghost of Mott is still alive." It is true that effigies of the man can be seen all over the city's built environment, from university buildings to park benches, effectively joining Flint's prosperity to the hip of Mott's aid. But that aid was also an effective technique to extend the Motts' influence over local and regional planning and policy decisions. And, in Flint, the Motts wielded extraordinary influence over how the city raised revenues and what public expenditures were funded. This influence continued to dominate city government decision making, including the fate of elected officials and the appointment of emergency managers, selected to champion the programs that the Motts thought worthy.

"I mean, it was just [one of] all of these bids to revitalize Flint that have failed over and over and over again," said a born-and-raised Flint resident in describing the master plan. "But, you know," she continued, "I don't think they were actually meant to be sustainable in the long run. They just garnered money from one arm of the Mott Foundation to another. They just keep handing each other money back and forth and then congratulating themselves on how great they are. And the city went, 'God, what would we do without them? You know, they've saved the city.'" Rather than save or revitalize Flint, a "civilizing" mission common to many charitable

Figure 14. Charles Stuart Mott pictured talking (down) to a Flint boy, 1940s. Charles Stewart Mott Foundation 2016.

Figure 15. A stoic Mott in front of the GM Building in Detroit, 1920s. Charles Stewart Mott Foundation 2016.

organizations, the Mott Foundation supposed charity has served to conceal a fundamental detail about Flint city government: the fact that critical taxing and spending decisions have and continue to be controlled by unelected bodies that shift the tax burden of their reforms to those least likely to benefit from or afford such (white) privileges. The debate over the recent arts and culture millage to support the Flint Cultural Center and other related nonprofit arts organizations provides a poignant example of Mott's influence.

"Rumor has it," the same Flint resident told me, that this [the new millage] was partly triggered by the Mott Foundation making noise, like it's going to pull out some of its funding, and that the Mott Foundation had dumped this $35 million into charter school, and then they want other people to support the rest of the Cultural Center. So it's very controversial right now.

"People have a lot of questions," another Flint resident observed, "about, you know, . . . we can't afford to pay our water bills," so many residents do not support additional tax assessments for the arts. "And then there is another group that's like, I don't like those assholes over there; they are elitists who I didn't elect to decide what to do with the $8 million a year of my money, you know? So I don't know—that's just another classic Flint story."

For many residents in Flint, urban redevelopment was quickly becoming the new frontier of environmental justice, where increasingly they were being written out of plans to rebuild their city. "It is a deliberate strategy," this resident insisted. "It is very deliberate. When you look at the policies under consideration, when you look at the practices in play, when you look at the larger cultural norms in the city, when you look at all those things together—it amounts to nothing more than gentrification." And, she made clear, the real strategy behind the charitable veil is to disenfranchise the Black community. "So . . . the C. S. Mott Foundation . . . are not very revered in the [Black] community. Even though they are trying to operate in the background," the resident concluded, "we know that they are one of the driving forces" of Black segregation and disenfranchisement in Flint. Scholarly research has also revealed the multiple ways in which access to the city and its services is increasingly becoming a matter of both white privilege and environmental justice.[25] The thing that sets Flint apart from other cities experiencing the same transformation is the way in which race, in particular racialized constructions of urban austerity, has played a crucial role in legitimating policies and practices that would simply not be tolerated in other white places. The following chapter employs a similar analysis to show how racialized austerity was once again summoned to force the largest urban bankruptcy in US history and take control of the region's most valuable resource—water.

5 Emergency (as a Paradigm of) Management

Many scholars have provided important empirical insights into the role of the courts in advancing and maintaining racial inequality in this county. For important reasons, the bulk of this work has focused on the criminal justice system.[1] This chapter focuses on the impact of another court—the federal bankruptcy court—in the adjudication of debt obligations in the predominantly Black city of Detroit. Under the directive of Emergency Manager Kevyn Orr, the city of Detroit filed for Chapter 9 bankruptcy protection on July 18, 2013, for debts estimated at $18 billion. Governor Rick Snyder had appointed Kevyn Orr, a bankruptcy attorney, in March of the same year. Both the amount of the city's default and the speed of this municipal bankruptcy were unprecedented.[2] The bankruptcy proceedings took sixteen months to complete, whereas the city of Vallejo, California, spent three years in bankruptcy, and Stockton, California, just over two years.[3] It is this timing and, as I explain below, manipulation of the debt burden that left many Detroiters believing that from the start, Emergency Manager Orr's mission was to *ensure* Detroit was declared eligible for bankruptcy, not to protect the city and its residents from it.[4]

Two divergent narratives have been cultivated to frame this unprecedented event. The first and dominant narrative paints a picture of a decaying and broken city unable even to keep its streetlights on. Into this situation was helicoptered Emergency Manager Kevyn Orr, faced with the Herculean task of bringing financial sanity to a city long neglected and mismanaged. And after careful deliberation of all available options, the bankruptcy attorney in charge was forced to restructure the city's unprecedented debt, in the process implementing a $1.7 billion revitalization plan. This narrative attributes blame for Detroit's problems and its eventual bankruptcy—the largest municipal bankruptcy filing in US history— to failures of city management, relentless spending, and even corruption of city officials. It's worth repeating that this same narrative was carefully enrolled to defend the appointment of the four emergency managers in Flint.

The second narrative, one shared by many Detroiters, is a little more complex and, I believe, also more convincing. This counternarrative suggests that Detroit's bankruptcy provided a persuasively colorblind defense of the state's use of austerity measures to systematically strip away Black assets and public infrastructure for the benefit of white political and economic elites. US bankruptcy judge Steven Rhodes presided over the city's bankruptcy proceedings; he confirmed the city's eligibility, plan, and settlement under Chapter 9 of the bankruptcy code. According to the "composite narrative" he put together in response to a long list of parties that objected to the outcome, "The bankruptcy was the intended consequence of a years-long, strategic plan. The goal of this plan was the impairment of pension rights through a bankruptcy filing by the City."[5] Investigative reporter Curt Guyette called the Detroit bankruptcy a "takeover." In one of many articles he wrote on the bankruptcy, Guyette argued that the legal proceeding was a concerted effort to use the state's emergency powers to obtain a ruling of municipal bankruptcy and thus evade the state's constitutional obligations to protect public workers' pensions.[6]

"It was contrived," a longtime Detroiter told me. "All the debt that the state *owed* to the city of Detroit, around $1.2 billion. And if you add all that the banks and the other deadbeat taxpayers that live outside the city [but] didn't pay, you are looking at about $1.8 billion that was owed to Detroiters." The real purpose of the bankruptcy was, this resident concluded, "to forgive, to provide amnesty, to renegotiate and give them tangible perks and pieces and parcels of land in exchange for this manufactured, contrived idea that we owe all of this money, when, in actuality, people owed us."

If the bankruptcy was contrived, as many people believe, how did it play out? Who was involved? And, if race was a factor, what role did it play? Everyone that I've talked to and everything that I've read, from detailed archives to newspaper articles, raise serious questions regarding the legitimacy of the state's emergency management law and the motivations of emergency managers appointed to balance the books of indebted cities. In this chapter, I reveal how forced austerity and discourses of Black corruption and disfunction were exploited to support the privatizing and pillaging of Black assets for the control and benefit of whites.

I'M AN ACCOUNTANT AND YOUR GOVERNOR

Rick Snyder was inaugurated as Michigan's forty-eighth governor on January 1, 2011. "So Republicans took control of the legislature in 2010, took the house of representatives, the governor's office. Just swept in," an Oakland County Intermediate School District employee I'll refer to as Joe recalled. "[Snyder is] not really a Republican. My Republican friends don't really own him. He's a business leader from Michigan; that's his power base. Universities, the *Fortune* 500 companies, the Fords, the DeVoses—that is where he comes from. That's who he is; that's who he represents."

Snyder's business ventures propelled him to the chair of Gateway Inc.'s board of directors. In 2007, when he stepped down and Gateway was sold to Acer for a song ($710 million), *Time* magazine ranked Gateway as one of the ten biggest tech failures of the previous decade. Perhaps this past failure should have been read as writing on the wall. But more than a lesson not learned, it illustrates how a white business leader's missteps are rarely attributed to his race, a privilege not afforded to Coleman Alexander Young, Detroit's first Black mayor.

Snyder also cofounded a venture capital firm and a digital health-coaching company. "He's got a really small inner circle," Joe continued. "It's not clear who advises him about the daily operations at the legislative

level. It was no surprise to us at all that he got into this trouble in Flint."
As a law student at the University of Michigan, Snyder crossed paths with
fellow law students Mike Duggan and Kevyn Orr. Apparently, Orr and
Snyder met over a snowball fight on campus and lived in the same quads
at U of M.[7]

"This guy was looking to run for president," Joe reminded me. "Crush
the unions in Michigan, fix Detroit, get rid of the business tax—he was
building a portfolio. He formed an exploratory group and had a political
action committee that was raising money [for his campaign]." Snyder's
political message had many deep-pocketed and influential backers, ready
to bring the financial medicine of Motown to every town. "He has now
diverted [that money] to pay for Flint, which is ironic." This was going to
be part of the great success of Michigan's turnaround, and at the heart of
it all was the Emergency Management Law. Yet implementation of the
plan hit a hiccup right away, particularly in Detroit, and has drawn serious
scrutiny ever since by advocates and critics alike. In spite of the doubts
and ample derision, the architects of Michigan's austerity program found
the legal apparatus and political allies to force their ideological and racist
agenda on the general public.

In his first month in office, Rick Snyder, among other actions, eliminated the Michigan Business Tax and replaced it with a flat 6% corporate
income tax on some 95,000 companies in the state, thereby reducing state
revenues by more than $2 billion when adjusted for inflation. "We're get-
ting rid of all the special-interest kind of items," Snyder claimed about his
first budget. Those special interests included children in K–12 public
schools, college students, welfare recipients, military veterans, people
serving prison sentences, and employees and clients of the Department of
Human Services. The rhetoric of the accountant-governor simply making
the "numbers add up" is contradicted by the vulnerable communities that
have been targeted for financial disciplining and the white businessmen-
in-arms engorged by such strokes of his colorblind pen. It was, of course,
the latter who immediately sprang to his defense when Snyder was criti-
cized for these early moves. In particular, the Mackinac Center for Public
Policy, the largest state-based free market think tank in the United States,
generously funded by the Devos and Walton families, the Koch brothers,
and other right-wing billionaires, implied that people targeted by the state

budget had somehow been abusing the system and therefore deserved to have their services taken away.

In defense of the governor's severe cuts to revenue sharing (the distribution to municipalities of a portion of sales tax collected by the state) Michael LaFaive, director of the Mackinac Center's Morey Fiscal Policy Initiative, said in 2011, "Things are tough all over, not just at the local level." To which he added, "I understand how easy it would be to get used to that [revenue sharing dollars] rolling in, especially when politicians are willing to ladle the gravy." This colorblind narrative has muddied the waters regarding the true fiscal crisis of the state; namely, its policy to systematically redistribute the tax burden from the white, elite, and mostly suburban class and shift it to the working poor and people of color who live in its cities. "Ladling the gravy" serves to hide the cruel truth of financial fascism: while white Michiganders and their supporting constituencies were given generous tax cuts, tens of thousands of low-income residents—mostly people of color, many of them dependent on social programs, many disabled and elderly—had government programs they desperately needed taken from them. Moreover, the strategic use of "ladling the gravy" depicted urban residents as welfare dependent and their leaders as unable to make tough financial decisions in difficult times. The deployment of this colorblind narrative to portray Black leadership in Michigan's struggling cities as being soft on finance reform provided the justification for placing more than half of the African American population in Michigan under emergency management law (compared with only 2% percent of the white population).

REVENUE SHARING

Revenue sharing is the process by which money from the federal government is transferred to state governments, or money from a state government is turned over to local governments. Federal-state revenue sharing began under President Richard Nixon with the State and Local Fiscal Assistance Act of 1972. This act created a system by which a portion of federal funds would be shared with state and local governments. In a speech he gave promoting the program, Nixon presented revenue sharing as a necessity for the proper functioning of local and state governments across the country. He described the distribution of federal funds as a means of "multiplying the centers of effective power in our country." Money from revenue sharing would be used, Nixon explained, to meet the needs of the people, to build "better schools and better hospitals and better police forces . . . [to] stop the alarming escalation in local and state property taxes, income taxes, and sales taxes."[8] Revenue sharing was not a federal government handout, a "gravy train" intended only for struggling cities, as LaFaive flippantly described it, but rather an essential policy intervention in assisting local and state governments. Forty years later, LaFaive, stoking the deep regional animosity in Michigan between white suburban political elites and the city they loved to hate, chose to weaponize the use of a genuine social program vital to local governments in providing much-needed services to the public.

Michigan's commitment to sharing revenue with local governments preceded Nixon's by decades. Since the 1930s, as much as 85% of money generated from the taxation of businesses with liquor licenses had been returned to the cities, villages, and townships of origin. In 1946 the state constitution was amended to require a portion of the state sales tax to be returned to local governments. Michigan renewed its commitment to revenue sharing when, in 1963, the new state constitution required that 15 percent of "all taxes imposed on retailers on taxable sales at retail of tangible personal property . . . shall be used exclusively for assistance to townships, cities and villages, on a population basis as provided by law."[9] In 1972, Public Act 212 changed the method by which state revenues were distributed from a per capita formula to one that accounted for a city's, village's, or township's relative tax burden and relative tax income. This revision was meant to ensure that need was accurately measured and not based on population alone. Revenue sharing in Michigan now falls broadly into two categories: constitutional and nonconstitutional, or statutory. The former cannot be revised without voter approval. Statutory revenue-sharing funds are earmarked by state law for local communities across Michigan to support essential local services, including law enforcement and firefighting, water systems, road maintenance, parks, and libraries. The fund amounts are calculated as a percentage of sales tax revenues collected at the local levels.[10]

Numbers differ on how much Michigan's austerity reforms cut revenue sharing. Some claim the total reduction between 2002 and 2016 amounted to $8.1 billion.[11] The Michigan Municipal League claimed in 2014 that the state had "managed to pinch over $6 billion in revenue sharing from local government over the last several years."[12] In many instances, the losses resulted in steep cuts to government staffing and public services that many poor and urban residents rely on.[13] From 2003 to 2013, state sales tax revenues actually went up from $6.6 billion to $7.72 billion, providing the state the opportunity to increase its revenue-sharing obligation. Instead, during the same period, the governor and legislature diverted at least $6.2 billion in statutory revenue sharing from local communities to pay for substantial tax cuts for businesses.[14] The city of Detroit ranked number one in the long list of Michigan cities losing shared revenue. Between 2002 and 2012, Motown lost $732 million from the state's cuts. That money could have prevented this majority-Black city (79.1% Black; 14.1% white) from state takeover by emergency managers. It could also have prevented the largest municipal bankruptcy in US history. Flint had $54.9 million taken from its budget over the same period; the city's deficit in 2012 was $19.2 million. With revenue-sharing dollars, Flint could have eliminated its deficit, paid off all $30 million of its bonded indebtedness, and still had over $5 million in surplus to invest in schools, transportation, police and fire protection, and other critical services. This majority-Black city (53.9% Black; 39.9% white) wouldn't have been taken over by four successive state-appointed emergency managers. The city wouldn't have needed to switch its water supply to the Flint River. Its residents didn't need to drink lead-poisoned water.

Cuts to revenue sharing were not enough for LaFaive and the Mackinac Center. The latter had for decades recommended eliminating all statutory revenue sharing and the personal property tax. And with generous donations from the Kochs' DonorsTrust and its affiliate, Donors Capital Fund, the Mackinac Center was able to keep their political fire burning. For example, between 2014 and 2016, the same period that Flint residents were drinking lead-laced water, the Mackinac Center received a total of $2,274,950 from DonorsTrust and Donors Capital Fund.[15] And in 2011, Governor Rick Snyder eliminated statutory revenue sharing altogether and replaced it with the Economic Vitality Incentive Program, whereby funding would have to be earned by local governments based on their ability to consolidate local expenditures and limit benefits in new-employee compensation packages.

The paradox of LaFaive and other austerity proponents condemning "ladling the gravy" was that the legislature, through its own efforts to balance the state budget while also dishing out massive tax cuts to the rich, raided the revenue-sharing trough and diverted that public revenue stream used to provide critical city services to private interests. In so doing, lawmakers caused the very financial insolvencies that then prompted state takeovers by emergency managers. The Michigan Municipal League referred to this scheme as the "great revenue sharing heist."[16] The ability to root the debt crisis in the social pathology of Black leadership and cities allowed the heist to occur in broad daylight. In Michigan, the true special interests are not majority people of color living in its segregated cities, as Governor Snyder intimated, but rather the corporations, industries, construction and other businesses that think tanks like the Mackinac Center represent. During this period the state was making "all sorts of [cuts], reduction in department staff, et cetera—for years and years and years," recalls an Oakland County school board employee. "Then I remember at the time saying, Someone is gonna die! The community health cuts, the human service cuts. We are cutting so far that people are probably going to die. And it just turned out to be something this bad."

MICHIGAN'S EMERGENCY MANAGER LAW

The role of Michigan's emergency manager law in the Flint water crisis has drawn serious scrutiny by advocates and critics alike. "The governor's own task force," explained Curt Guyette of the Michigan chapter of the American Civil Liberties Union (ACLU), "in its report, [concluded] that the primary cause of this totally avoidable man-made crisis was the role played by the Michigan Department of Environmental Quality (MDEQ) and the role of the state's Emergency Manager Law."

> In fact, [the task force] recommended that the law be re-evaluated as a result of what happened in Flint. It's beyond dispute. Those two facts are

really beyond dispute, and the fact that it was the governor's own task force. The governor who was a champion of this Emergency Manager Law, the governor who appointed the director of the MDEQ, and the governor who established the campaign on the idea of running government like a business. The people he appointed to investigate the causes of the Flint water crisis came to this conclusion. I think it's . . . beyond debate at this point.

Yet Snyder refused to say, "I own this, I made a mistake," explained a political pundit. "He says, you know, 'we should have done this differently, it's too bad this happened, but let's move forward.' And that the state government is the reason this happened." The governor was never charged, and no convictions have resulted from the numerous pending criminal charges arising from the Flint drinking water crisis, which underscores how effectively the judiciary ensures the impunity of white supremacy.

While the governor and his team were trying to distance themselves from the Flint water crisis, other policy wonks and advocates were quietly meeting to rethink the emergency manager law. One such event was the invitation-only Emergency Manager Law Research Forum, hosted by Mary Schulz and Eric Scorsone, both from Michigan State University Extension's Center for Local Government Finance and Policy. Many consider Scorsone a key architect of Michigan's Emergency Manager Law. Those close to him commented that he might be reconsidering his original premise about the efficacy and fairness of preempting local democratic decision making in order to force municipal financial reform. Nevertheless he continued to champion its necessity in correcting the financial problems of local government. Schulz and Scorsone began the forum at 4:30 p.m. on September 22, 2016, at the Chateau on the River in Trenton. The forum's goal was to assemble a mix of people from various municipalities with a wide range of experiences with emergency management in Michigan and have them propose changes to the Emergency Manager Law. There were too many people at the forum, an invited participant remembered, and too short a time (two hours) for any meaningful analysis of people's experiences or development of concepts. "It was, however," according to this participant, "principally a good way for Eric to get 'filler' for his forthcoming 'white paper,' I think. From that standpoint, he did well."

The evening started with introductions, and then the participants, as instructed by Eric, were to engage in a "good dialogue; we want all the ideas out there," as he put it. In attendance were county executives and budget directors, city controllers and mayors, and a few academics. Last to introduce themselves were four personnel from the Pew Charitable Trusts, a nonprofit, nonpartisan research organization based in Washington, DC. "I work with a team of people that has done extensive research on states intervening in local governments," explained one of these Pew staffers. "Michigan being one of our target states that we focused a lot on. When I first heard the term 'emergency manager,' I thought it was the person that dispatched the paramedics to, but since then I learned all the ins and outs of it, talked to your governor, everybody involved in it, and Eric."

Knowledge of the meaning and potential impact of emergency management as a legislative tool is shared across a wide swath of government, industry, and the academy, whether or not the participants, as in the Pew staff's case, have much knowledge about the subject matter. "I picked up a paper from Pew on the [Pew] foundation's 'research' on this EM stuff," a participant and city administrator told me. "I paged through it, and my impression is that even they are way light on this stuff." In effect, those charged with understanding the impact of this policy instrument, according to this former emergency manager, were both ill informed and ill prepared for the assessment.

For Scorsone, this gathering presented a research opportunity to learn from the experiences of folks from various levels of government responsible for implementing emergency manager efforts in the state. One thing he made abundantly clear to all invited guests was that this forum would not question, much less denounce, the strategy of state takeover of municipalities in Michigan or to ascertain to what extent the strategy worked any injustices on the Black communities in the cities the state controlled. Rather, what was up for discussion were potential reforms, tweaks, to the existing legislation. For Scorsone, this forum presented an opportunity to develop Emergency Manager Law 2.0, a second generation of municipal austerity reform. This and other forums like it shed light on the collaborative efforts involved in shaping racial capitalism. And in the state of Michigan, the land grant university played a pivotal part in assembling the actors and writing the doctrine that produced the state's most egregious civil rights violation.

KICKING THE CAN DOWN THE ROAD

The law was never intended to be a cure for municipal insolvency, explained Michael Stampfler, former emergency manager of Pontiac, Michigan. Twenty years of experience as city manager in Casselberry, Florida; Talladega, Alabama; West Warwick, Rhode Island; and Portage and Pontiac, Michigan had taught Stampfler that state takeovers usually sell off resources and assets that could help keep a city viable, which serves to only worsen the economic climate in the local communities affected by the law.[17] For Stampfler, Michigan's emergency management legislation did not address root issues or introduce new mechanisms that might achieve long-term financial solvency for the communities involved; rather it kicked the can of municipal insolvency down the road.

Many of the communities forced into state receivership in Michigan since 2000, including Flint, Ecorse, Highland Park, Benton Harbor, and Pontiac, remained there over multiple budgetary cycles. In Flint, which went through four emergency managers from November 2011 to April 2015, the authority of the mayor and city council was reinstated only when the fourth and final emergency manager order was repealed by the state in January 2018. In Stampfler's experience, Michigan's emergency manager law cannot achieve a lasting cure for the problems facing many financially troubled communities. "Improving the community's ability to stand as a financially viable and economically stable municipality, post receivership," he writes, "will require more than tactics such as balancing the books by selling off community assets."[18] You have to change the economic system that supports these communities, and nobody is focusing on that. "So, you can expect that it's just going to keep on going, kicking the can down the road." In the absence of greater and more careful investment, such hastily cobbled-together legislation will lead again to financial distress and receivership, rather than achieving a lasting cure for the problems facing many communities.[19] Stampfler compares it to the ancient practice of bloodletting, draining cities of the financial blood they need to fight the disease of urban disinvestment.

In truth, the Emergency Manager Law was never expected to cure the financial problems of Michigan's cities. "It's strictly a papering [over] to get the numbers to add up, Stampfler explained to me, "and at the end of the day, they are going to recycle this thing. It might take three years" or longer. Emergency management might even get politicians reelected, and "that is what they are looking at." But there is no cure being put in place, Stampfler affirmed. The law's purpose, in effect, is to take debts strategically accumulated in one place and turn them into credits for others in another place. This balance sheet of racial capitalism never balances. "If you are going to cure this problem," Stampfler continued,

> You have to do something more than balance the books. In my view, it's like, what new economic situation or system are you going to infuse into these places that gives people hope, that gives people jobs, that changes the way the community is functioning? You pulled the rug out from under them, whether it's by removing revenue sharing, strategic racism, or whatever? Just balance the books and give it back to those people that are still there and say, good, have a go at it? No. I think, you really have to spend a lot of money in infrastructure to get it ready to go on its own again. And these economies are totally broken, and it's just a recipe to do the same thing again. It's been going on for years and years and years.

THE NEOLIBERAL AUSTERITY COMPLEX

In the development and implementation of the Michigan Emergency Manager Law, academic influence like Eric Scorsone's has been immense. He is among a growing number of academics and think tanks helping to shape Michigan's neoliberal policy agenda, which continues to target cities of color, while presenting their deadly ideas as disinterested academic research.[20] In July 2014, just months after Flint's emergency manger Darnell Earley authorized the city to switch its water supply from Detroit to the Flint River, the Mercatus Center at George Mason University released Scorsone's working paper "Municipal Fiscal Emergency Laws: Background and Guide to State-Based Approaches.". The Mercatus Center is one of several university think tanks that investigative journalist Jane Mayer highlights in her book *Dark Money*. Since the 1980s, Mayer writes, Koch enterprises and other pro–free market organizations have made George Mason University an academic beachhead for preaching anti-regulatory policies, effectively turning the Mercatus Center into an extension of the Kochs' lobbying operation.[21] George Mason's economics department, Mayer reports, became a hotbed of controversial theories that began to channel Americans' tax dollars toward projects that greatly advantage the rich.[22] We can now add Michigan State University's Department of Agricultural, Food, and Resource Economics to the list of university departments supporting the Kochs' lobbying operation. The guise of public choice and the racialization of austerity, not to mention the war on drugs and welfare reform more generally, have been combined to make urban austerity an easy sell to white suburbanites, who benefit from tax cuts that deprive urban governments of much-needed revenue.

Perhaps it is no surprise, then, that Scorsone's working paper on municipal fiscal emergency laws did not include an analysis of the ramifications of massive tax cuts and rising government debt on the solvency of local government. In fact, Scorsone blames the implementation of municipal fiscal emergency laws on the emergence of public sector collective-bargaining laws in the 1960s and public sector unionization more generally. "The degree of fiscal stress that municipalities across the country face," Scorsone wrote, is a "given," compelling states to continually test new solutions.[23] Scorsone sought to normalize the deeply authoritarian and ideological source of this form of state interventionism by sorting out which states have explicit municipal fiscal emergency laws and which ones do not (34 don't have them, according to Scorsone), which states have passed special legislation (Massachusetts, New York, and Connecticut) and which states (13) have passed laws that deal in a general way with municipal fiscal emergencies.[24]

"Michigan's law," Scorsone wrote, "is a *good* example of the interaction among various laws in understanding the causes of and potential resolutions to fiscal crises" (emphasis added). The law's most recent iteration, Scorsone acknowledged, allowed "the emergency manager to ignore and set aside union contracts and establish new pay and benefits as well as work rules." Scorsone concluded that extreme municipal fiscal distress remains rare, however: "Where municipal fiscal emergency laws exist, generally speaking, they respond to poor management, local incompetence, and perhaps even corruption."[25] This depiction of elected officials as greedy, self-interested, and corrupt is consistent with the Kochs' anti-government libertarianism and free market absolutism. The fact that the populations of cities under emergency management in Michigan were on average 71% African American suggests how this deeply authoritarian and ideological form of state interventionism is aligned with white supremacy.

A year earlier, Scorsone wrote a fact sheet explaining the state's most recent emergency manager law, the Local Financial Stability and Choice Act (Public Act 436, 2012). Scorsone wrote that the new "law was passed because the Michigan Legislature and Gov. Rick Snyder felt that a replacement was needed for the now-defunct 2011 Emergency Manager Law (Public Act 4 of 2011)."[26] The fact sheet acknowledged that PA 4 had been rejected by voters in a November 2012 statewide referendum, but it depoliticizes this overwhelming rejection by Michiganders and does not examine its constitutionality or possible racist overtures. Scorsone argued that the need for a new law was deemed "critical because of the fiscal crises being experienced in cities such as Detroit and Flint, and school districts such as Highland Park and Muskegon Heights."[27] But Scorsone conveniently omitted from his explanation of the fiscal crisis that enveloped these majority-Black spaces how the state had created the necessary conditions for municipal bankruptcy. In Detroit's case, the road to bankruptcy was years in the making. The state used predatory forms of financing and cultivated parasitic forms of governance to target Black assets, jobs, and neighborhoods in the city. This distinctive form of racialized capitalism was propagated through countless think tanks, academic programs, legal organizations, lobbyists, and business interests. And, in Michigan, it took a fiscally conservative venture capitalist who billed himself as "one tough nerd" to put this political project into practice.

·   ·   ·   ·   ·

The history of appointing managers to help financially troubled municipalities dates back to 1988 in Michigan. That year, Public Act 101 created both the financial emergency status and the emergency financial manager (EFM) position to help with the specific financial plight of the city of Hamtramck. Two years later, the practice was expanded with the enactment of PA 72, which allowed an EFM to be appointed for any local governmental unit, including school districts. Beginning in 2000, Michigan governors, both Republican (John Engler) and Democratic (Jennifer Granholm), started appointing EFMs to right the fiscal ships of Hamtramck, Highland Park, Flint, Ecorse, Pontiac, Benton Harbor, Three Oaks, and Detroit Public Schools. In nearly all those cases, Curt Guyette of the Michigan ACLU wrote in 2014, "African-Americans were the majority of residents."[28] At one point, the EFM over Detroit Public Schools (DPS) tried to exert authority over the curriculum. This particular transgression was indicative of the self-assured hubris of state-appointed managers eager to test the limits of their newfound authority. It also suggests the clear antipathy toward government that so many of them shared. The Detroit Board of Education sued the state, charging that the emergency financial manager, Robert Bobb, had overstepped his authority. The court agreed that the law restricted the EFM to addressing issues directly related to financial matters. For those seeking to stretch the reach of their state-appointed authority, this ruling was a significant setback.[29]

Two months after he took office, Governor Snyder signed into law the Local Government and School District Fiscal Accountability Act (PA 4). "It was widely seen as a response to the ruling in the DPS case," wrote Guyette. The new act greatly expanded the authority of appointees, as reflected in the change of their titles from "emergency financial manager" to simply "emergency manager."[30] "No state in the country," Guyette explained to me, "had had a law that put so much power into the hands of just one person. These appointees could cancel collective bargaining agreements and other contracts, disregard existing local ordinances, create new laws, sell off public assets, and eliminate the salaries of local elected officials. They also decided how much authority, if any, duly elected officials retained."

"They became increasingly more harsh and repressive and regressive as time went by," recalled Debra Taylor of We the People of Detroit. "And it hasn't mattered which governor, it doesn't matter whether it's been a Republican or a Democrat in office. Quite frankly, we are tired of being redlined and subprimed." Taylor, together with thousands of other Michigan citizens, launched a public backlash against PA 4. Individuals and organizations worked to collect more than 225,885 signatures—65,000 more than the 161,000 needed to place a referendum on PA 4 on the ballot.

In a well-researched article, Curt Guyette provided a deep dive into the secret tactics and backdoor dealings that took place between the governor's team and legal coconspirators, including Jones Day, the third-largest law firm in the world (with 2,407 attorneys and gross revenues of $1.6 billion in 2012), and Miller Buckfire—a private investment banker and consultant based in New York City.[31] Guyette's investigation revealed the length to which this group used old friendships, business associations, and legal alliances to skirt judicial precedent, stretching both fact and truth to contrive Detroit's bankruptcy. As soon as citizens started collecting signatures, Jones Day attorneys, in concert with Miller Buckfire, began strategizing with the governor and his team a contingency plan in case the petition for a referendum succeeded. At that time, Guyette noted, Jones Day was offering its services to the state for free—so lucrative was the potential of bankruptcy for them.

"Jones Day's hand is deeply entrenched in this contrived bankruptcy," Monica Lewis-Patrick told me. The state hired the firm to be the city's *restructuring counsel.* Emergency Manager Kevyn Orr has been a Jones Day partner (and at the writing is partner in charge) since May 2000.[32] Jones Day also provided legal representation to most of the global banks that then held most of Detroit's total municipal debt of over $12.9 billion, including UBS AG, Citigroup, Goldman Sachs, Bank of America's Merrill Lynch, and Muriel Siebert and Company, an affiliate of the SBS Financial Group. Jones Day also represented some of the biggest media and media-related companies in the country, including the McClatchy Company (formerly Knight-Ridder), which owns the *Detroit Free Press.*[33]

"What you will find is," Lewis Patrick warned me, "it is very difficult to get an opposing view to much of the mainstream media" about the Detroit bankruptcy, because Jones Day represents most of the city's media sources, including "the *Free Press* news and channels 2, 4, and 7."

"So that is a big part of what we are up against": a total media blackout when it comes to questioning the legitimacy of the city's bankruptcy process. "You should know," Lewis Patrick informed me, "that Jones Day also represents Veolia, [which] advised Flint and Detroit that they can drink poisoned water. Its total control. So all the decision-making, the contracts that were developed, all the referendums, the RFPs [requests for proposal], everything was drafted by Jones Day" to ensure that the state's austerity playbook was followed. "Much of their news is repetitive," Lewis Patrick went on, "so a news story you see on channel 2 you also read in newsprint. It's all an effort to 'scare us all' and promote 'their predatory practices.'"

Both Miller Buckfire and Jones Day were also advising state treasurer Andy Dillon on tactics.[34] For Jones Day, Detroit's insolvency was an opportunity to push forward the firm's thesis on the jurisprudence of municipal pensions and to make a whole bunch of money while doing so.

BUILDING A THEORY

In 2011 Jeffrey Ellman and Daniel Merrett, both attorneys in the business restructuring and reorganization division of Jones Day, authored an article titled "Pensions and Chapter 9: Can Municipalities Use Bankruptcy to Solve Their Pension Woes?" published in the *Emory Bankruptcy Developments Journal*.[35] Ellman and Merrett wrote: "Perhaps the single largest problem facing municipalities today is the dramatic and growing shortfall in public pension funds." This was the result, they contended, of municipalities' freedom to choose pension funding methods and policies. "The result has been several decades of increasingly *rich benefits packages,* often resulting from negotiations with a municipality's collective bargaining units, coupled with a *less-than-rigid fiscal approach* to paying for those benefits."[36] Yet, for all its scholarly appearance, the article advances no political theory about municipal bankruptcy; rather, it advocates a political agenda to dismantle public pensions and disarm unions' collective bargaining power. This now-nationwide campaign was bankrolled by anti-pension nonprofits funded by key conservative supporters, including the Olin, Koch, and Scaife foundations. "Money is funding most of your largest well-funded research projects in the country," Debra Taylor pointed out. Their beachhead strategy, journalist Jane Mayer wrote, involved funding prestigious law and economics programs across the country in an effort to support faculty willing to devise theory that fortified their political agenda and then train the next generation of legal and economic thinkers in a new philosophical approach to the state fiscal crisis.[37] The Olin Foundation alone, Jane Mayer reported, spent $68 million underwriting the expansion of "Law and Economics programs in American law schools between the years of 1985 and 1989."[38]

Ellman and Merrett's article, along with a growing repository of other articles, books, special collections, and policy briefs, has provided proponents with scholarly authority to advance a conservative campaign against welfare policies and unions, their favorite whipping boys for what ails freedom and American democracy. Their article posing as academic research is a treatise written by two bankruptcy attorneys addressing how best to operationalize their raison d'être. This playbook, adopted to the letter by Jones Day and its associates, affiliates, and allies, focused not only on slashing benefits to state employees but also assigning blame for the city's financial woes. The problem, we are told, was that public service workers' benefits, negotiated by collective bargaining units and mismanaged by elected officials—mostly Black officials—were now simply too expensive and had to be right-sized. Such gross oversimplification speaks to the extent to which political theory has morphed into pure ideological gobbledygook.

Emergency managers played a vital role in translating conservative political rhetoric into action. Louis Schimmel was appointed emergency manager of Pontiac in September 2011. Beginning in 2000, Schimmel had served as EM of Hamtramck for six years. Before that, in 1986, he was appointed to oversee the city of Ecorse's finances after it landed in state receivership. Wherever he took office, Schimmel aggressively implemented the state's mandate to nullify labor contracts and privatize public city services, which included everything from firing first responders to privatizing city cemeteries, effectively selling off any and all city assets. In Flint, for example, the city-owned Santa Claus figure was auctioned off. By 2014, many of Schimmel's assignments were back in debt and under the direction of a new emergency manager ready to again follow the state's mandate. Just before his turn at Pontiac's city treasury, Schimmel was an adjunct scholar and director of municipal finance at the Mackinac Center for Public Policy. In 2005, the conservative policy promoter published an essay by Schimmel that called for an expansion of the state's emergency financial manager law (Public Act 72, 1990) to, among other tasks, impose contract changes on public-employee unions and "replace and take on the powers of the governing body."[39] When Republicans gained control of both the executive and the legislative branch in 2010, the Mackinac Center reprinted Schimmel's article.[40] Schimmel's recommendations were adopted verbatim into Public Act 4 in 2011, greatly expanding the power of both school board and city emergency managers.

"So you have this really pretty bizarre chain of events," as ACLU spokesperson Guyette described it to me,

> where you have a law [Public Act 4] that is clearly anti-democratic in the sense that it takes away the power of locally duly elected officials and puts it in the hands of one appointed official. People living in the state saw the law as clearly anti-democratic, and through the democratic process of the referendum, rejected it. And the response on the part of the governor and the state legislature was to come back with a very similar law, crafted in a way that made it not subject to the democratic process, and passed it during a lame duck session of the legislature.

It was clear to all those concerned that the road to the largest municipal bankruptcy in US history went right through the Emergency Manager Law, PA 436, and no amount of citizen mobilization was going to stop them.

Dispensing with political theory altogether, Ellman and Merrett confidently wrote of widespread optimism that Chapter 9 can provide "a real, workable solution *to the overwhelming and seemingly unassailable pension obligations* of many municipal debtors."[41] Others, however, have suggested that there is vehement disagreement over the legality of reducing pension benefits this way. Setting aside the moral implications of actively strategizing to default on contract obligations to city employees who have dedicated their entire working lives to public service, Ellman and Merrett conclude, "The reality is that this area of the law is largely untested in the courts, and very little is certain."[42] In other words, anything is possible for those wishing to push boundaries. The law to be tested was the Michigan constitution itself. In Michigan and some other states, employee pension plans and retirement systems of the state are contractual obligations that cannot be taken away.[43] However, under Section 365 of the US Bankruptcy Code, a "trustee, subject to the court's approval, may assume or reject any executory contract or unexpired lease of the debtor."[44] Ellman and Merrett hopefully speculated that courts would understand the state's pension obligations as "executory."[45] This interpretation would give the trustee—in this case Detroit's newly appointed emergency manager—with the federal bankruptcy judge's approval, the choice to assume, alter, or terminate contractual obligations protected by the Michigan constitution. Ellman and Merrett's optimism was realized when Judge Steven Rhoades ruled that federal bankruptcy law trumped public employee pension protections embedded in the Michigan constitution and approved the filing with a speed rarely seen in such proceedings.

One hundred and nine parties filed objections to the city's eligibility to file for bankruptcy, and none swayed the court's ruling. Objectors argued that the bankruptcy violated both the US and the Michigan constitution. In response, the court certified the matter to the US attorney general, permitting the United States to intervene. The AG filed a brief in support of the constitutionality of Chapter 9. Because the constitutionality of a state statute was in question, the court also certified the matter to the Michigan attorney general. Similarly, state treasurer Andy Dillon also filed a response in support.[46] Both officials judged Chapter 9 to be constitutional as applied in this case, and the court ruled that the governor's authorization to file Detroit's bankruptcy under PA 436 was valid under the Michigan constitution.

The court ruled, however, that the city had not negotiated with its creditors in good faith, implying that the prebankruptcy negotiations the city had undertaken to resolve disputes were not sufficient to satisfy the "good faith" requirement. Specifically, the court found that the city's vague proposal to its creditors did not provide them with sufficient information or enough time—some thirty days—to make meaningful counterproposals.[47] The court also noted that the explanations provided by the city bordered on disingenuous, providing "little opportunity for creditor input or substantive discussion" (119). "Was the City of Detroit's bankruptcy filing a 'foregone conclusion' as the objecting parties assert?" the Court asked. "Of course it was, and for a long time" (135). Yet, while "acknowledging some merit to the objectors' serious concerns about how City and State officials managed the lead-up to this filing," the court concluded that the city's petition was filed in good faith (140). In effect, while the court clearly blamed the hurried and contrived bankruptcy on the state's neoliberal measures, it also supported the private appropriation of public assets otherwise destined to support Black lives, revealing the extent to which the court system was deeply embedded in this phase of racial capitalism, which forces Black residents to shoulder the burden of righting the city's financial transgressions while freeing up capital for city creditors, real estate moguls, and business interests to invest as they wish.

RACIALIZED AUSTERITY

While Ellman and Merrett suggest many fathers sired municipal bankruptcy, they clearly blame the deviant behavior of urban leaders, and their collective bargaining units, leaders who were now indulging in the fiscal spoils of their transgressions.[48] They characterized city employee pensions as lavish, in this and other ways suggesting that the recipients were somehow not quite deserving of their compensation packages. Before the bankruptcy, general retirees received a yearly payment of less than $19,000—hardly lavish. Moreover, the authors made no mention of the thousands of city positions eliminated during the Mercado-Feikens era, displacing thousands of municipal workers. Public jobs have frequently been the only avenue for women and workers of color to get secure employment. Ellman and Merrett nowhere alluded to the fact that a large percentage of those who would lose their pensions were Black middle-class people, many of whom had worked their entire life to secure basic retirement income. Many of them belonged to the first generation in the history of Black wage labor to be eligible to earn retirement income. The authors didn't have to be so explicit. Their article is much more a reflection of their racialized class interests than it is a sincere analysis of the pension obligations. Conspicuously absent is any mention of white flight, disinvestment, the reduction in state revenue sharing, or any of the multiple forms of racialized dispossession and financial fascism embedded in their "theory" of municipal bankruptcy.

The numbers, Curt Guyette wrote, are indeed slippery concerning the reputed deficit leading to Detroit's municipal bankruptcy.[49] "The numbers kept rising," explained a Detroit resident. "It started off with under a $100 million deficit. Then it went to a $145 million and then it went to $165 million. And then they trumped up more debt because they were determined to sell off the city's assets, including Belle Isle Park, which is the jewel of the city of Detroit, and to set the Water Department up for privatization."

Detroit's insolvency and bankruptcy filing, as Wallace Turbeville, senior fellow at the liberal think tank Demos, described it at the time, was highly inflated and, in large part, simply inaccurate.[50] Moreover, to get out of bankruptcy, the city needed to address the shortfall in its annual cash flow, whether it was $145 million, $165 million, or $198 million as the emergency manager projected, not its total outstanding long-term debt, which the EM pegged at $18 billion. If my bank insisted that I pay back my entire home mortgage tomorrow, I too would file for bankruptcy. Among the many inaccuracies used to inflate the debt was to add as a liability of the city the $5.8 billion the DWSD owed. Yet the DWSD's debt was not a liability of the city's general fund, which served more than 3 million people across all of southeastern Michigan.[51]

"But you also have to go back and fill in the blanks," Monica Lewis-Patrick reminded me. "Over forty-four pension labor unions negotiated in *good faith* to actually make concessions of about $180 million over a ten-year period. They were also willing to concede another $120 million per year." Together "that would have been more than enough [to cover the] shortfall the governor and the state had said that Detroit was in."

"They also could have renegotiated the healthcare benefits of the city employees," she continued. At the time, "the healthcare package was $300 million to BlueCross BlueShield. We could have created a cost savings of $200 million annually by renegotiating with five other nationally noted insurance firms that were willing to offer us the same plan for $100 million annually." So, instead of taking the $200 million annual cost savings, Kevyn Orr and his negotiating team stayed with the higher-priced healthcare plan in order to raise the debt obligations and force the bankruptcy. "It was all sensationalism . . . to legitimize an illegitimate process, covering over" their real intentions. As it turned out, the largest reduction of the bankruptcy debt came in the form of health care cuts—about $4 billion.[52] Instead of retirees being enrolled in health insurance plans with a 20% copay, under the new plan retirees receive a $125 monthly stipend.[53] "On top of the healthcare cuts," Curt Guyette reported, general retirees "also suffer a 4.5 percent reduction in their pensions."[54]

Even more egregious, according to Lewis Patrick, was that the EM constructed a paradigm in which the retirees—who "became employed under the honorable Alexander Coleman Young's administration, primarily African Americans"—were at fault and should therefore shoulder the burden of the bankruptcy's real impact. In addition to medical cuts, retirees would also see reductions in their annual cost of living (COLA) increases. "They even clawed back funds that they had saved in their own mutual annuities and accounts," she emphasized, "saying they earned too much interest on their annuity savings accounts." The recoupment of alleged overpayments into annuity savings accounts amounted to more than $190 million being taken from retirees who participated in the program from 2003 to 2013.[55] As bad as this deal was, as Guyette noted, it might have been a lot worse if pension cuts had been even higher, as Kevyn Orr threatened if a settlement wasn't swiftly agreed to.[56] This dominant narrative about who is to blame for the financial meltdown is telling given that "the city's pension contributions in particular did not play a role in pushing it into bankruptcy."[57]

"Most of these cities are just stumbling along," a former emergency manager told me. "For the most part they can paper over their mistakes. Had revenue sharing been cut by 10% or 5% or something [like that], you probably would not notice as much." However, coming on the heels of the Great Recession, these massive cuts to revenue sharing plunged the city into a cash flow crisis.[58] In addition, the city also provided significant tax subsidies—as much as $20 million—to private interests, such as Dan Gilbert, the billionaire founder of Quicken Loans and Bedrock Detroit, and Ilitch Holdings, owner of Little Caesars Pizza, to spur the redevelopment of downtown Detroit. Gilbert even received lucrative federal tax breaks to encourage new investment in low-income communities.[59] "You can't continue to run it [Detroit] when we have our tax revenues going down the tubes," the ex–emergency manager concluded about the impact of tax cuts on financially struggling cities. But the bitter paradox of snatching interest payments on annuity savings accounts from city retirees while dishing out massive tax cuts to city billionaire land developers underscores the fact that Michigan's urban austerity was never simply about money; it was also about ascribing blame.

LIBOR'S RACIALIZED CAPITALISM

In 2005 and 2006 the city, at the direction of federal judge John Feikens, entered into hedge arrangements with UBS AG and Merrill Lynch Capital Services (later acquired by Bank of America)—both clients of Jones Day— to assume $1.44 billion of unfunded pension liabilities.[60] At the time, the plan was celebrated by investment pundits as a cutting-edge fiscal innovation that would supposedly save the city hundreds of millions of dollars from rising interest rates, thus averting widespread layoffs and also providing a convenient safe haven for investment banks to dump their predatory mortgage-backed securities in the precrash years.[61] The deal included an "interest rate swap" to fund debt obligations of the DWSD that had accrued over several decades largely because of subsidies to suburban water infrastructure and diminishing city tax revenues. The swap reflected a bet that interest rates would rise. After interest rates plummeted as a result of the 2008 crash, DWSD was forced to pay $537 million in swap termination payments to banks.[62] To pay the termination fees, DWSD increased water rates and, in 2012, took out $489 million in further bonded debt.[63] To show the banks that it meant business, DWSD foisted the largest residential water shutoff program in US history on the most vulnerable among the citizens it was supposed to serve. Given that the debt service now equaled more than 40% of DWSD revenue, nearly half of Detroiters' water payments were going to pay debt service to the questionable and potentially illegal predatory bank deals.[64] Many of those banks were implicated in the LIBOR-rigging scandal, in which many major financial institutions colluded in reporting false interest rates to manipulate the markets and boost their own profits. Billions of dollars were stolen from cash-strapped cities like Detroit, and this theft was a major source of the city's debt crisis. Yet few have acknowledged these criminal actions as part of the explanation for the city's financial collapse.

Those same banks—remember the mantra "too big to fail"—collected billions of dollars in bailout money and then went on to reap rewards from the financial crisis they created. Moreover, we know now that these banks targeted African American cities like Flint and Detroit to find home buyers willing to sign subprime mortgages. "Between 2004 and 2006," *Rolling Stone* reported, "a full 75 percent of mortgages issued in Detroit were subprime." In other words, three out of every four! "By 2012, banks had foreclosed on 100,000 homes, which drove down the city's total real estate value by 30 percent and spurred a mass exodus of nearly a quarter million people."[65] This sort of racialized financial dispossession is truly unprecedented in US history. Many who stayed were left *underwater,* having mortgage balances greater than the values of their homes. Across the county African American and Latino American borrowers were disproportionately harmed by the foreclosure crisis.[66] A study published in 2010 by the Center for Responsible Lending estimated the total number of African Americans and Latino Americans who lost or were in imminent danger of losing their homes to have been 734,950 and 1,067,610, respectively. Among owner-occupants, the center estimated that "7.9% of African Americans and 7.7% of Latinos who received loans to purchase or refinance their primary residence between 2005 and 2008 have lost their homes to foreclosure [since the market collapse], compared to an estimated 4.5% of non-Hispanic whites."[67] "Whatever their past faults," Curt Guyette wrote, "municipal employees and retirees didn't cause people and businesses to flee the city and had nothing to do with the predatory lending and mortgage-industry Ponzi schemes and the resulting foreclosure tsunami" that helped push cities like Flint, Detroit, and hundreds of other cities all across America toward insolvency.[68] This could have been a time to hold contractors and banks accountable for the billions of dollars they siphoned from the city's publicly shared resources, which had sedimented decades of racialized social existence. Instead, dog whistle politics and fictitious jurisprudence willingly racialized what became the inevitable path to insolvency, covering the layers of financial fascism with which the road to bankruptcy was paved.

Even as Detroit mayor Dave Bing and his administration were "imposing furloughs and health-care cuts on some staff and negotiating benefits cuts with others, the city, acting under the direction of the state, signed a $1.8 million no-bid contract with Miller Buckfire" to serve as counsel for the city in the bankruptcy proceedings.[69] "It is incredibly sophisticated," Monica Lewis-Patrick said of this type of racialized capitalism. "They recruited this bourgeois Negro, which is not a new phenomenon, but they strategically picked people that had kinship and relationships to certain communities so that they could claim that 'these people would not harm these communities.' So even if you can't vote, or we set aside democracy, you are still represented [by this] one African American." The governor appointed Kevyn Orr as Detroit's emergency manager on March 14, 2013, and the following day Jones Day began working toward authorizing bankruptcy proceedings for the city. Detroit filed for bankruptcy on July 18, after the governor authorized the emergency manager's decision to do so.

At stake was not simply who would be left holding the cities bag of toxic debt but also the very future of municipal bond markets in this country. For that reason, this bankruptcy hearing attracted and held the attention not only of every Detroit household standing to lose its pensions, homes, and much else but also of Wall Street, which had come to trust the municipal market as a safe—read: low default risk—cash cow. In addition to a low risk of default, municipal bonds offer unique tax advantages. Under present federal tax law, the interest income from most municipal bonds is exempt from federal income taxes, and most states exempt the interest on in-state bonds from state income taxes as well, which makes the after-tax yield earned on municipal bonds higher than similar (in credit quality and duration) investments.[70] In the absence of other forms of revenue, municipalities have sold bonds to raise money for public purposes such as constructing water and sewer systems, schools, highways, and public buildings. The total size of the municipal bond market in 2018 was approximately $3.8 trillion, 71% of which was tax exempt.[71] As of June 11, 2018, the state of Michigan was tied with one state in having the seventh largest amount of tax-exempt municipal bonds outstanding.[72] Detroit's contrived bankruptcy was a clear signal that the municipal bond market would perpetually remain a stable and trusted *growth machine* for finance and capital.[73]

.   .   .   .   .

Notwithstanding the claims and insinuations of Jones Day attorneys and political talking heads Ellman and Merrett, "state pension funds," as *Rolling Stone* reported, "were more or less in decent shape prior to the financial crisis of 2008."[74] And the city's financial crisis was caused by a fraud-riddled banking industry, of which many lawbreakers were defended by Jones Day. "In fact," as *Rolling Stone* noted, "prior to the crash, state pension funds nationwide were cumulatively running a surplus."[75] A surplus, in spite of the fact that many states regularly failed to make their required contributions to pension funds. That shortfall in funding in previous years, economist Dean Baker with the Center for Economic Policy and Research wrote in 2011, "is not the main reason that pensions face difficulties now." That rests, according to Baker, squarely with the downturn in the economy and the stock market following the collapse of the housing bubble.[76] Baker affirmed that most states faced pension shortfalls that were manageable and would likely not bankrupt them, particularly if the stock market did not undergo another sudden reversal.[77] To use *Rolling Stone* reporter Matt Tibbi's words, politicians, pundits, think thanks, and in Detroit's case, emergency managers have used scare tactics, questionable arithmetic, and "lavishly funded PR campaigns to cast teachers, firefighters and cops—not bankers—as the budget-devouring boogeymen responsible for the mounting fiscal problems of America's states and cities."[78]

It was a strategy, explained Monica Lewis-Patrick, that "takes public wealth and converts it to private wealth. They are letting contracts to family and friends and a network of people to control essential assets—essential to life. You are talking about privatizing health, you are privatizing prisons, you are privatizing water, you are privatizing parks, you are privatizing education. And this all becomes wealth for those who are already very wealthy and those who aspire to be even more wealthy." This strategy has been effectively implemented following a well-known script. And for its efforts, Jones Day was rewarded with a $150 million check when the case wrapped up. Yet hidden in the exchange of legal tender is the calculated cruelty and straight-up meanness of stealing basic social protections that working-class folk have labored their entire lives to secure. Moreover, the absence of any analysis of the economic violence and personal suffering that arises for pensioners from such actions only serves to further normalize Black and brown suffering as these residents are further denied both voice and basic entitlements. The state's real fiscal crisis is the burden that unfair and unearned advantages for the few entail on the rest of us. What happened in Michigan suggests that a city's financial destiny is not for the majority to decide, and with the right players in the right roles, statist reforms can swiftly move a city from debt management to financial fascism. All one has to do is meld spurious political theory with racial politics. No city has filed for bankruptcy since Detroit did in July 2013.

6 Environments of Injustice

All these people that have done these wonderful things in
the community, and they have just been crushed and hurt.
When you get to know them personally, it is just devastating on a personal level. I am just so angry . . . at how many
people have been destroyed or nearly destroyed. Tendaji
Ganges and Michael Fernandes, and Ananth Aiyer. And all
the other people that died from the Legionella.

—Flint resident (2019)

In this chapter, I describe some of the interlocking and compounding
ways in which people have suffered from exposure to unsafe drinking
water. We have very little detailed knowledge about how people experience racialized water insecurity in this country. Not having water can disrupt one's livelihood, unsettle one's neighborhood, close one's school, and
forever change one's life. It is the multidimensional character of this
human suffering that makes it so difficult to fully comprehend: physical
impairment is often accompanied by psychological fallout; economic
stress has to be juggled along with institutionalized discrimination; and
calls for justice are drowned out by narratives that continue to dehuman-
ize people of color and justify their abject suffering by implying they had
it coming to them. One of the more than two hundred emails released by
the office of Governor Rick Snyder about the Flint water crisis revealed
that a state nurse told a resident in January 2015, regarding her son's
elevated blood lead level, "It is just a few IQ points. . . . It is not the end of
the world."[1] The bigoted assumption by this government agent underscores a widely accepted belief that this population, a priori, is cerebrally
inferior and that any further harm by lead poisoning would be minimal.

As I explain later in this chapter, government response, whether medical or educational, has reinforced this bigoted worldview, which holds that it is pointless to spend more money on medical treatment and educational programs for students who cannot achieve much anyway. These comments and responses by government officials speak volumes about just how much Black lives really matter. Listening to residents explain their experiences, one begins to understand the intersecting and multiple ways in which poisoned water and water shutoffs have inscribed a new color line in Michigan cities.

REPRODUCTIVE ENVIRONMENTAL INJUSTICE

I'm sitting in Kendra and Shawn's living room. They have been kind enough to spend the afternoon with me. Kendra is a well-known activist in town and lectures at one of the six colleges in Flint. Shawn is the stay-at-home dad. This family is living the water crisis on a daily basis. There is a broken washing machine in the driveway, and holes in the ceiling through which pipes have been replaced. Kenda starts with a story of a dear friend: "She miscarried with twins. And she came home from the hospital after miscarrying for the second time to find a letter informing her that pregnant women should not drink the water, and she was devastated. She lost one [child], then the other . . . and she still lives with that, 'I killed my babies. It was my fault.'"

We discuss at length how devasting it must have been for her friend. Such misfortune is difficult to imagine, and added to the immediate shock is a lifetime of guilt and regret with no hope of closure. Also, the friend's poverty has left her with little access to much-needed services, deprivation made worse by the state's deep cuts to social welfare programs, eliminating critical health services she desperately needs. This woman's painful struggle underscores the injustices associated with intersecting oppressions of race, class, and gender.[2]

"She got pregnant again and had another miscarriage," Kendra tells me. "And now she feels the lead has poisoned her for life, and the lead has damaged her body, and she has all these health problems going on." The loss of a child is a parent's worst fear. To lose three children is simply unthinkable. Yet the mental and emotional trauma that this and other women had to endure has effectively been erased from the public record. In the absence of an array of support structures that many privileged white folks take for granted—counseling services, community support, health benefits, and just plain sympathy—the state's austerity measures have left these women of color truly abandoned.

The ominous fact that state-sanctioned austerity disproportionately impaired the reproductive capacities of women, particularly women of color, underscores the gendered aspect of this intergenerational violence. In effect, in reducing the number of children born to mostly women of color, lead poisoning in Flint, Michigan, has resulted in state reproduction regulation. This agenda is reminiscent of coerced government sterilization of poor Black women.[3] But rather than being injected with a long-acting contraceptive, all the women had to do in Flint was drink their tap water.

"I am a single [Latinx] mother, a single parent, with an infant. When I was pregnant with my daughter . . . nobody told me that the water was not drinkable." Community organizers in the Latino community reported many stories such as this woman's during the water crisis. "They were unaware of the water crisis," one community organizer told me in reference to another mother. "They had not had access to clean water for the entire life of their eleven-month-old." This mother had been consuming the water and breastfeeding her child. The child had been bathed in the water and had rashes and a number of other health problems. Another Latinx mother told the Michigan Civil Rights Commission, "It wasn't until January 2015 that someone came to my home, volunteers from the Hispanic community, nobody from the city, to tell me I have to be using a filter. I did not use a filter until then."

For nearly nine months after E. coli, total trihalomethanes (TTHMs), and lead were found to be contaminating the water, this Latinx mother breastfed her child. Visibly upset, she told the commission, "It is wrong for her to breast feed from me because she gets some of my lead too.

"Any parent has always been told that breast-feeding is the best thing to do for your child," she continued, "but to know that you have poisoned your child from your own body. It is painful.

"My baby took three months to get her vision, [and] her progress has been slow.

"I do not have cable in my home. I barely have internet at $14.99 a month to be able to educate myself on what is safe for my baby. That is not right," she proclaimed.

It is hard to imagine how a mother survives with this knowledge, with this guilt. Moreover, her experience underscores the stark fact that we cannot possibly understand environmental injustice in Flint without also foregrounding this government assault on women of color's procreative freedoms. Detroit has one of the highest rates of infant death in the United States, while Flint has higher rates of stillbirths, preterm births, and low birth weight when compared to the rest of the state. The weaponization of drinking water was used to reduce the number of children born to poor women of color by lowering, if not eliminating, their reproductive potential. In effect, the long-term consequences of being exposed to lead in utero or during early childhood reflects a new kind of environmental biodeterminism, a self-fulfilling prophecy, of sorts, whereby the next generation of children of color are saddled with compromised learning and flattened aspirations as a result of this toxic exposure.[4]

YOUNG AND OLD

For those US citizens who have health care and can afford good health insurance, living with lead poisoning is a different experience than for those without. "I have a rheumatologist, a gastroenterologist, [and] a neurologist, . . . because the seizures haven't stopped. So it's constant doctors' appointments for me and the kids, and my biggest worry is my children." This mother's eldest child, she explains, "almost didn't pass [his grade] last year. He can't remember—his biggest thing is he can't remember the assignment he did the night before. So he's having a hard time. But we are working with him. We usually do his homework again over with him in the morning, just as a reminder. But it's his memory. But it has gotten better, because we are doing all sorts of detox."

The lasting physical burdens from lead poisoning have been debilitating for residents, particularly children. Constant migraines and regular convulsions make daily living unpredictable and horrifying. The mother quoted above is faced with scheduling numerous doctor visits and medical examinations that take time and cost money. Copays add up quickly, and appointments are often available only during work hours, forcing many parents to take sick and personal days to seek medical help they or their children, or both, desperately need. Adding to these burdens is the psychological trauma of not knowing what to do or who can help. As a parent, however, this woman worries not only about her own health but about the immediate effects of lead poisoning on her son. The depth of worry about her children is difficult to convey. Every parent in Flint knows that there is no safe level of lead exposure. Those who have experienced lead poisoning of their children have helplessly witnessed their child struggle with attention deficiency, irritability and aggression, and lethargy. Some parents have also reported physical delays in their child's growth, stomach problems, and bone and joint pain. Parents struggle to get answers from the medical profession, and many of them are frustrated with the lack of knowledge and treatment for this environmental toxin. Trying to balance their own symptoms with their children's, many parents are desperate for answers and help.

But children are not the only ones whose lives have been compromised by lead. The elderly suffer too. "My dad is a citizen," a Latinx woman told the Michigan Civil Rights Commission, "yet he speaks very little English. He worked so hard until he got sick. He doesn't work anymore—he can't work. His whole body ails. My body hurts [too]. He is now taking six different medications to counter his bacterial infections on his skin and in his lungs." The Flint water crisis caused many health problems for the elderly. The fact that many of them already suffered from compromised immune systems put them at additional risk of infections like Legionnaires' disease and pneumonia. Moreover, in the rush to test children's lead levels, the elderly population was simply overlooked or unable to get to clinics. Many were not able to get to the water point of delivery (POD) stations, either, leaving their fate in the hands of able-bodied friends or family members. Those without either friends or family had to reach out to their church, if they belonged to a congregation, or the Red Cross. Even folks who had transportation had a hard time lifting and bringing the water back to their homes. "I hurt my wrist carrying a case [of water] from the Fire Department," a senior woman reported.

"As all of this stuff is going on," a local water activist told me, "my sister got sick and died" from drinking the water in her house. Before she got sick, he "wanted to get her house tested. I felt guilty because I dropped the ball. And I still carry that guilt. I'm telling you, I've never seen nothing like this. One minute you go over and she is fine; the next minute she's got blotches all over, she's all swelled up from the steroids she got. It's like, this ain't good. I almost well up . . . because my sister."

They were close. And this brother had deep regrets about his inability to help his sister in her time of need. Other family members, too, watched in disbelief as close relatives succumbed to exposure to Legionella or became sick from lead poisoning. Attending funerals of loved ones while also dealing with personal troubles associated with contaminated water underscores the emotional impact of guilt and loss experienced by so many in Flint.

ONE BOTTLE AT A TIME

Living with contaminated water means making decisions one bottle at a time, decisions not just about drinking the water but about other uses as well. A Flint resident shared, "I cannot shower in my house. It takes me hours to bathe my daughter because I have to warm up her water." As tap water is no longer safe, this young mother must pour bottled water into a kettle and then heat the kettle, several times for each bath. "And then my electricity bill just increased—really? And now they are charging us over $200 a month for water" that is poisonous.

Coping with the Flint water crisis was never just about poisoned water. It was also about the joint vulnerabilities that were hard to predict, let alone manage. The daily anguish was draining. A Flint resident explained: "When we get up in the morning, we have to think about every movement we make. How do we brush our teeth, wash our face, careful not to get it into our tear ducts, not inhaling it, cutting down on taking a shower." These daily decisions lead to constant fear and chronic stress, which can compound already-stressed immune systems. The cumulative burdens associated with both the labor and increasing costs of health care and childcare become yet another aspect of living with poisoned water.

Some activists have referred to the Flint water crisis as another Tuskegee experiment, referring to the 1932 Tuskegee Syphilis Study. The parallels are striking: an isolated African American community, intentionally poisoned by a government agency while state officials looked on, even when an appropriate and safe response was available. Eventually, public opinion swayed state policy, yet the victory came too late to prevent needless suffering and premature death among many African Americans and people of color. To paraphrase critical environmental justice scholar David Pellow, Flint is just another example of the expendability of an entire population "marked for erasure and early death."[5]

DIVIDE AND CONQUER

Another hardship that many have faced during the Flint water crisis is family separation. This inhumane act captured the media spotlight when the Trump administration separated asylum-seeking parents from their children at the US-Mexico border. This cruel behavior resulted in the premature death of many people seeking asylum and left the fate of thousands of children, many of them infants, in limbo. Yet this unconscionable act is nothing new to American imperialism. Native American families were systematically torn apart as whites first settled and then colonized Turtle Island. Both the United States and Canada adopted a "civilization" policy whereby Indigenous children were snatched from their families and forced into off-reservation boarding schools, where they were taught English and Christianity. Aboriginal students on both sides of the colonial border were also forced to cut their hair, wear "Western" clothes, and adopt Anglo-American domestic and agricultural practices, all while being taught that their culture was backward and subordinate. Nor is this policy something that happened in the country's distant past, as the last residential school in Canada closed in 1996. Owners of enslaved people in the United States routinely practiced family separations in slave auctions, ripping children from their parents, and lovers from partners. Centuries of this cruel tradition, to paraphrase James Baldwin, ensured that all over this continent people of color died first of a broken heart and then from broken bodies.

In Flint and Detroit, the entire institution of Black motherhood has been under assault as the traditional source of support from blood mothers, grandmothers, aunts, and other woman-centered networks was slowly dismantled. A Flint resident told the Michigan Civil Rights Commission,

"My daughter is pregnant right now. But she is living outside of the city. Normally that child would be living with their mother." For the child's safety she was being raised in a suburb outside Flint by distant relatives. In addition to the emotional turmoil, this separation of mother, child, and community also causes added financial burdens in the form of additional housing, transportation, food, and childcare costs that would break the bank even of most upper-middle-class white Americans. As a Black mother told the Commission, "It's not just the lead: there's the mental drain" of breaking up the family, breaking the intimate bond between mother and child, and the guilt that so many parents, but mothers in particular, live with. Equally troubling is the fact that limited access to doctors and health care services have all but ensured that some children and fetuses were simply not counted among those exposed to lead poisoning, because they were not tested, further normalizing the scope of harm to this truly vulnerable population. This state-sanctioned violence strikes at what Mohawk midwife Katsi Cook has referred to as environmental reproductive injustice: "Environmental justice and reproductive justice intersect at the very center of woman's role in the processes and patterns of continuous creation."[6] In the Flint water crisis, the state abandoned the reproductive lives of women of color while clearly supporting that of others.

ADDING INSULT TO INJURY

In addition grappling with health struggles, some women in Flint felt humiliated when seeking emergency food and water during the crisis. "When we go to the water PODs [points of distribution]," a woman told the Commission, "they look down at you, like, 'You're here again?' I have an infant, my father, and myself, and six cases of water doesn't last us a week even if we tried."

Others reported having to show identification before receiving water at the PODs. Moreover, most distribution sites were open only during specific hours, 9:30 to 12:30 in some cases. "When you are working 9 to 5," the woman explained, "you can't make it, [especially] when you only have one car. And you don't have food in your house . . . but the places that are providing free food . . . are only open during the working hours."

Flint has a poverty rate over 40%, underscoring the cumulative impact of no water and no food on the city's already vulnerable population. Again, the very people who are seeking basic needs during this time of crisis are the ones shut out by a system that fails to recognize their very existence. For scholar Nancy Scheper-Hughes, this sort of intentional institutional neglect symbolizes "a culture of institutional efficiency and indifference" that sees these vulnerable populations "in all likelihood as 'better off dead.'"[7]

A dearth of credible information also left residents frustrated and angry. "We don't know who to believe," one resident said. "We have been lied to for two years . . . and for over a year we were screaming and nobody was listening. I have been to three different meetings and been given three different stories about flushing, boiling the water, what the lead is doing to the pipes." Some people were conflicted about flushing water becuase of the added costs to their already high water bills. Immediately after the switch in supply source on April 25, 2014, residents complained about the water quality. There had been several boil water advisories, as the city remained in violation of the Safe Drinking Water Act because of persistently high TTHM (total trihalomethanes) levels for almost eleven months. Prolonged exposure to TTHMs may cause problems with the kidneys, liver, or central nervous system and may increase the risk of cancer.

"I was waiting to meet with council member Eric Mays," documentary producer Abby Ellis told to me. "'I've got this meeting,' he tells me, 'you should come to it.' I didn't know what it was. I stumbled in at the very end of it."[8] During the meeting, council member Mays approached the board. "His hands were shaking," Ellis remembered; "he was really upset, and he kept saying, 'people are dying.' It was really upsetting." Shortly after this meeting, Flint city council member Wantwaz Davis posted on his Facebook page that the deliberate poisoning of Flint residents by the state-appointed emergency manager was a form of anti-Black genocide.

THE LATINX COMMUNITY TAP

The Latino community is not highly visible in Flint, and throughout the water crisis they continued to be left in the dark as government health agencies refused to translate warnings into Spanish. Also, US Immigration and Customs Enforcement (ICE) used the water crisis as an opportunity to infiltrate the city, employing stop-and-frisk measures to find, detain, and deport undocumented people in the Flint area. They were the last ethnic group to be notified that their water was not safe to drink and the first to be penalized for it.

"In August of 2015," sixteen months after the city was forced to switch to the Flint River, "I received a letter at work," Camilla Torres told me, "informing the institution to not use the water—there are high levels of lead, and the city was trying to treat it." At the time, Camilla worked at the Hispanic Technology Community Center at Mott Community College. She asked her mother if she had received a similar notification at her house. Neither her mother nor anyone else living on the east side of town had been advised not to drink the water. "I knew the water was coming out really dirty. It was either yellow or dark brown. We started boiling the water, because we thought it was bacteria." But, using Google, Camilla found out that the contaminant was lead, and she started advising folks in the Latinx community not to drink the water. Shortly thereafter, Camilla told me, the United Way started to distribute filters. "They had an event on the campus of UM Flint. But they were asking people for identification, which excluded many in the Hispanic community. I eventually spoke to someone at the United Way, and they agreed to give me 60 filters without identification."

While Camilla was still employed at the Hispanic Center, "I told them, there is an issue with the water and such, [and] they told me, well, that's not your responsibility; we don't do anything with water." It was clear to her that Mott Community College was not interested in helping the Hispanic community, so "I resigned, and I became a full-time volunteer with the collaborative [Genesee County Hispanic Latino Collaborative] at that time. Families [started] coming to me and asking me, 'What's going on—the water is not coming out clean; it smells; it burns. My hair is falling out. My kids are suffering from rashes.' I was like, OK, we have to do something."

At that time, nothing was translated into Spanish. Camilla reached out to the Detroit Hispanic Development Corporation, and "they translated all of the documents that they could find regarding lead on the state's website. They translated all of the documents, because at that time, it was just me. I didn't have a computer, I didn't have anything. We didn't even have an office." Camilla held information meetings "with the families at Tim Hortons, McDonald's, their homes, [and] at the church, St. Mary's. We need[ed] to have a place to have water delivered. But then we ended up getting kicked out of there [St. Mary's], because they didn't like all of the water donations and media going there." Camilla explained to me that in addition to making water available, she had set up a workshop where families could talk to immigration lawyers about their visa issues. The church didn't want any press associated with immigration, so they kicked the activists out. "Of all the churches," Camilla reflected, "you would think the Catholic Church will be for that, right? Totally [the] opposite." When push came to shove, it appeared, segregation in houses of worship would not be limited to Sundays, as Martin Luther King Jr. once observed, but would also be enforced in time of need.

The Catholic Church was not the only institution to deny help. The expansion of Medicaid to Flint children and pregnant women excluded the undocumented. Conversely, folks who lived in white suburban neighborhoods but worked in the city were eligible for this program, but undocumented children and pregnant woman living in Flint and regularly drinking it's contaminated water were not. When Camilla pleaded with a senior-level staff member at the Department of Health and Human Services about a waiver, "they said, no," Camilla recalled. "Till this day we don't know how many [Hispanic] children have high levels of lead. Either they were tested once and then not tested again, or they were not tested because of the parents being asked for documentation." Effectively, when Flint's medical resources were extended to residents, it was done in a manner that reinforced the contemporary racial order, removing resources from people of color and claiming that only legal (read: white) residents were eligible for social assistance that was only needed because of government malfeasance.

To make matters worse, "border patrol ended up showing up," Camilla recounted. "We were told ICE was providing security for the federal government building" in which Flint's Social Security office is located. "But then [we were told] the federal government was here meeting with the state, the city," and ICE would be providing additional security.

"But then they were parking here on the east side, blocks away from our families, [and] then if you fit the criteria of maybe being undocumented, they will [would] stop you, and ask you for documentation. They were going to the stores [too], parking there, and they picked up two families. To this day, we don't even know where they are—where the kids [are]."

Camilla also related that "one of the schools called ICE on one of the families, because they [the children] went and asked for water [at school], because they didn't want to go to the pods. I said, 'How can you be so heartless when you know we are going through a crisis?' Especially [given that] the only place that children should be feeling safe is at school, and you call ICE on their parents?"

For many undocumented people, the suffering from lead poisoning and Legionella was increased by a state that refuses to admit any responsibility for its wrongdoing. "They face other health issues," a resident explained, "because a lot of them don't have the right documents. You have to be a citizen to get Medicaid," and without universal health coverage, many victims of lead poisoning have no access to the health care they desperately needed. Moreover, fear of deportation exacerbates the denial of the right to reside in the United States. "What happens," undocumented people asked, "if I am here illegally, I get deported, and I have to take my US-born child with me?" This child, a US citizen, is facing a lifetime of health battles stemming from lead poisoning, and there is no way to get the medical assistance they urgently need in their parents' home country.

Both fear and stigma remain elevated in the Hispanic community, as their vulnerabilities—including lack of reliable access to water, food, information, shelter, and health care—during this racialized environmental crisis were used to ratchet up the deportation of undocumented people, many of whom have lived in the United States for decades. Some of the children deported were born in Flint. The threat of deportation has been front and center in undocumented people's lives as the entire state of Michigan has become a highly patrolled ICE border zone. Moreover, the Trump administration made the fate of undocumented people all the more uncertain. And what is the fate of children born in America to undocumented parents? Are they too now subject to family separation? For those "lucky" families deported together, a lifetime of battles begin, as most of them will not get access to appropriate medical assistance in their home country. Poisoned by administrative design, removed from their means of livelihood, and then abandoned to far-off regions, Flint's undocumented residents have been subjected to the blatant violence of an

American economic system all too ready to externalize human destruction and skirt social responsibility.

HOUSING AND FORECLOSURE

Flint's deeply rooted vestiges of Jim Crow have not only ensured that the city's water crisis disproportionately harmed people of color but also that their misfortunes would once again become the impetus to reinscribing the synergies of racial segregation into the folds of its postindustrial imaginary. "I may live in a low-income neighborhood," one Flint resident reflected, "but I consider this my home, my safe place that I provide for my child." For this single mother, home ownership was her American Dream come true. "What people saw as poor was a dream come true because it was the first time we could afford a home. A home, not a house. My house may be . . . the worst on the block but it is the best one for me because my baby gets to live there, and I know she is with good people."

Like many immigrants' story, hers is one of struggle, perseverance, and finding one's community, one's place in American society. But the water crisis has left many Flint homeowners financially underwater, as home values plummeted to less than market value. One woman bought her house for $80,000. Now, after the water crisis, it is worth $20,000. All three of her children have been tested positive for lead poisoning. Possible foreclosure is the latest hardship that this and thousands of other Flint residents must struggle with as water liens and underwater mortgages have left many hanging onto worthless investments, and others homeless after they walked away from their shattered dreams. "I own two homes in Flint," explained Debra Taylor at the third public hearing on the Flint water crisis.

> Both of those homes were part of my retirement plan. Governor Snyder has shattered what I have worked for, for decades. How many other thousands of homeowners here in Flint can sell a house right now? What is it worth? Have you looked at the real estate? The wealth of most Black people has come with home ownership, and that wealth has been stolen by this government. We are tired of being redlined and robbed of our hard-earned money.

The 2008 housing crash, a result of Wall Street's reckless mortgage market manipulations, hit segregated cities like Flint particularly hard. About 75% of real estate value in the city was lost almost overnight.[9] And just as Flint's housing market appeared to be recovering, state austerity measures launched the despondent city into the water crisis, further eroding housing property value. In March 2016, CNN reported that Flint had the highest vacancy rate in the country, with 1 in 14 homes vacant. "The problem is even worse in some areas in the city's center where 1 in 5 homes sit empty."[10] From 2012 to 2017, housing values in Flint plummeted, stripping millions of dollars in household wealth from homeowners. By 2017, a little more than three years after Flint officials switched city water sources and exposed residents to lead-poisoned water, the vast majority of homes in Flint had dramatically decreased in value. The average price of a home in the United States in 2017 was $193,000; in Michigan, the average was just under $127,000. But the average home price in Flint in 2017 was just $13,000—a little over a tenth of the average in surrounding white suburbs. But housing value data also reveal that not all homeowners were affected equally. For example, in 2012, almost half the houses in Flint, 1 in 2, were valued at less than $50,000. By 2017 the percentage had increased to 72.3%, almost 3 in 4 houses, underscoring the disproportionate loss of wealth in poor neighborhoods.

Those looking to sell or buy during or after the water crisis were confronted with another environmental injustice: the discrimination on the part of local real estate associations and lending institutions working together to deny the sale or purchase of housing owned by African Americans in particular zip codes.[11] "Real estate agents don't show houses in the 48503 zip Code," a local resident told me. "They steer them away from our neighborhood to more desirable neighborhoods, like Carriage Town," then a rapidly gentrifying neighborhood adjacent to downtown. In some neighborhoods you couldn't buy a house; in other neighborhoods you couldn't sell one; and, as is often the case with redlining, price didn't matter. Residents observed that realtors were not showing houses in predominantly Black neighborhoods. As a result, houses in their neighborhoods sat on the market longer, further depreciating their value. Vacant housing has led to further depreciation as lawns are left unkept and houses dilapidate.

Table 3   Change in values of owner-occupied housing in Flint, 2012–2017

Values of owner-occupied housing units	2012	2014	2017
Less than $50,000	49.6% (+/–1.8)	63.8% (+/–1.6)	72.3% (+/–1.7)
$50,000 to $99,999	37% (+/–2.2)	27.5% (+/–1.6)	21% (+/–1.7)
$100,000 to $149,999	7.3% (+/–1.1)	4.4% (+/–0.8)	2.9% (+/–0.7)
$150,000 to $199,999	3.5% (+/–0.8)	2.3% (+/–0.7)	1.9% (+/–0.6)

SOURCE: US Census Data Profiles.

Banks and mortgage companies had a similar strategy of leveraging Flint's housing crises, buying up bundles of properties at discounted prices, eager to both recoup their losses and, once again, profit from an undervalued housing market. As previously mentioned, in 2008, 53% of Flint residential housing stock was owned by investment companies, 29% was owned by real estate companies, and 16% was privately owned. Of those investors, 22% were out-of-state companies, 21% were located in Michigan, 27% in Genesee County, and 23% in Flint.[12] "Banks don't lend in this area," a Flint resident informed me. The Federal National Mortgage Association, commonly known as Fannie Mae, temporarily removed homes it owned in Flint from the housing market in 2015 to conduct water tests.[13] In predominantly white and gentrifiable neighborhoods, lending institutions would foreclose on a delinquent property, take possession, and resell the property on the open market, whereas in predominantly African American neighborhoods lenders simply abandoned the house. In effect, housing investment after the water crisis was systematically channeled to middle-class white neighborhoods, while predominantly Black neighborhoods were intentionally left to blight and the discretion of the Land Bank.

Flint residents who rent have also been subjected to housing injustices amid the city's water crisis. Legal Services of Eastern Michigan was receiving three hundred calls a week about water and landlord-tenant issues during the water crisis. Tenants wanted to break their lease and find safe housing, as many landlords were not providing potable water. However, many renters were anxious that their efforts to terminate their lease would result in loss of their Section 8 vouchers. The Section 8 Housing Choice Voucher Program is the federal government's largest plan for helping very-low-income families, the elderly, and the disabled to afford decent, safe, and sanitary housing in the private market. Under the voucher program, families are provided a rent subsidy and required to sign a lease with a landlord, then the local public housing agency (PHA) pays housing assistant payments directly to the landlord. By law, a PHA must provide 75% of its vouchers to applicants whose incomes fall below 30% of the area median income. The median household income in Flint in 2018 was $31,509,[14] and 30% of that figure is $9,452.70. The Flint Housing Commission administered approximately seven hundred Section 8 Housing Choice Vouchers at the time. However, breaking their lease would mean that a tenant would lose their rent subsidy. Faced with the reality that their dwelling was uninhabitable, however, many were forced to abandon this program and find costlier housing elsewhere. Moving across town or to the suburbs also meant extricating children from their neighborhood schools, community, and friends, adding further distress to an already frantic situation.

SCHOOLING

Speaking at the first public hearing on the Flint water crisis on April 28, 2016, Art Reyes, a former commissioner of on Hispanic/Latino Commission of Michigan, informed the Michigan Civil Rights Commission of one particularly disturbing story. "Just the other day I was talking to a local resident who was explaining how her son was suspended fifty-six times this year." He is a first-grader. By comparison, the previous year, before the water crisis, he had been suspended only once. Research shows that lead poisoning results not only in lower IQ scores but also in learning and behavioral problems in school-age children.[15] Lead poisoning may perhaps also explain why this boy's behavior at home also noticeably changed. We are seeing significant impacts in the health and education of children who have not been given adequate social services, explained Reyes to the Commission. "Short, medium, and long-term help, including wraparound education and health services" were desperately needed, he explained. Decades of research have found that exposure to even low levels of lead can profoundly affect children's growth, behavior, and intelligence over time. Studies have linked elevated lead levels in blood to learning disabilities, problems with attention and fine motor coordination, and even violent behavior.[16] In 2017 the school district landed in the bottom 5% of districts statewide on a range of school and student performance measures, and the Michigan Department of Education has categorized it as a "chronically failing school."[17]

In response to the public health crisis, the state directed the Flint Community Schools and the Genesee Intermediate School District (GISD) to form a partnership with the Michigan Department of Education and the State School Reform/Redesign Office. The partnership agreement put in place several time-sensitive goals. Benchmarks in the first eighteen months included raising student attendance rates to 88%, reducing the number of out-of-school suspensions by 5%, and increasing reading and writing proficiency by 5% as measured by state assessments. If the benchmarks are not met, the Flint schools face closure or come under GISD control. Additional consequences for noncompliance would include significant changes to instructional and noninstructional programming, and the termination of at least 25% of teachers and support staff. According to state officials, the partnership agreement was designed to maximize and retain local control.[18] Ridgway White, president of the C. S. Mott Foundation and one of the partners named in the agreement, said his nonprofit organization signed off on the agreement "because we care about Flint kids."[19] But caring would require what educational scholar Lilia Bartolomé called a "humanizing pedagogy" that "respects and uses the reality, history, and perspectives of students as an integral part of educational practice."[20] Instead, partners to the agreement have used the learning and behavioral problems of children subject to lead poisoning— low test scores, attendance, and suspension—to reform K–12 public education in Flint.

Similar forms of public school capture happened in Detroit after its bankruptcy and in New Orleans after Hurricane Katrina. In Michigan, taxpayers poured nearly $1 billion a year into charter schools, but state laws regulating charters are among the nation's weakest.[21] The Mott Foundation, which, historian Andrew Highsmith writes, has consistently looked to racial segregation as an indispensable component of community education, also opened a charter school in Flint.[22] Charter school reform has been shown to be segregating and is often termed "separate but improved." In districts that participate in school choice programs, white and more affluent parents have fled as poorer minority kids have come into their schools, exacerbating de facto segregation.[23] The loss of career teachers— that is, teachers who are more likely to be committed to and capable of culturally relevant pedagogy—and local support staff is yet another example of the cumulative harms flowing from the city's lead poisoning.

Parents have had enough. On October 18, 2016, a class action lawsuit was filed on behalf of fifteen children, ages three to seventeen, each of whom was exposed to lead in Flint. Plaintiffs alleged that they were denied the special-education services they needed, and were entitled to under the federal Individuals with Disabilities Education Act, the Americans with Disabilities Act, and Michigan state law.[24] "In the wake of the Flint lead crisis, Flint children face an unprecedented educational and civil rights disaster," the 133-page complaint stated.[25] "It is impossible to overstate the resounding effects of the failure to provide meaningful education opportunities, and to provide them now."[26] Not doing so, the complaint alleged, would permanently foreclose Flint children's opportunities to reach their potential. Instead of providing these resources, the Michigan Department of Education has cut funding for teachers, staff, and special education services, citing a $10 million deficit. The state's primary concern, once again, is the huge potential costs these children of color will impose on stressed budgets and burdened taxpayers, rather than the children's immediate needs and long-term welfare.[27]

·   ·   ·   ·   ·

The Flint water crisis clearly demonstrates the necessity of access to safe and affordable drinking water in our lives and the multiple and dire consequences that can occur when that access is taken away. Physical illness is only one. Water is not just a utility (like cable or internet access). If your water gets cut off, you can't take a shower, run the laundry, or wash your hands or dishes easily in the sink. In effect, your home becomes unusable. If water access is compromised, renters can be evicted. According to Child

Protective Services, a family without running water can't provide a fit home for a child. Thus, losing your water might also mean losing your children.

Research has shown that housing insecurity can lead to employment instability. In Flint, back taxes and overdue water bills contributed to an unprecedented number of home foreclosures, forcing many families to relocate. Flint children had to endure family separations or relocation, both of which inhibit their feeling of safety and belonging and capacity to cultivate relationships, develop a sense of self-worth, and learn in school. For many of the youngest and most vulnerable Flint residents, these social ills came on top of those stemming from lead poisoning from contaminated water. In many ways the home is *the* social determinant of health. In Flint, policies of racialized austerity made it impossible for many people to live in a safe home.

7 The Water Is Off

I hail from a city where the water is off.
45's on Flintstones, where they're picking us off.
They thought they had us cornered but they'd pissed us off.
Now we have come together, who would have thought?

I hail from a city where the water is off.
45's on Flintstones, where they're picking us off.
They thought they had us cornered but they'd pissed us off.
Now we have come together, who would have thought?

I witnessed her soul slither violently from her body
Denial pressed tightly upon her lips
She fixed her face to tell me she wasn't thirsty
That her babies weren't 30 days away from being ripped from
    her custody

I could sense desperation in her teardrops
She was lying to me about water
Fearing to keep her babies near
She almost let me leave them waterless
And I wanted to hug her
But I knew that her pride was the only ounce of protection that
    she had left to muster
Barely hanging on, as if the reaper had granted another chance,
If she could just pull herself together

Why do folks got to beg for water?
Hiding behind scarlet letters spray-painted to mark their
    negligence
I wonder what she thought of me standing there
With the fate of her family stuffed inside my trunk

I left three gallons of water and walked away
There were 10 more mothers for us to hydrate that day.

I hail from a city where the water is off.
45's on Flintstones, where they're picking us off.
They thought they had us cornered but they'd pissed us off.
Now we have come together, who would have thought?

—Tawana Petty

"Shutting off water and denying hundreds of thousands of people access to water," Monica Lewis-Patrick of We the People of Detroit asserts, has resulted in serious, incalculable, and irreparable harm. "These are the political crises and water wars that we hear about in places like Cochabamba, Bolivia, and other parts of the [developing] world. But we are having the "same struggles here," she said.

> My mother is a twenty-four-year military veteran. She's a retired master sergeant. And as soon as I told her in 2014 about what was happening with the water shutoffs in Detroit, she said, "Honey, you know, you are at war." And I said, "I don't understand." She said, "Shutting off water is an act of war. Any time we want to seize another country, we shut off their water and food supply." I want you to sit with that for a minute. When you cut off a community from access to water, whether they know it or not, they have just entered into war.

Access to safe water is a human right. This basic entitlement was aptly articulated on World Water Day in 2019 by Audrey Azoulay, the director-general of UNESCO.[1] Moreover, under international humanitarian law, it is prohibited *"to attack, destroy, remove, or render useless objects indispensable to the survival of the civilian population, such as foodstuffs, agricultural areas for the production of foodstuffs, crops, livestock, drinking water installations and supplies and irrigation works."*[2] The International Criminal Court deems *intentional deprivation of materials indispensable for survival, such as food and water, a war crime.*[3]

"Do you know," Lewis Patrick points out, "you are just as poisoned if you can't properly hydrate yourself as if you drank contaminated water? Because after five days, usually you are not sticking around long enough to know what the end will be."

Between 2014 and 2016, the Detroit Water and Sewerage Department (DWSD) deliberately shut the water off in more than 80,000 homes and buildings in the city, leaving more than 200,000 Detroiters, including some of the most vulnerable and disenfranchised, without water. The city was expected to conduct an additional 18,000 shutoffs in 2017.[4] "What Monica didn't tell you," Debra Taylor said, "was that she worked with the local coalition of activists and nonprofits to plan the UN visit here [by the special rapporteurs for the United Nations High Commissioner for Human Rights] and actually organized the tour that they took to see the impact [of water shutoffs] on families without water. It has been the activists the whole time." We the People of Detroit along with other activists brought Catarina de Albuquerque, the United Nations Special Rapporteur on the Human Right to Water and Sanitation, and Leilani Farha, the Special Rapporteur on the Right to Adequate Housing, to Detroit in the fall of 2014. During their visit, they went to different parts of Detroit and met with people whose water had been shut off, as well as others who were struggling to pay expensive water bills to avoid shutoff. They listened to stories from single mothers with low income, older persons, and people with disabilities and chronic illnesses.

Both UN officials expressed concern regarding the "unprecedented scale" of water shutoffs affecting the "most vulnerable and poorest" of the population, a predominant number of whom were African Americans. Leilani Farha, the expert on the right to adequate housing, expressed concern that children were being removed by social services from their families and homes because, without access to water, their housing was no longer considered adequate. These water shutoffs, Farha added, are "in violation of treaties the US has ratified."[5] The investigation concluded that the Detroit mass water shutoffs were "a violation of the human right to water and other international human rights."[6] The shutoffs posed immense harm to victims, including health problems, threatened removal of children from homes, and loss of housing through foreclosure.[7] Thousands of households were living in fear that their water might be turned off at any time without due notice, the special rapporteurs found. In many cases, unpaid water bills were being attached to property taxes, increasing the risk of foreclosure in already-depressed neighborhoods.

"The water shutoffs are a public health crisis of enormous dimensions," Dr. Wendy Johnson, director of the La Familia Medical Center of New Mexico. Speaking at the Damon J. Keith Center for Civil Rights in Detroit in 2017, Dr. Johnson clarified, "To me it is astonishing and unconscionable that the previous Director of Public Health for the City of Detroit, Dr. El-Sayed, and the current Public Health Director, Dr. Khaldun, have said nothing publicly about the public health effects of these water shutoffs." A preliminary study conducted by citizens and researchers at the Henry Ford Global Health Initiative found that patients who lived on blocks that experienced water shutoffs were 1.55 times more likely to be diagnosed with a water-associated illness.[8] One possible public health concern is MRSA (Methicillin-resistant *Staphylococcus aureus*), a bacterium that causes infections in different parts of the body, infections much more likely to occur in a person who can't practice basic hygiene. For people with chronic diseases such as diabetes, a lack of water can be life threatening. For someone with heart disease, dehydration is a risk factor for heart attack and stroke. Lack of water also worsens the effects of childhood illnesses such as gastroenteritis. "You don't have to be a public health official to know these things," Dr. Johnson asserted, "but if you are a public health official, it is your duty to know these things, and respond to the community, and I really think it is a dereliction of duty on their part" not to inform the public.

"What we know in Detroit," Monica Lewis-Patrick told me, "is that it took organizers and leaders, much like what happened in Flint, to prepare the data and the research to alarm their neighbors and their own government" of the public health crisis impacting their community. Many citizens in Detroit felt déjà vu as some in the medical community told activists they were trying to politicize the data. "I am disheartened by the reaction of activist groups," wrote Marcus Zervos, an infectious disease specialist with the Henry Ford Hospital. "We approached this issue as an exploratory effort into the possible public health impact of water shutoffs, understanding that the results would only be preliminary and shape the framework for a future comprehensive cause and effect study."[9] Although they agreed with the results, public health agencies continued to down-play their correlation with the more than six hundred hepatitis A cases in the city. To have done so would have implicated the city of Detroit and the DWSD in another man-made public health crisis like that in Flint. And then there's the fact that the Henry Ford Hospital does a lot of business with the city. Currently, the Henry Ford health system owns more than two hundred buildings in Detroit and is working on a number of new developments, many of which will require the city's support for permits and zoning.[10] Yet, in a city where the poverty rate is just below 40%, the city, bent on urban austerity, continues to promote the privatization of water regardless of the human harm it inflicts on Detroit's most vulnera-ble populations. Activists in Detroit, as well as the United Nations, have repeatedly proclaimed, "That ain't right."

A coalition of organizations held an impassioned protest outside the headquarters of the Detroit Public Schools Community District on September 4, 2018, the first day of the school year. School officials had just announced that water would be shut off to all 106 Detroit public schools, affecting nearly 50,000 children, due to high levels of lead and copper found in the water, even though administrators had known of the contamination weeks before schools were to open. Taking the bullhorn, Joanna Underwood spoke to the crowd about the long-term poisoning of Detroit's children. "We all know that the state took over public schools in Detroit because of low testing scores," Underwood said. "Well, maybe that was because they were drinking poisoned water. Why have our children been underperforming in schools? Maybe it's because they were drinking poisoned water.

"They got high concentrations of lead in Benton Harbor, they got lead poisoning in Pontiac, [and there is] lead poisoning in Eastern.

"What is the predominant factor?" she asked.

"All of those are predominantly Black cities. For those of you that tell me it's not about race, let me tell you something: you go to hell, because it's *all* about race. They poisoned our babies and that is what it is. That is telling the truth and calling it what it is."

The conditions that I have seen in Flint and Detroit are hard to com-prehend. Houses boarded up with people living in them. No heat or run-ning water in the middle of winter. Discarded appliances strewn on lawns and driveways. "We've gone through four dishwashers since the water crisis," a Flint resident told me. Holes in ceilings where pipes have been replaced. Makeshift kitchens and partly demolished bathrooms. Beneath the physical pain and mental strife lies a white supremacy–based culture that maintains indifference on the surface by actively hiding the intentionality of the state's malicious decisions.

In Flint and Detroit, the Michigan governor and state agencies made decisions with the intent to destroy people of color by exploiting their "group-differentiated vulnerabilities."[11] But this glaring case of ethnic and racial environmental injustice was not limited to government actions but was also reinforced by other actors including school boards, churches, family service providers, and the police. In many ways, the government-instigated water crises provided an opportunity for these institutions to sharpen their racist bite, to refresh their imperial mission in order to shore up American-style apartheid and urban segregation more broadly.[12] We know this now. These intentional practices and policies killed people and caused serious harm to others. Yet the full spectrum of the systematic trauma that these communities have faced will never really be understood. The state government and its backers deliberately inflicted "conditions of life calculated to bring about physical destruction."[13] They imposed measures intended to prevent births and forcibly removed people of color from their communities. This is why people in Flint and Detroit charge genocide. Today, as in the past, forces around the globe are pioneering some of the core structures of everyday genocide in the camps and colonies of modernity, and Flint and Detroit are the beta tests in this most recent phase of racial capitalism.

.   .   .   .   .

Water is critical to maintaining a safe home. You can't live in a house without it. If your gas or electric heating gets cut off, you get cold. So you put on a coat or blanket. If your cable is disconnected, you stop watching television. But if your water gets cut off, you could be evicted or you could have your children taken away. If your water is poisoned, your house becomes lethal when you drink from the tap. "In languages all over the world," sociologist Matthew Desmond writes, "the word for 'home' encompasses not just shelter but warmth, safety, family—the womb."[14] The home remains the primary basis of life; it is where meals are shared, quiet habits formed, dreams confessed, traditions created.[15] Housing stability leads to employment stability. Housing instability can impair a child's health, their ability to learn, their capacity to cultivate peer groups, and their sense of self-worth. In many ways the home is *the* social determinant of health. All of the suffering in Flint and Detroit is shameful, and in both cases, as in so many other cases of harm done to people of color, it was also completely unnecessary.

8 Shut Off and Shut Out

Gentrification is often associated with positive collective economic outcomes for local communities—benefits eventually realized with the strategic placement of a Starbucks, Chipotle, or Whole Foods in the neighborhood. In reality this new frontier of environmental justice is the result of particular people and groups employing racialized extractive practices involving land and other capital in order to transform neighborhoods in ways that suit their economic and ideological interests.

This chapter explores how one postindustrial urban center, Detroit, has revamped its local economy. Detroit proves to be a particularly instructive case, in part because private interests and nonprofit organizations allied with one another to frame the revitalized city as an object of white possession. What also sets Detroit apart from other forms of urban renewal is the use of racialization to target both the livelihoods and the assets of the city's predominantly Black residents. In Detroit, not only did private interests use the popular rhetoric of "livable," "sustainable," and even "start-up" to transform the city in their image, but they also cultivated a colorblind imaginary to hide the latent displacement and "greenlining" effects of the transformation. As in previous chapters, I rely on activists and community organizers in Detroit to help me explain how gentrification in their

Figure 16. "Turn on Water! Shut Down 'New Detroit.'" Sign displayed by protesters in front of the Frank Murphy Hall of Justice. Photo by We the People of Detroit.

neighborhoods and their city manifested as racial capitalism. Their efforts, their struggle, is to both analyze and resist the intersecting social and political affronts that present methods of institutional racism as common-sense urban planning. Their praxis is part of an ongoing intellectual and lifesaving effort to provide an explanatory framework that can be used to resist this new racial formation as it works to target other places and peoples around the globe.

·   ·   ·   ·   ·

The most obvious thing one notices when one exits Interstate 75 onto Trumball Road en route to St. Peter's Episcopal Church is the condition of the roads. A combination of broken brick, torn-up asphalt, and deep pot-holes makes driving in one lane nearly impossible. Arriving at the church early, I sat on the stairs up to the main doors. It was midmorning on this summer day, and Michigan's all-too-familiar humidity was starting to rise. Other men also seeking shelter amid the increasing heat joined me on the church steps.

"In the basement," a man told me, "is a kitchen." We walked down the stairs together, and I beheld a makeshift cafeteria providing breakfast for a large number of people. More people came and went as we talked. "Meals on Wheels," Stan told me. "Been here forever, since the sixties. One of a kind." We took his breakfast back outside to join an assembly with others forming on the grass. "I'm at a homeless shelter at the present," he told me. "Things will get better, I hope." We moved back to the steps, where the shade and concrete made the rapidly rising summer heat of Detroit seem tolerable for the time being, and were careful to leave a path open for others to come and go. As we sat and talked, I counted the police cars that drove by. One, two, three, four. Soon I lost count.

Kitty-corner to the church is the Onassis Coney Island restaurant, where the parking lot is full of Fords and GMs. White folks walk in and out of the restaurant, many carrying leftovers and a meal to go, oblivious to the world that exists across the street, beyond the patrolling police cars. Directly across the street from the restaurant is a fenced vacant lot, where the old Detroit Tigers stadium used to be. There are plans to construct a state-of-the-art community center, the Police Athletic Center, in this excavated hole, I am told. "Yet it is doubtful that it will serve many in this community," reflected Tom, a young white pastor at the church. "It is turning out to be another Brooklyn here," he told me, referring to the recent invasion of $400,000 condos and destination bars, restaurants, and shops in this fast-gentrifying neighborhood.

A few blocks east, in Midtown Detroit, one can buy sushi at a new Whole Foods store—an exemplar of neighborhood gentrification—or dine at Grey Ghost Detroit, a modern, hip, and popular spot that offers pricy steaks, craft beer, and cocktails to those who can afford it. This definitively white space is not only blocks but worlds away from St. Peter's and its meal program. In this gentrified space, bars, brew pubs, coffee shops, and restaurants dot the landscape. The roads are newly paved and kept free of garbage. Exclusively white, local patrons are also afforded the option of leaving their cars at home and avoiding the hassle of parking them, thanks to the new M-1 street car, servicing a 3.3-mile stretch of Woodward Avenue—the heart of Detroit's new, young, and hip nightlife.

In many ways, crossing an intersection in Detroit, or another postindustrial city in America's Rust Belt, is analogous to going to another country. And in Detroit that "country" is often dubbed "Gilbertville" (after Dan Gilbert, the owner of Quicken Loans). Yet it is worth asking how it is, in the absence of openly racist policies such as restrictive covenants, racial zoning, redlining, and segregated schooling, that these two segregated areas have come to exist adjacent to yet unaware of each other in postracial America? Many politicians and pundits have attributed the problems of Flint and Detroit to the rapid deindustrialization that affected many cities in the US Rust Belt. It wasn't too long ago that Flint had the highest per capita income in the United States, or that city planners looked to Flint as a paragon of city infrastructure and development. For example, Flint reported the highest median income for young workers in 1980, according to US Census figures, followed by Detroit.[1]

Today, drivers of environmental racism have invoked a wholly color-blind narrative to justify urban development in the private interest,[2] effectively enabling white elites such as Dan Gilbert to use nonracial language to advance not only their economic interests but their ideological views as well. This veiled racism points to both the culture of Black leaders and their cities' burgeoning economic debts to justify another phase of discrimination against people and cities of color. But it also depicts white elites' vaunted moral superiority as somehow in line with the public good rather than as exploiting the current conditions of racialized uneven development. And in Detroit, Michigan, white elites are not only remaking the city into a twenty-first century growth machine, but also selecting who belongs and who has access to the city's new environs.

.   .   .   .   .

I am at St. Peter's Episcopal Church to meet Monica Lewis-Patrick and Debra Taylor. We the People of Detroit's office is on the third floor of this historic building. Walking up the stairs, I glance up at portraits of Mahatma Gandhi, the leader of India's nonviolent independence movement, and American abolitionist Frederick Douglass. These forerunners of civil rights movements past, I think to myself, must inspire these current civil rights leaders. Today, the two leaders of grassroots organizing are meeting with a group of architecture and planning students from New

York University. She identifies first as "an activist," Monica Lewis-Patrick tells the students, "because it allows me to speak my truth, represent my community in a very rigorous, robust way. And I am unapologetic about that representation." We the People of Detroit came into existence in 2008, fighting for mayoral control as the organization recognized that deep pockets and outside interests were rigging local elections. "Some of what does not get spoken of is that 50% of the acquired wealth in the city of Detroit was extracted and stolen during the bankruptcy. Eighty percent of the bankruptcy was placed on the backs of the pensioners. The average pension in the city is $19,000. Many Detroiters had anywhere from 22% to 33% of their pensions taken." Activists like Monica Lewis-Patrick saw the bankruptcy as a vehicle to redirect money and power from mostly Black leaders and city employees to whites while making no direct reference to race. "I think up until 1997," Lewis Patrick observed, "we had the highest home ownership per capita in the country." The point being, "we had a history of paying our bills and paying our taxes and owning our homes. Many of us had home ownership in our families for generations. Some as many as three, four, five generations. So we took a lot of pride in owning our houses."

I think Monica Lewis-Patrick felt it was important for the students to hear a counternarrative to the one repeated in the media about who was responsible for the city's financial problems. I don't think it was lost on her that these privileged, mostly white students were here to gather information about Detroit's infrastructure woes in an effort to offer academic solutions. Detroit was their research project, and they came equipped with all sorts of good intentions. But before they could offer solutions, Lewis Patrick needed to orientate their intellectual gaze toward the real men, the white patriarchs, behind the curtain of Detroit's private interest–induced bankruptcy. It was her moment to set the record straight.

"Many of the millionaires and billionaires are looking at anywhere from a twelve- to thirty-year tax abatement," Lewis Patrick explained. "Many of them were able to have their debts forgiven, money that [they] owed . . . the city of Detroit. Much of that debt was restructured around this contrived bankruptcy, so it was beneficial to the banks and to the wealthy person[s] that had an interest in the city." In fact, according to city documents obtained through the Freedom of Information Act, businesses and government-owned properties owed nearly twice as much in overdue water bills than residences: $41 million compared with $26 million for homes. But only 680 of the approximately 10,000 delinquent nonresidential accounts were shut off in 2015, compared to the 23,300 homes denied water.[3] The state of Michigan alone owed the city $5 million in unpaid water charges for the state fairgrounds on Woodward Avenue.[4] Joe Louis Arena, home of the Detroit Red Wings, and owned by the late billionaire Mike Ilitch, owed $82,255 as of April 2014. Ford Field, where the Detroit Lions play, owed more than $55,000. City-owned golf courses owed more than $400,000. "All of that was able to be forgiven or renegotiated," Lewis Patrick told the students. Instead, the city went after residential customers who were more than sixty days late and owed at least $150. If the city was genuinely concerned about lost revenues, it would have gone after delinquent commercial customers, which carried a larger share of the unpaid bills. But they didn't. Instead, they blamed the city's poor and mostly Black population. Embedded in this decision was the question, *who* is worthy of "water welfare" from the city. And while it was clear that the mostly Black Detroiters would be targeted for water payment delinquency, race was never explicitly used in adjudicating the city's water policy.

ONE IN THREE

In reality, Lewis Patrick explained, "there was a master narrative created that everything in Detroit either was criminal, corrupt, [or] dispensable. I think Kevin Orr called us dumb, lazy, happy, and rich." Orr and others regularly enrolled these code words and phrases to portray what they saw as a culture of incompetence and immorality. This pathology, they intimated, was the sole reason for the city's financial ruin and the hardships that many city residents were currently experiencing. This colorblind narrative that blamed Black Detroiters for their problems provided the justification for city fathers like Gilbert, Mike Illich, and John Hantz to pursue their privatization agenda while depriving certain residents of an element essential to life.[5] "We saw water shutoffs go from somewhere around fifteen hundred shutoffs a week to as high as eight thousand shutoffs," Lewis

Patrick told the student group. "At one point, at least one in three Detroiters were either living without water or in jeopardy of not having access to water. Right now, we still think that number is as high as one in five. They don't know. The city can't [won't] tell you."

But right before the bankruptcy, Lewis Patrick affirmed, "what residents began to see was a change in the decision-making structures regarding how the city's water department was 'managed,' how decisions were made, how contracts were let out. And what we saw was a lot of secret backdoor deals . . . being made." A series of federal judges made these changes, which "weren't transparent to the public." However, these types of decisions "should have been open, according to the Open Meetings Act." For example, Lewis Patrick explained, US district judge Sean Cox established the Root Cause Committee in an attempt to overhaul the Detroit Water and Sewerage Department. Local activists believed that the committee, which was composed of four executive officials, was another effort to concentrate decision-making power and expand the role of private interests in the city's water department. "So I know all of you think that . . . Detroiters [were responsible for the city's problems]," she said, "but, no, it's also been . . . government at the state and federal level" and private elite interests that "have leveraged their power in all of these spaces where we used to be able to say there were checks and balances."

THE DETROIT WATER AND SEWERAGE DEPARTMENT

Certain people operating in particular government agencies have, as sociologist Jill Harrison carefully demonstrates in her ethnography of the US Environmental Protection Agency, undermined the critical environmental justice advocacy of community organizations.[6] In Detroit, Gary Brown is noteworthy. "Mr. Brown is a retired police lieutenant," Debra Taylor began. "He now heads up the Water Department." Brown's career spanned more than two and a half decades with the Detroit Police Department, ending with his position as deputy chief of the Professional Accountability Bureau in May 2003. Brown was elected to the city council in 2009 and served as the president pro tempore. During his city council tenure, he was a member of Judge Cox's Root Cause Committee, which proposed converting the Detroit Water and Sewerage Department (DWSD) into a regional water authority, the long-held dream of suburban political leaders. Judge Cox ultimately rejected the proposal, because he found the revenue projections in the committee report to be based on "pure speculation." "The transfer of one of . . . Detroit's largest assets at this juncture," Cox wrote in his order, "could potentially force the city into bankruptcy or have other highly undesirable consequences."[7] Brown then resigned from the city council and took the position of chief operating officer under Emergency Manager Kevyn Orr during the city's bankruptcy, where he earned $225,000 a year and helped to shepherd the eventual regionalization of Detroit's largest asset. In October 2015, after the bankruptcy was completed, Gary Brown became the DWSD's director and CEO.

"In our mind," reflected Taylor, "the advancement of Gary Brown was akin to militarizing the water department." To begin with, his expertise was in police tactics and training. "He has no management experience of any major city division or department." And the only reason he ascended to the head of the water department was "because he assisted Governor Snyder in ushering Detroit into . . . bankruptcy. So he walked away from his council seat in order to get about a quarter of a million–dollar job annually with the emergency manager. And then he transitioned from working for the emergency manager to heading up DWSD." There were so many individuals like Gary Brown, Taylor lamented to me, willing to place their own political aspirations and personal agendas ahead of the communities they are supposed to be serving.

METRO DETROIT

Stereotype threat has also been used to invigorate Detroit's financial disciplining. "If you watch the media," a member of an affordable-housing group told me, "they are talking about crime. They use this terminology of 'Metro Detroit'" to engender white fear of a Gotham-like chaos created by Black masses out of control. "You had award-winning journalists . . . giving radio shows . . . every day . . . tell[ing] you all the crime that had happened. It's been 20 years of us being [represented by the media as] "the crime capital of the world," this person explained. "But this is not true.

"If you look at the statistical data, we were not [the crime capital]. If you look at the crime data, they have actually reworked the wording [of what constitutes criminal activity] since Clinton to where many of the crime issues or categories were collapsed into [total] incidents. So an incident could be anywhere from a traffic violation to a rape."

And, while some of the crimes accounted for are indeed serious, the lumping of heinous incidents together with minor infractions and counting every one as a "crime" works to create racialized hype. Governor Rick Snyder similarly referred to Flint as "murdertown" to justify cutting both public services and retiree benefits while increasing funding to the city's police force. "If you look at Detroit now and listen to the news, you still have that mantra of crime. How inundated we are with crime. It's not true. If you watch the media, much of the things they are talking about—half of the stories happened outside of Detroit. Some of the heinous crimes that they talk about didn't happen in Detroit."

The constant rhetoric about crime and chaos created this kind of Stockholm syndrome for Detroiters, new and old, so that they too started to live in fear. People looked to "particular zip codes that were extremely Black and dark" and asked that their streetlights to be turned on. And, contrary to evidence that increased lighting deters crime, city fathers used this opportunity to hand over the city's lighting infrastructure to the utility giant DTE Energy.

DTE ENERGY

"Our lighting actually was a revenue generator for the city. The city of Detroit sold lighting services to the hospital . . . to the museum . . . to the casinos. So it generated revenue," a resident told me.

"And then of course, what did DTE do?" the resident went on. "They took concerns of public safety and turned it into a strategy to extract more profit from the struggling city. [We] paid them $154 million to take it. And then they turned around and said, 'This is such ill repair, we can't do anything with this,'" implying that city mismanagement was in part responsible for the collapse of its public utility. DTE Energy's private sector solution was to request that the city take out a $160 million bond issue to invest in the city's infrastructure. "So then they went and met with the governor—'they' being the head of DTE—and brokered a deal without it going to a vote of the citizens," even though any structural changes to the city's infrastructure or any major utilities deal was supposed to go to a vote of the people, the resident explained.

"So then we go from $154 million to another 160—what is that?—$314 million that we paid to still stay in the dark," this resident affirmed. "[We used to have] over 88,000 lights in the city, now we are reduced down to about 33,000, which means there is whole sectors of the city, pitch black." As a result of this sale to DTE, city residents paid twice as much for fewer lights.

Dave Bing, then the mayor, who was on the board of directors of DTE Energy until 2005, was integral in turning the public lighting system over to the company he had served.[8] During his tenure as mayor, 20 percent of the city's workforce was laid off, decimating fire protection, public transportation, and essential infrastructure services like water and electricity. In 2010, Mayor Bing collaborated with major corporate interests to downsize Detroit "by relocating residents from neighborhoods deemed to be underpopulated or poor for investment."[9] By the time Emergency Manager Kevyn Orr was appointed to initiate the largest municipal bankruptcy proceeding in US history, Bing had already negotiated the sale of the public lighting system to DTE, as well as the sale of a long list of other public assets to corporate ventures. And the ease with which EM's shadow government mobilized for corporate interests in the city was enabled in part by the racist narrative that it was not so much the infrastructure that needed fixing as the mostly Black personnel who were (mis)running the public sector.

"You also have many people that are benefiting from public sector services providers, like the Department of Human Services, Michigan Workforce Development Board, and the Department of Health and Wellness," a fair housing advocate explained to me. These are government agencies or public sector programs that "have been privatized," a person associated with the Detroit People's Platform told me. "So many people that should be advocating with the community for [essential services] to be restored to a public space," he continued, "those persons have now been co-opted into becoming private managers of those [government] entities. So, it's sort of a backdoor way of payoffs, if you will," that has changed politics in the city. "Many of the council people," he explained, elected to represent city residents, have "ushered in this totally reptilian approach to governance." Persons like Saunteel Jenkins, who "just walked away from her seat and then walked into a six-figure job. I think she makes about $235,000 a year. She made $67,000 a year as a council person." As a council member, Jenkins approved a consent agreement in 2012 that deepened state control of the city's finances. She also supported creation of the new Great Lakes Regional Water Authority. Both free market "solutions" drew criticism from union workers and other city residents concerned about the privatization of water services, the influence of white suburban interests, and excessive state influence over local city affairs. Mayor Mike Duggan and Emergency Manager Kevyn Orr praised Jenkins's neoliberal agenda. But it was her role over subcommittees that extended lighting and heating contracts with DTE that have some questioning her real motives. "We estimated that the city needed about $2 million to install and update the city's lighting," a city resident recalled. "Instead, we ended up indebting ourselves [to DTE Energy] to the tune of about $160 million to get a third of the lights that we have now. And, of course, she [council member Jenkins] did not recuse herself from any of those decisions, and then her payoff is to give her this cushy job, after she has made those decisions." In November 2014, Saunteel Jenkins resigned from her city council position to become CEO of the Heat and Warmth Fund, a charity that provides millions of dollars a year in utility bill assistance to low-income households.[10] The nonprofit organization provides a substantial portion of its assistance to individuals in the form of direct payments to energy and utility companies. Financial statements reveal that in 2017, DTE Energy received $7,113,656, or 80% of its total direct payments, from the Heat and Warmth Fund; in 2018, the figure was $10,700,693 in direct payments from the nonprofit, or 76% of DTE's total assistance payments. [11]

HANTZ FARMS

Companies profited handsomely from characterizing the city's Black neighborhoods as in need of fixing by the private sector. In the fall of 2013

Detroit emergency manager Kevyn Orr approved a purchase agreement for 1,500 noncontiguous city-owned lots on Detroit's east side to Hantz Farms LLC. "It's my understanding that he was able to get his property to the tune of 10 cents per foot," a community organizer told me. According to the Associated Press, the discounted property purchase by John Hantz, a Detroit resident who runs a network of financial services businesses, would allow him to clean up vacant lands and demolish blighted buildings.[12] "Mr. Hantz offered us trees," in exchange for our land, the community organizer told me. "He was going to put trees in the city. I don't know about you, [but] I don't know anywhere where trees are brought back in the community for people. I think it's a good enhancement, and we love green space in Detroit. Walks on the riverfront. But there was nothing about that [private sector initiative] that was beneficial to Detroit."

Moreover, the land sold to Hantz Farms was already being cared for, and in some cases being farmed by, the city's majority-Black residents. "Detroiters [had been] cutting [those] yards for fifteen to twenty years. Some as many ten and fifteen parcels every week. They couldn't buy the parcel next to them and they were willing to pay market value," the community organizer told me. Among those in the community who were actively cultivating usable land, this redlining strategy was all too familiar. Historian Pete Daniel has chronicled how the US Department of Agriculture denied Black farmers loans, information, and access to farming assistance programs during the civil rights era.[13] This government assistance not only kept many small white farms in business during economic downturns but also transformed many into highly profitable, stable, and successful family farms.[14] These racist policies, Daniel writes, resulted in a 93% decline in the number of Black farmers in the United States between 1940 and 1974.[15] In fact, the number of small farms (fewer than 50 acres) has steadily increased since 1974.[16]

Today, a significant percentage of farms in the United States, almost 40%, are small. The fact that most of these farms are owned by white people is not an accident but a function of agricultural policies that redlined Black farmers. Reckoning with the effects of redlining policies and practices in the United States is often limited to discussions of housing, transportation, and infrastructure; however, similar redlining efforts transformed both rural and urban farming environs to exclusively white spaces, as well. For Black farmers this was not just a matter of being evicted from once-flourishing farms; it also meant food insecurity and economic hardship. Also erased from the landscape was the local farming knowledge that Black folks used to cultivate the land they worked. "So these are the things that made us really understand that this was more about race" than about helping Detroiters restore their infrastructure or planting trees, the community organizer reflected. Moreover, what was heartbreaking for many Detroiters was that an opportunity to "move us more toward a green economy, a green infrastructure, has now gone [and been directed] as a subsidy to millionaires and billionaires." And while city leaders' neoliberal efforts to rejuvenate the ailing city never explicitly mentioned race, a clear racial hierarchy was tied to their development plans, whereby rules and norms for land acquisition and property owner-ship continued to be a function of one's skin color.

VEOLIA

"And so, right before the emergency manager took his space [assumed office], what they began to do is they began to cut back" on the water department's responsibilities, the community organizer said, and "they began to bring in companies like Veolia, which is known around the world as one of the worst water managers in the world," to assess the city's water systems. "They [Veolia] have had their hands in many of the destructive practices that are happening around water in Boston, in Baltimore, and in Flint." Veolia might be best described as a true neoliberal monster, with Hydra-like tentacles working assiduously to privatize water, transporta-tion, and energy infrastructure around the globe. This privatizer in chief of public services has a long and infamous history of union busting, pro-viding inadequate services, cultivating systems of inequality and profit, and in the case of Flint, poisoning people. Globally, the Moratorium NOW! Coalition writes, "managers at Veolia-controlled plants have been charged with corruption, bribery, embezzlement, kickbacks and falsifying reports."[17] They show up whenever urban centers are in some kind of financial crisis and use these moments of distress as opportunities to seize the city's utilities. They have mastered the process of transferring public resources into private hands for private profit making. Veolia was hired to "consult" for the city fathers during the bankruptcy in support of the interests of many developers, businesses, and banks, activists informed me, pushing a consultancy model that creeps into the management and control of local municipal services. In Michigan, Veolia has provided a conduit for advancing a host of radical, far-right-wing causes of the De Vos family and its friends, including anti-union and anti-tax efforts. The family has given more than $44 million to Michigan's Republican Party, GOP legislative committees, and Republican candidates since 1997, making it the largest donor in Michigan.[18]

The power and influence of the DeVos family empire in Michigan is perhaps second only to those of billionaire Dan Gilbert, chair of Rock Ventures and Quicken Loans (now Rocket Loans). The DeVos empire also comprises vast real estate holdings, as well as sports teams—something else it has in common with Gilbert and Illich—and it funds cultural events and contributes to university and college endowments.[19] For years, the DeVos family owned Peter Island, part of the British Virgin Islands. The DeVoses also own one of the world's largest yachts, have helicopter pads at their homes, and travel in their own private airplanes. They exert political influence by sitting on the boards of major economic development organizations and conservative policy groups in the state, including the Right Place, the Econ Club of Grand Rapids, the One Kent Coalition, the West Michigan Policy Forum, Grand Action, and the Regional Air Alliance of West Michigan.[20] They have spearheaded coalitions that lobbied against a state business tax and renewable energy and bankrolled any and all efforts to weaken public sector unions, to privatize public education, to eliminate LGBTQ rights, and to take power from local government through emergency management policies.

In March 2014, nearly eight months after the city of Detroit filed for bankruptcy, Emergency Manager Kevyn Orr issued a request for proposal from potential operators of Detroit's water and sewer systems. The private operator Veolia responded to that request and then submitted a final binding proposal. Later that year, as part of the formation of the Great Lakes Water Authority, Veolia was again hired to assess the water and sewer systems. In December 2014, it released two reports about the DWSD. Then, in May 2016, the Board of Water Commissioners for

DWSD approved a $2.3 million contract with Veolia for field services and meter operations.

"They also had their hand in the M1 Rail," Monica Lewis-Patrick pointed out. Transdev Services Inc., formerly Veolia Transdev, signed a five-year, $15.5 million contract with the city to manage the six-vehicle 3.3-mile streetcar system—the Q Line—that connects downtown to midtown Detroit along Woodward Avenue. These contracts were let even though Veolia's anti-labor policies have led to strikes in England, Canada, France, and the United States. In water delivery, Veolia is known for breaking state contracts and overcharging residents. At a time when cities all over the world are taking back their water and transport systems from Veolia in a concerted effort to restore public control, improve operations, and lower costs to residents, emergency managers in Detroit and Flint employed Veolia in order to translate a neoconservative agenda advanced by the De Vos empire and others to weaken public sector unions, undermine worker rights and benefits, and privatize the delivery of public services.

Lewis Patrick is mindful in drawing attention to the Q Line. The public transit project has been dubbed the "streetcar named disaster," not only for usurping public funds for private interests but also for epitomizing how urban development in the private interest perpetuates environmental racism in the city. First, the US Department of Transportation provided $37.2 million in capital funding for the project. Another $41 million in public money came from the state of Michigan, Wayne County, Wayne State University, and the Detroit Downtown Development Authority. In total, 42 percent of the transit project's startup costs, including those for laying the rails and buying the streetcars, came from public and quasi-public money.[21] Yet it was the development interests of billionaire city fathers like Dan Gilbert and Roger Penske that ultimately benefited from this publicly funded project, which provided boutique streetcar transit to the city's downtown and midtown white residents and left a quarter of the city's poor residents, mostly of color—many of whom don't have a car—stranded.

The streetcars "were a silly idea," Mayor Dave Bing told the *Detroit Free Press* in 2019. "We need reliable transit that reaches the neighborhoods, where people most need it." Bing's opinion was consistent with the research that shows that new streetcars do not improve accessibility for transit-dependent populations in most cities. In Detroit, these mostly Black residents need transit connections across the city to get to their jobs. Yet city fathers used their immense influence and command of racial ideologies to persuade local governments to cede important long-term infrastructure decisions to private interests for the latter's financial gain. In fact, journalist Steve Neavling reported, one M-1 Rail committee member said they didn't believe buses would spur "economic development" as well as light rail. And "another committee member, cited anonymously, conceded that buses would have been more effective for Detroiters, but 'rich, white people don't ride buses.'" This colorblind ideology has been an effective strategy in leveraging dollars that were part of the community development block grant program that should have kept Detroiters in their homes. Instead, free land and hundreds of millions in stimulus dollars were given to billionaire and avid Trump supporter Dan Gilbert and his real estate and development company, Bedrock Detroit, to redevelop the city's downtown and midtown districts. This form of political graft is not unusual among those with both power and ambition, but its deployment in Detroit is particularly egregious.

TOXIC FINANCIAL ASSETS

It is only when one digs deeper into the city's now-blighted Black neighborhoods and crumbling streets, absent of both streetlights and streetcars, that the real impact of this modern redlining project is fully revealed. Quicken Loans payday outlets may dot the streets of south Woodward Avenue, but the company had a newly uncovered role in the nation's subprime mortgage crisis: it targeted Black and brown communities with toxic mortgages. Between 2004 and 2006, homes underwritten with Quicken Loans had a foreclosure rate of 34%, and around half of those foreclosed houses, journalist Tom Perkins wrote in 2017, are now blighted.[22] In Virginia, Quicken Loans was fined $11 million for writing loans on properties appraised in excess of their fair market value, a scheme that ultimately left homeowners holding underwater mortgages. The US Department of Justice filed a lawsuit in 2015 alleging that Quicken Loans made hundreds of improper loans through the Federal Housing

Administration (FHA) lending program.[23] Since 1934 the Federal Housing Administration (FHA), which today is part of the Department of Housing and Urban Development (HUD), has insured the home loans of participating lending institutions. Today, Quicken makes more FHA loans than any other institution in the country.[24] Under the program, if the borrower later defaults on their mortgage, the holder of the loan can file an insurance claim to cover its losses.[25] In Quicken's case, $500 million of defective mortgage loans were issued, leaving HUD and the taxpayer holding the bill. These illegal practices seem to be business as usual for the Detroit-based Quicken. For example, in 2015 it settled with the Federal Deposit Insurance Corporation for $6.5 million for allegedly selling "soured loans" (mortgages that had ended in foreclosure).[26] "So, much of the development that Dan Gilbert is participating in [today]," Monica Lewis-Patrick explained, "he already knew that there was going to be a major financial crisis around predatory lending practices as it related to urban centers and communities of color, because he had participated in it." It was Gilbert and other "millionaires and billionaires," Lewis Patrick and other Detroit activists I spoke with argued, who created the very conditions from which they then profited. To date none of these white criminals have been charged. Rather, they have been praised as the saviors that put Motown back on its feet.

In addition to major giveaways and tax abatements to millionaires and billionaires, the internal dynamics of firms like Quicken Loans prove equally instructive in understanding how this new form of redlining was being put into practice in Black cities like Detroit. According to the *Detroit Free Press,* multiple lawsuits have been brought against Quicken Loans by its mortgage-loan officers regarding overtime pay. In 2011, the company won a class action lawsuit that involved four hundred former employees, because federal rules at the time didn't require it to pay overtime.[27] However, the Center for Public Integrity found that "Quicken executives managed by bullying and intimidation, pressuring [its loan officers] to falsify borrowers' incomes on loan applications and to push overpriced deals on desperate or unwary homeowners."[28] In addition, ex-employees "accuse the company of using high-pressure salesmanship to target elderly and vulnerable homeowners, as well as misleading borrowers about their loans, and falsifying property appraisals and other information to push through bad deals."[29] These internal dynamics, most of which are hidden from the general public, highlight contemporary corporate practices, not unique to Quicken, that have targeted vulnerable communities for toxic financial assets. This financial dispossession of vulnerable communities helps to explain the disproportionate drawdown of Black and brown wealth since the subprime mortgage crisis. This corporate culture has been motivated in part by a white supremacist ideology that works to perpetuate the material realities of racial oppression in cities like Flint and Detroit. Such rule bending practices are indicative of a white corporate attitude that posits the promise of home ownership to poor people of color is not one that any white lender must keep.

Yet, for Gilbert and his talking heads, the reactionary backlash to accusations of racial bias and discrimination was as immediate and scathing as it was predictable. Gilbert has called out anyone who dared to question his use of public funds as either immoral or jealous. These public funds could end up paying for most of his downtown redevelopment projects. In response to a judgment in West Virginia that fined Quicken $2.7 million for defrauding a borrower, Gilbert took the high road, claiming that his company was the true victim in the case. Gilbert called a lawsuit filed by the Department of Justice in 2015 a "witch hunt," an attempt at government overreach, and an assault on business freedoms. Also that year, he sent a scornful tweet calling investigative journalist Steve Neavling "dirty scum" and classing him among the "lying venom filled wannabes" of the city over a story Neavling had authored and Gilbert didn't like.[30] A 2015 blight investigation report by the *Detroit News* evoked a similar blistering response from Gilbert, who tweeted that the article was "shoddy, lazy journalism." Equally concerning, I feel, has been the media's response to Gilbert's bombastic outbursts. For example, in response to his criticism of the 2015 blight investigation, the *Detroit News* printed a follow-up piece in which Gilbert was given the opportunity to defend his company's lending practices. Similarly, Yahoo deleted a negative story after Gilbert complained.[31] Such aggressive derision and slander have become the go-to tactic used by Dan Gilbert, Donald Trump, Rick Snyder, and other patriarchs of racial capital. It would appear that another quality these white hypermasculine elites have in common is a fragile ego, a form of toxic masculinity, ever ready to lash out at any and all detractors who dare to question their white male privilege. Instead, those asking important questions are depicted as irresponsible and immoral, as one Quicken representative told journalist Tom Perkins: "Characterizing Quicken Loans as being responsible or associated in any way with the 'foreclosure crisis' in Detroit, or anywhere else in the country, is irresponsible and reckless."[32] Instead, Gilbert and others believe that their intentions fit with the general societal goals of revitalizing the abandoned city and that any detractors are either envious or irresponsible.

Rather, Gilbert, like most ruling class elites, find fault with the victims— in this case, the homeowners, most of whom are people of color, who lost their homes to foreclosure. "It's very hard to make any causation between these loans and the fact that [homeowners] walked away or could not afford the payments and some eventually became blighted," Gilbert told the *Detroit News*. Even though homes underwritten by Quicken Loans had a foreclosure rate of 34 percent between 2004 and 2006, Gilbert is convinced—or, perhaps more accurately, would like to convince us—that responsibility for widespread foreclosures lies with the individual homeowners in this majority-Black city who simply "walked away" from their most significant asset, and not his company and its predatory lending practices. Safeguarded behind colorblind rhetoric in a culture of white supremacy, Gilbert can defend his economic and political interests while lashing out against "irresponsible and reckless" critics and blaming the mostly Black homeowners for their own misfortune. Yet, as journalists Christine MacDonald and Joel Kurth reported. more than one in three homes were foreclosed over ten years in Detroit, roughly equal to the total number of housing units in Buffalo, New York (136,664).[33] The blighted proportion of these bank-foreclosed homes has cost city taxpayers $500 million over the ten years.[34]

But the Gilbert-led agenda not only remade Detroit into a more desirable place for his companies' mostly white middle-class employees. Gilbert has also led private support for the city's efforts to demolish dilapidated properties, creating new profit streams from his little Havana of racialized capitalism. "I know that they talk about how Detroiters destroyed the housing stock. Well, we have footage and we have hours and hours of film where there were demolition companies and private contractors that came into the city, targeting certain neighborhoods." The point for this community activist was that private sector developers targeted specific neighborhoods for redevelopment. Homeowners did not walk away.

"If you look at who is behind these urban reforms in Michigan, they are accountants, lawyers, and businesspeople," Monica Lewis-Patrick pointed out. "The governor has repeatedly stated that he is an accountant *and* a politician. It is a business model to govern, and everything I have seen about it has failed. We call it the modern day Tuskegee experiment," she concluded. Emergency managers are supposed to create financial security. Instead, what they really created amounted to *financial sovereignty* for a new generation of private sector reformers. This manufactured crisis was part of a larger concerted effort to "buy low and then sell high." They cultivated "this national narrative for . . . years that everything in Detroit was broken . . . [and] there was nothing of value, nothing of worth," a community organizer explained.

Every step of the way, the operators of this anti-democratic form of governance have left no public stone unturned by their private sector bulldozer. The stealing of pensions, the closing of schools, the restricting of public debt from refinancing, and the cutting back of health care coverage were some of the many anti-democratic efforts that citizens I spoke with readily identified as part of their city's new urban economic disciplining (read: extraction). In its wake was a tsunami of environmental racism that left many devasted and others simply fed up. "They even took away food and cash assistance," a resident told me. The latter helped some people pay their light or water bills. "Those things have been taken. Assistance for the unemployed has been reduced," another resident affirmed. Together, these cuts to social welfare programs have created a pressure cooker of poverty and scarcity. Welfare reform has continued to make it difficult for Blacks and other people of color to access public assistance, no matter how small. Yet in Michigan there is no limit to the excesses of corporate welfare—that is, as long as it remains colorblind. For many, the policies of urban austerity created the perfect storm of opportunity and profit. And the master narrative that Detroit was "coming back" has legitimized the targeting of those supposedly responsible for the city's troubles—"the least and the lost," as one activist characterized them.

THE HARDEST HIT FUND

The Hardest Hit Fund (HHF) is a federal mortgage payment assistance program to help unemployed and underemployed homeowners with foreclosure prevention and neighborhood stabilization. The program was initially successful, helping many families in Detroit harmed by the subprime lending crisis to keep up with the mortgage payments. However, "what happened is," a fair housing community organizer explained to me, "you had several political persons as well as Dan Gilbert and others go meet with President Obama and offer to him a 'win-win strategy.'" The Gilbert-led coalition persuaded the president "to divert those [federal tax] dollars" from their intended use—unemployed homeowners and those with underwater mortgages—toward blight removal in the city.[35] The argument these city fathers put forward was clear: the city's economic recovery would be best served by targeted blight elimination in the city rather than by helping mostly Black homeowners with mortgage assistance payments.

The Detroit Blight Removal Task Force was created with HHF dollars and tasked with the development and implementation of a blight removal plan for the city. The task force's three cochairs were Glenda Price, president of the Detroit Public Schools Foundation; Linda Smith, executive director of U-SNAP-BAC (United Streets Networking and Planning: Building a Community), and Dan Gilbert. According to the website Data Driven Detroit, the cochairs "organized a team of experts from all levels of government, the private and nonprofit sectors, and the foundation community to provide insight on the topic of blight elimination." Cutting through the colorblind gobbledygook is difficult, but, effectively, this "collaborate effort" produced a mapping project that extended Gilbert's and other elite's efforts to transform the city according to their vision by targeting Black neighborhoods for gentrification. The task force's mission, according to its website, is "to develop a straightforward and detailed implementation plan to remove every blighted residential structure, commercial structure and public building, and clear every blighted vacant lot in the city of Detroit as quickly as possible using an environmentally-conscious approach. The plan's recommendations will focus on creating economic opportunities for the city and its people, as well as dramatically improving the safety of residents and first responders."[36]

For white investors and those white homeowners considering a move back to this now-cool, hip, and reinvigorated Detroit, this mission statement read as a clear dog whistle. Specifically, as a result of the reboot, crime, with which this majority-Black city has long been associated, would be a thing of the past, and first responders, specifically police, will ensure that white property would be strictly protected. For many years Starbucks was the emblem of gentrification in transition neighborhoods. Whole Foods too. Increasingly, bike lanes, street cars, and parks also fill this urban space. In Detroit, another slogan signaled the return to city living: *law and order.* "So what that said to me," Monica Lewis-Patrick explained, was that

> it was more important for the young, white hipsters . . . to come into the city. That they had a space and a place to be more than the people that had stayed and paid when everybody else had ran from the city. I don't know about you all, but that doesn't stick well in my craw, as my granny would say. Just doesn't feel good. That you can say that my community should die, because you just decided that you want to come back.

THE MOTOR CITY MAPPING PROJECT

The Detroit Blight Removal Task Force's "come back" plan used preliminary data collected from the Motor City Mapping Project, a property survey of the 380,000 parcels across the 139-square-mile city, an area larger than Manhattan (22 square miles), Boston (48 square miles), and San Francisco (46 square miles) combined. Information on its website (now defunct) indicated that the survey was implemented by Data Driven Detroit (D3), an affiliate of the Michigan Nonprofit Association (MNA), in conjunction with Loveland Technologies and "the Quicken Loans family of companies."[37] Other funders included the Michigan State Housing Development Authority (MSHDA) and the Skillman and Kresge foundations. The original survey, completed in 2009 by D3, evaluated the condition and occupancy status of 350,000 residential parcels in Detroit. As with the federal Home Owners Loan Corporation redlining maps of the

Table 4 Breakdown of structure condition, Motor City Mapping Project

	Publicly owned (71,125)*	Privately owned (186,629)**
Good (green)	5,259 (34%)	115,238 (85%)
Fair (yellow)	4,608 (30%)	14,252 (10%)
Poor (orange)	3,693 (24%)	4,607 (3%)
Demolition recommended (red)	1,747 (11%)	1,616 (1%)

*15,327 structures + 55,787 lots

**135,742 structures + 50,861 lots

Table 5 Breakdown of structure occupancy status, Motor City Mapping Project

	Publicly owned (71,125)*	Privately owned (186,629)**
Possibly occupied (yellow)	739 (5%)	6,316 (5 %)
Partially occupied (gray)	12 (less than 1%)	84 (less than 1%)
Occupied (green)	3,417 (22%)	109,901 (81%)
Unoccupied (red)	11,147 (73%)	19,414 (14%)

*15,327 structures + 55,787 lots

**135,742 structures + 50,861 lots

1930s, a battalion of surveyors—"a dedicated team of 200 resident surveyors and drivers," as D3's website put it—performed windshield sociology to classify each residential parcel.[38] With this data, organized and evaluated by real estate developers and mapping professionals, and funded by federal and nonprofit agencies, each building structure and lot in the city was assigned a grade that reflected its condition and occupancy. That condition of each building was then indicated on color-coded maps. Structures classified in good condition were denoted in green on the map. Structures classified as fair were colored yellow. Structures in poor condition were colored orange, and those in need of demolition were shown in red (see tables 4 and 5).

As with previous redlining practices, this real estate mapping project relied on a network of white real estate developers, lenders, and appraisers to inventory and assess the city's housing. Also like past redlining tools, these maps were used to direct federal dollars intended to stabilize a recession-rocked housing market toward preserving racial segregation, intergenerational poverty, and environmental degradation. Gone, however, was the 1930s HOLC redlining vernacular that specified the "infiltration of negroes," "Mexicans," or other "undesirable" populations for discriminatory housing opportunities. Instead, colorblind prompts regarding a neighborhood's built structures and their condition served as contemporary redlining tools for directing federal funds to white homeowners, real estate interests, lenders, and businesses. The mapping projected reported, a housing advocate explained, that "over 90% of the housing stock of the city was in good to fair condition. That meant that many of the homes only needed some basic upkeep or restoration, like windows, doors, heating systems, hot water heaters, some plastering, some basic electric work, some basic plumbing, to bring those houses up to a livable standard."

These restoration efforts would have been greatly enhanced had Michigan's Housing Finance Agency (HFA) directed the financial assistance from the HHF program to those homeowners in need. The distribution of interest-free loans, for example, would have helped homeowners struggling to make their monthly mortgage payments stay in their homes, preserving home ownership in Black neighborhoods and ensuring property tax revenues that the city needed while also improving the housing stock of neighborhoods hardest hit by the subprime mortgage crisis. In 2010, the HHF extended to the state of Michigan more than $761 million in federal moneys to provide such assistance.[39] "What they did [however] is allow those houses to sit," a housing advocate told me. "And then they [started to] talk about how Detroiters destroyed the housing stock." The colorblind rhetoric became a formidable tool for the continued exclusion of Black communities from the city's development efforts. The Michigan State Housing Development Authority (MSHDA) created a nonprofit housing corporation, Michigan Homeowner Assistance (MHA), to design programs and oversee the distribution of the HHF funds in Michigan.

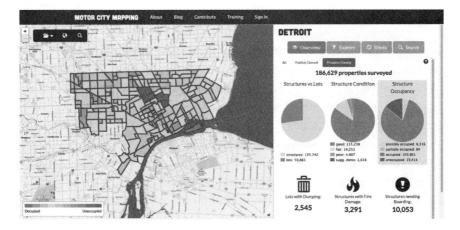

Figure 17. Motor City Mapping Project.

In 2009, the city's mapping project was converted to a digital platform (fig. 17). Key to this advancement was the donation of two hundred tablets by Dan Gilbert's Rock Ventures. The tablets came preloaded with a "blexting" app (a blend of "blight" and "texting"), which systematized blight cartography throughout the city, enabling any appraiser, regardless of expertise or training, to gather and record blight data with ease. Datasets included historic designation and eligibility, ownership, current and future land use, tax delinquency, and foreclosure status.

In total, the philanthropic arm of Quicken Loans and other nonprofit allies donated more than $2 million to create these online digital mapping tools and interactive resources to steer the development of infrastructure, services, and housing in the revitalized city. In effect, Gilbert brought the entire weight of his excessively influential charitable-industrial complex to rebuild Detroit in his image. To anyone living in these struggling neighborhoods the lesson was clear: federal assistance that was supposed to help them and their neighborhoods deal with the fallout of the subprime mortgage housing collapse was being diverted toward the redevelopment interests of city elites, and in some cases, they were the very same corporations that were, in part, responsible for the subprime mortgage crisis in the first place. The similarities to the 1930s redlining maps and project are striking.

PROJECT GREEN LIGHT

To protect these gentrifying efforts and to ease the fears of new white gentrifiers, all Detroiters now live with constant surveillance. In 2016 the
Detroit Police Department (DPD) entered into a public-private partnership with Guardian Alarm Company, telecommunications giant Comcast,
and local businesses and associations, including BOMA (Building Owners
and Managers Association) Metro Detroit, the Eight Mile Boulevard
Association (8MBA), and the Detroit Land Bank, to introduce a real-time
crime surveillance program called Project Green Light.[40] According to the
city's website, the project is "the first of its kind, blending a mix of real-
time crime-fighting and community policing aimed at improving neighborhood safety and strengthening DPD's efforts to deter, identify, and
solve crime."[41] Under this mass surveillance program, businesses and
associations pay to have flashing green lights installed on or near their
property. Each lit green sign, bearing the words "Green Light corridor and
the city's logo indicates 24/7 police surveillance, implying "You are being
watched" to Black or other persons of color and "You are safe here" to
white people (fig. 18).[42] The deep irony that a city which couldn't afford to
keep its streetlights on has found ample resources to fund private security
cameras should not be lost on anyone. Moreover, for many, the constant
flashing of lights has become a neighborhood nuisance and has raised
health concerns associated with stress, anxiety, and hypertension for people constantly being watched.

Since its launch in 2016 the program has expanded to more than two
thousand cameras at more than seven hundred businesses, including public housing, recreation centers, school campuses, grocery stories, and
medical facilities.[43] The city's website offers an interactive map, along
with a smart app to inform people of their whereabouts, as well as a hyper-
link to the Detroit Police Department (fig. 19), just in case. Facial recognition technology has been part of the city's surveillance system since 2017.
The city continues to use facial recognition software in spite of research
that indicates it regularly misidentifies people of color. Sighting recent
research, the *Washington Post* reported, "Asian and African American
people were up to 100 times more likely to be misidentified than white
men, depending on the particular algorithm and type of search. Native

Figure 18. Green Light Corridor sign, Detroit. City of
Detroit 2020.

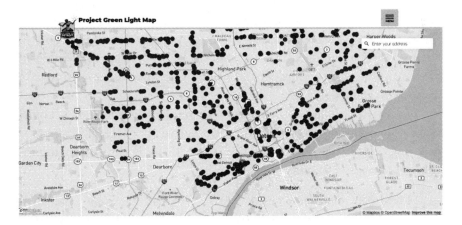

Figure 19. Project Green Light map. City of Detroit n.d.

Americans had the highest false-positive rate of all ethnicities, according
to the study, which found that systems varied widely in their accuracy."[44]
To date, the use of facial recognition technology has led to the wrongful
arrests of two Black men in Detroit, Robert Williams and Michael Oliver.
In light of this research, California recently banned the use of the software
in police body cams. Michigan has not. In fact, Project Green Light is only
one layer of the panopticon that surveillance cameras have made of this

majority-Black city. The hundred-plus buildings that Dan Gilbert owns downtown are all monitored with the cameras of his own company Rock Security. They all feed to his corporate headquarters but also have a direct line to the police department. "Likewise, a separate system of streetlight cameras, and even drones, is under development," community activist, pastor, and author Bill Wylie-Kellermann writes, underscoring the extent to which systems of BIPOC surveillance are embedded in white gentrification.[45]

.   .   .   .   .

"My granny used to say, 'You can't piss on me and tell me it's raining,'" Monica Lewis-Patrick tells the group of architecture students visiting from New York University. "You cannot piss on Detroit and still convince me that there is not good in us, and ability and innovation. We put the world on wheels. We are the arsenal of democracy. We didn't come to Detroit [just] to build cars. . . . We came to Detroit fleeing the tyranny of the South. Rapes and murders and lynchings that were happening on a daily basis [there].

"That is why we fled to places like Detroit and Chicago and St. Louis: looking for a better way" [of life for future generations]; looking for that one rung on the social and economic ladder that you cling on to, to provide some sense of stability to one's family.

> My grandparents moved here in 1952; they had twenty-one children. They had worked in the coal mines of southwestern Virginia, so they weren't somewhere being fat, happy, and lazy. Some of the hardest work you can do in the world is coal mining. In the world! So, my grandfather, he didn't own his first house until he was about sixty-three.

And purchasing a home was no easy feat for a Black man in the 1960s as redlining, racial covenants, zoning, and other forms of what historian Carol Anderson has referred to as "white rage" worked to derail Black advancement. Buying a home in the "wrong" neighborhood (read: white) in some cases, Anderson notes, often led to tragic outcomes for aspiring Black families.[46] But in "buying that house in 1963," Lewis Patrick explained, "from there we were able to acquire some wealth. Today his children either have a trade or several degrees. We are doctors, we are lawyers, we are secret service agents." In other words, makers, *not* takers.

Today, moneys set aside to help families harmed by the financial downturn—mostly families of color—have been diverted to once again incentivize white people. Hardest Hit Fund moneys have been redirected to the redevelopment of downtown and midtown Detroit to bring people— white people—back to the city. "And it did incentivize many people to return to the city," Lewis Patrick admitted, particularly people employed in eds and meds, people who "work for the hospitals, work in the arts, and the museums, work for educational institutions. They were seriously incentiv- ized to move to midtown and downtown."

HOW GENTRIFICATION WORKS

"I will give you a perfect example" of how gentrification works in Detroit, Lewis Patrick explained. "I used to live in Lafayette Park. Lafayette Park is one of the most noted architectural neighborhoods in the city, also still probably one of the best maintained"—a prime location for gentrifiers. "And what we saw happening in 2009 is, there were these white folks coming from all over the country" to check out our neighborhood. But white folks, she explained, "don't come up in the hood and just look at stuff. They don't. They are coming to speculate. And so we started telling government and others, you know, this seems to be strange. There were just forty white people walking in my neighborhood at 10:00 at night. That seemed strange. Or coming in and biking. Those are things gentrifi- ers do." She and other residents were having these conversations about "major potholes in the road," but the city was putting bike lanes in, which "seemed strange. Those are moves of gentrification. And so, because we started seeing that," neighbors got together to strategize about how to "start speaking to it."

They decided to attend city-sponsored meetings and other forums of block clubs, community groups, business owners, and faith and school leaders. Lewis Patrick and other grassroots activists found, however, that the meeting organizers "were only inviting the people that were new to the city to come and have discussions about moving the city forward, or collaborative ventures or things that 'we could do together.'" When longtime residents showed up at these venues in an effort "to be seen," Tawana Petty, blogger for *Data for Black Lives*, observes, they were usually marginalized in the proceedings, allowed a mere thirty seconds to make a public comment.[47] "I find it always strange," Lewis Patrick reflected, "because we would get in these public meetings, and they . . . act like they don't know anything about gentrification or structural racism or environmental racism. It's almost like, If we don't talk about it, maybe it will go away." Thus, instead of focusing on including the actual community at these town hall meetings, city advocates presented corporate and business interests with "very glossy brochures and very sleek Power Points." To those anti-gentrification activists who witnessed what went on at these meetings, the strategy was clear: "they marginalize the voices of community," as Lewis Patrick put it. Moreover, upon raising the issues, in "pushing back," as Petty phrases it, community activists were characterized as "just distraught because we didn't have bootstraps or something like that."

Many of the organizations hosting these "community efforts" were supported by the charitable arm of Dan Gilbert's Rocket Mortgage empire. In 2020, for example, the Greater Palmer Park Community, a group "dedicated to the holistic improvement and advancement of the entire area," received $150,000 from the Rocket Giving Fund, whose moneys are raised through the Rocket Mortgage Classic, a golf tournament on the PGA tour.[48] Similarly, $122,320 was distributed to the Birdies for Charity program to help verified nonprofit organizations raise awareness of their organizations. These two disbursements make up a small percentage of the $2.7 million raised by the Rocket Mortgage Classic in 2020 and distributed to the city's nonprofits.

"And so these are some of the dualities and complexities that we are seeing in the city right now." Money and resources are pouring into Detroit. But all of that investment is directed exclusively to white lives and livelihoods. A lot of this has been driven by using race, Lewis Patrick told me, because "it is so divisive, it just is."

> Even if people are desirous of being in an inclusive environment, what begins to happen is that if you are young and you are white, then you are

incentivized to . . . move into the city. If you are Black and you have been here and you are trying to just hold onto your house, there is no help for you. There are no resources available for you. So it's forcing two realities, one where people are downtown dancing in the streets because they have got a job and a new house and a new car and $40,000 in the bank, and then [the other, where] it's creating a whole different dynamic and racial tension in the [Black] neighborhoods. Not because people don't embrace diversity and all of what that richness includes. But it's because you have decided that others can come in while you are pushing me out. So it's a perfect picture of gentrification and they are not beyond using genocidal tactics to do that.

In many ways Lewis Patrick's reflection echoes the 1968 Kerner Report on the causes of racial disorder in the United States. The Kerner Commission found that racial inequality was created and maintained by white society.[49] Today in Detroit, as well as other major cities in this country, gentrification brings a new form of racial capitalism that continues to move the nation "toward two societies, one black, one white—separate and unequal."[50] In this new economy, environmental injustice is not limited to physical displacement but extends to economic well-being as well, as both wealth and income opportunities become systematically debased. For example, those able to find employment are generally limited to minimum-wage service sector employment. This is why efforts to raise the minimum wage are so vital to environmental justice efforts in Detroit and elsewhere in the United States. If a large segment of the economy available to BIPOC communities is the service sector, their ability to afford basic needs—food, shelter, and water—is contingent on a fair wage.

PUBLIC SCHOOL CLOSINGS

"The other thing that we saw in our neighborhoods were the alarming increase in 'school closings,'" a resident explained. "I'm sure you already know this," he told me, but "when you close a school, it's one of the worst assaults you can have on a community." Most of the public schools in Detroit were closed after the emergency manager takeover, leaving 89 bona fide public schools open in 2016 out of 261 in 1994, "depriving entire communities of the institutions that once anchored them," wrote columnist Diane Bukowski.[51] Bukowski quoted school board member Elena Herrada as saying, "Seventy-seven school buildings have been bundled and given to the City of Detroit to pay an alleged water drainage debt. Art, music, and math teachers have been cut from the budget. Teachers have had their pay cut and their health care benefits slashed."[52] "They have actually put us on a pathway to have all of our schools close and eventually everything would be charterized," a parent told me. "It is a way to commodify everything," consistent with a capitalist agenda and the push to privatize all public services.

Rich donors once again led the movement to privatize public education in Michigan under the guise of "schools of choice." In particular, the DeVos family empire, the largest single donor to Michigan electoral politics, has backed every single reform and every single elected public official advocating privatizing education in Michigan. In addition, the DeVoses have given dearly to major right-wing think thanks, including the Mackinac Center for Public Policy, a leading architect of Michigan's emergency manager Law, right-to-work legislation, and other anti-union and anti-tax efforts in the state. The DeVos family was also deeply involved in the creation of the West Michigan Policy Forum, a nonprofit organization focused on advancing a pro-business policy agenda in Michigan. As secretary of education under the Trump presidency, Betsy DeVos was personally rewarded for the family's support of the Republican Party, giving the empress of West Michigan the opportunity to take her racist corporate-education agenda to the national level.

These efforts brought about the state capture of Detroit Public Schools (DPS), the largest school district in the state. And from March 2009 to February 2016—seventeen years—the DPS was under the control of a governor-appointed emergency manager. When Robert Bobb was appointed as the first emergency manager, the DPS had a $139.7 million deficit. By 2016, after four emergency managers had come and gone, the district's deficit had ballooned to $515 million.[53] During this time, DPS saw no improvement in the education outcomes of its students. While that outcome might reasonably have been predicted given the fact that none of the emergency managers had any background in education, it also appeared that the EMs' goal was never to balance the district's budget but rather to privatize public education delivery writ large in the city. "My initial focus was on covering the bankruptcy," Curt Guyette, the Michigan ACLU's investigative journalist, told me in the ACLU's downtown office. "I started writing about the water shutoffs, which were occurring in Detroit as part of the bankruptcy process. Then I wrote about the Education Achievement Authority," which was a unique school district, "a brainchild of the governor's that was created through an interlocal agreement," a little-used legal loophole.[54] This state takeover of the DPS was accomplished outside the legislative process through an interlocal agreement between the emergency manager and the Eastern Michigan University Board of Regents, all of whom were gubernatorial appointees. The Educational Achievement Authority (EAA) was also governed by gubernatorial appointees and modeled after the state of Louisiana's takeover of the New Orleans public school system following Hurricane Katrina's devastation of the city.

"The Education Achievement Authority has been a disaster since day one," Guyette told me. "I conducted an investigation, . . . through filing the Freedom of Information Act requests." The EAA took fifteen schools out of Detroit Public Schools, twelve of which the authority ran directly and three it converted to charter schools. Had there not been an emergency manager, Guyette emphasized, the DPS would never have agreed to the state takeover of its school system. "Because it took 10,000 students away and the state funding that goes with all those students—in excess of $7,000 per student. Millions and millions and millions of dollars in funding were taken away from DPS with the loss of those students. Had it not been an emergency manager unilaterally making that decision, DPS would have never agreed to do it." Moreover, the EMs took the lowest-performing schools in the city, whose "students [were] most in need of every benefit that could be given them in order to improve . . . students who were for the most part years behind their peers," and turned them into charter schools. Currently there are as many Detroit children in charter schools, about 71,000, as in public schools. And there is increasing pressure from the DeVoses and other elites in Grand Rapids to convert the entire Detroit district (which is 95 percent African American) to charters.[55]

ELI BROAD

As with the New Orleans model, a constellation of national organizations converged on Detroit to support the EAA. All of the teachers in the fifteen schools were fired. "It could be seen," Guyette noted, "as attempt to help bust the unions or at least certainly weaken the teacher's union." The EAA relied heavily on Teach for America (TFA) to supply nonunionized instructional staff. Originally conceived with good intentions, Teach for America gave young recent college graduates the opportunity to help curb teacher shortages plaguing America's least-resourced and generally urban public schools. But a recent ProPublica report suggested that Teach for America has now evolved into an arm of the charter school movement.[56] "I believe [TFA] supplied as many as 50% of the instructional stuff. [And] it was [all] funded by the Broad Foundation," Guyette told me. Named after billionaire Eli Broad, the foundation is one of the nation's leading charter school boosters. "I think he donated 10 million to help fund it." Much of the money was derived from his shares of stock in American International Group. Better known as AIG, the finance and insurance giant was implicated in the 2008 financial crisis, having indulged in "all kinds of unconscionable bets," according to Ben Bernanke, who then chaired the Federal Reserve. In the wake of the global financial tsunami that ensued, AIG received a taxpayer bailout of more than $170 billion. And even as it declared a loss of $61.7 billion for the fourth quarter of 2008, the largest corporate loss in history, the delinquent company paid out $165 million in executive bonuses, which was part of a larger total payout reportedly valued at $450 million.[57]

Nearly 10 million homeowners in the United States lost their homes to foreclosure sales between 2006 and 2014 thanks to the predatory lending practices of companies like AIG. In total, the Federal Reserve estimates that American households lost $7 trillion in home equity as a result of the housing crisis.[58] Banks specifically targeted people of color for subprime loans even when they qualified for prime loans, later leaving communities mostly of color holding the bag. From 2005 to 2009, the median net worth of Black households fell by 53% to $12,124, and of Latinx households by 66% to $18,359, compared to a net worth drop of 16% (to

$113,149) for whites.[59] The Center for Responsible Lending estimated that African Americans lost 240,020 homes and Latinos lost 335,950 homes between 2007 and 2009.[60] Others living in subprimed neighborhoods and communities were also adversely affected by depressed home values. Local governments' efforts to raise property taxes used to fund schools, police and fire departments, and other public services were also drastically hampered by this latest phase of racialized capitalism. And into this economic void stepped individuals like Eli Broad who exacted their fortunes from the subprime mortgage crisis they manufactured and then sought to privatize education and other public services.

The Los Angeles–based philanthropist Eli Broad, like other powerful supporters of the charter school movement, served for a time on Teach for America's board.[61] Broad and his foundation directly and indirectly backed political candidates favorable to their agenda. He has also created an academy where future school administrators are trained to run public schools around the country *his* way. His zealous, multimillion-dollar plan to expand the number of charter schools in his hometown of Los Angeles, the nation's second-largest school district, has drawn much scrutiny. Yet, in part due to his sole influence, LA as of 2016 had more charter schools than any other district in the country, representing 23% of the district's student population.[62] The Broad Foundation is a partner of Betsy De Vos's American Federation for Children, a "national advocacy organization promoting school choice, with a specific focus on advocating for school vouchers, scholarship tax credit programs and Education Savings Accounts."[63]

In Detroit, however, the Education Achievement Authority and its proponents not only changed who taught students in K–12 classrooms but also course content and assessment. "The keystone of the EAA was a computerized learning [platform] system," explained Curt Guyette, "using a software called Buzz, which was produced by a private company in Utah," Agilix Labs Inc. "These kids . . . in need of quality education, the best education possible," Guyette pointed out, "were actually used as guinea pigs to test and develop this education software that was just not ready." With major taxpayer financial support, the EAA teamed up with Agilix and the School Improvement Network to test this new learning platform. Documents obtained though the FOIA reveal that over the course of two years, teachers and students were being "used as whetstones to hone a badly flawed product being pitched as cutting-edge technology."[64] Repeating a pattern, the state helped create a situation that made high-quality public education in Detroit an abomination and then used the resulting poor performance as justification for privatizing the public service, all the while exploiting teacher and student labor to develop and refine the software that the EAA then marketed to other municipalities.

Guyette cited a report, published the week of our interview, that the EAA owed Detroit Public Schools $14 million in rent. "They owe $14 million, $12 million of which is rent for those schools that hasn't been paid. And the chancellor of the EAA had secretly asked one of the emergency managers to forgive that debt." The *same* emergency manager who had been in charge of Flint and had directed the city to switch its drinking water supply to the Flint River: Darnell Earley. Afterward, the governor appointed him to be the emergency manager of the Detroit Public Schools. "So the person that was directly responsible for the lead contamination of the city's water supply, which caused irreparable harm to kids who suffered, had their IQs lowered, have learning disabilities and behavior problems as a result of the lead contamination—that person has been put in charge of the education of 46,000 Detroit Public School students."

The end goal was clear: nothing short of a complete overhaul of public education would suffice, and what resulted was a sort of pseudoscientific startup laboratory for private practitioners to cultivate and refine their learning platforms. Once again, the people who built and held up the city for a half century would be the ones pushed out or pushed down, subjected to shocking harm in order to establish new political possibilities for those that counted money as more important than people.

> And so, what they have done is they have leveraged their power in all of these spaces where we used to be able to say there were checks and balances. They have taken all of that away under the auspices of—the adults are in charge now, which is, for us, very offensive code language that Black folks can't lead themselves, that we don't have the capacity or the intellectual ability to be self-governed.

The deep irony pointed out by this Detroiter is that city and state leaders justified this form of racial dispossession by saying it would make the city a better place. The subtext being a better place for white people to belong to and live in. Many people have mixed emotions about gentrification. Considerable change of any form is never easy. This chapter highlights the historical factors shaping gentrification and the resultant environmental racism that has shadowed the city's transformation. I emphasize the power structures, networks, and alliances that have steered this history as it was being made. And integral to every idea, proposal, and plan in Detroit were racist constructions that posited white people as somehow more deserving than nonwhites. Motown too was now a place built by and for whites to work, live, and play. Skin color in gentrifying environs in the United States has become, to paraphrase Michel Foucault, a technology of racial power, a marker connoting rights to the city. And, having identified the significance of skin color in demarcating the boundaries and affordances of gentrification, white elites in Detroit milked it for all its white supremacy worth.

In Detroit, a financial fascist's agenda manufactured a bankruptcy in order to restructure corporate debt. Capital freed from debt—absorbed by taxpayers and longtime citizens of Detroit—was then used to refashion the city and thereby further benefit elite interests. Elites have amassed millions—in Dan Gilbert's case, billions—from the subprime mortgage crises and other predatory lending practices that targeted poor people of color. A simple drive down Woodward Avenue reveals the many Payday Loan stores that dot poor Detroiters' neighborhoods. These predators are now charged with saving the city they dismantled. How noble. As if their philanthropic efforts could somehow overshadow their selfish schemes, corporate transgressions, and the breaking of social norms. In each case, we see that local elected officials have been bought off by corporate heavyweights—sometimes it doesn't take much—and then gone on to be handsomely rewarded by the very people who are stealing the city from its citizens, from the people, that is, they were elected to serve. This profoundly conservative vision of cities has been staffed with "bourgeois architects, planners and self-styled 'urban gurus' [who] "advance a darkly troubling vision of urban planning" for the exclusive use of white metropolitans.[65] What Monica Lewis-Patrick and other Detroiters described to me are the very same conditions that lad to the civil unrest and eventual riots in Black neighborhoods in major US cities, including Detroit, in 1967. And what they have described is a ticking time bomb.

9 We Charge Genocide

"We charge genocide," declared Monica Lewis-Patrick during the public comment period of the Michigan Civil Rights Commission's hearings on the Flint water crisis in 2016 (fig. 20). These hearings, held in the grand ballroom of the University of Michigan–Flint's historic Northbank Center, on the north bank of the Flint River, marked the third and final public hearing on allegations that the city's residents were the victims of discrimination in the lead contamination of the city's public water supply. Specifically, the Commission examined to what extent environmental racism was a central factor in the city's drinking water crisis. The hearing offered a chance, albeit a limited one, for the victims to comment publicly. For many residents waiting their turn to speak, the hearing was a chance to set the record straight. A chance to counter the dominant narrative that they were exaggerating the harm, or were unable to fully understand the complexity of the crisis, or were somehow responsible. A chance to hold up to the state the suffering and pain it had caused decent citizens rendered expendable by racial capitalism.

It had been a long day for Lewis Patrick. Most of the mainly white, predominantly male experts who were invited to give official testimony as part of the hearing's procedures had left hours before. It was now past

Figure 20. Monica Lewis-Patrick and Debra Taylor testify at the public hearing on September 8, 2016. Michigan Department of Civil Rights.

7 p.m., and the audience in the ornate downtown Flint landmark consisted now only of citizens, most of them women and people of color. Most of them, like myself, had been here all day. We were all very tired. It might have been the fact that the public at this public hearing were only now given a chance to speak that angered Lewis Patrick. All day, she and other residents had listened to technocrats give another lengthy history lesson about environmental racism in Flint—a lesson residents had learned all too well, not through academic debate or text but by living it every day during the water crisis. "These outsiders," a resident explained to me, "beholden to a particular academic arrogance, don't have a clue what you have endured." Lewis Patrick, like all those who had waited to be heard, was given three minutes to speak to the Commission: three minutes to give sworn testimony; three minutes to get their stories officially documented; three minutes to explain to the Commission how the Flint water crisis had impacted their lives. Just three minutes to bear witness.

What we know [is] shutting off water is an act of war . . . poisoning water is also an act of war. What we know from the water research that we have done is that the water issue in Detroit and Flint are not separate. What we know is happening around the globe is that anywhere where water and land are adjacent and poor people own it and control it, [it] is being seized, privatized, or commodified in some way.

We, together with researchers from University of Michigan, Wayne State University, Michigan State University, the University of California, Berkeley, and other universities [places where Black women have historically been excluded from[1]] [have] joined ranks to put the evidence together and drive it by citizen's research to show that the policies of water, . . . from the water rates to how water is being controlled, is racist.

The words of this frontline community member underscore the degree to which we need to rethink important renderings of harm when theorizing the legacy of environmental racism in the United States. The multiple scales of intergenerational harm through which ethnic and racial environmental racism continues to function in this country impel us to recognize its genocidal nature.[2] Here, activists point to the processes of large-scale theft, specifically the theft of water and the precarious conditions of life that result. Since the beginning of the US empire, African American scholar Harold Cruse reminded us more than sixty years ago, Black people in the United States have been living under domestic colonialism. Today, activists in Flint claim they are living under global colonialism. Their struggles, both activists and Cruse insist, must be seen as part of the worldwide anti-colonial movement.[3]

The activists who attended the public hearing knew that this was not the first time the charge of genocide had been levied against their government. Beginning in 1968, the American Indian Movement (AIM) adopted the Raphaël Lemkin's concept of genocide to explain the systematic extermination, removal, assimilation, and religious and cultural persecution of Native Americans since European contact. The Black and Chicano liberation movements, the Puerto Rican and Hawai'ian independence movements, and groups within the US antiwar movement also used the discourse of genocide.[4] In 1951 a petition, edited by civil rights attorney William Patterson and colleagues, was submitted to the United Nations charging the United States government with genocide against African Americans. "We maintain" Patterson and his colleagues wrote, "that the oppressed Negro citizen of the United States, segregated, discriminated against and long the target of violence, suffers from genocide as the result of the consistent, conscious, unified policies of every branch of government."[5] Using Lemkin's conceptual framing, Patterson and his collaborators described genocide as a multifaceted social system that results in case after case after case of harm, dehumanization, exclusion, and premature Black death. The petition was endorsed by more than ninety signatories, including W. E. B. Du Bois. On the day of the hearing before the Michigan Civil Rights Commission, activists were once again charging genocide for the poisoning and premature deaths of African Americans in Flint.

"The city was abandoned" a local journalist explained to me. "I think the way that I am trying to make sense of it [is,] like, I think there is an incentive for essentially killing the city, right? The city is on the verge of death, and I think that you have a state that would soon push it over the cliff and not have people live there. . . . I'm trying to use my words carefully. It's like, I think you have a government that would just as soon see Flint cease to exist as a city." In effect, they suggested that the Flint water crisis was not a simple matter of government failure but an intentional act to kill the city, including its inhabitants. "It just seems like they are trying to push us off a cliff," another resident said, echoing the journalist. Yet the charge of genocide rarely gets much consideration in this country despite its continued genocidal history.[6] One could contribute its absence to American exceptionalism, which continues to ignore the fact that racial oppression and discrimination—whether in the form of slavery, Jim Crow, or (now) neoliberalism—have always been at the center of US economic institutions.

A FAR MORE EXPANSIVE DEFINITION

It is worth noting that the United Nations Convention on the Prevention and Punishment of the Crime of Genocide, which was adopted on December 9, 1948, on the heels of the Nazi war crimes trials—was not simply about the Holocaust. Genocide, according to the UN Convention, is "any of the following acts committed with intent to destroy, in whole or in part, a national, ethnic, racial, or religious group, as such: a. Killing members of the group; b. Causing serious bodily or mental harm to members of the group; c. Deliberately inflicting on the group conditions of life calculated to bring about its physical destruction in whole or in part; d. Imposing measures intended to prevent births within the group; and e. Forcibly transferring children of the group to another group."[7] In addition to genocide itself, punishable acts defined in the Convention include conspiracy to commit genocide, direct, public incitement to commit genocide, attempt to commit genocide, and complicity in genocide.[8]

In his seminal book on the Holocaust, *Axis Rule in Occupied Europe*, Raphael Lemkin combined the Greek word *genos* (race, tribe) and the Latin -*cide* (killing) to form a new word: *genocide*. Lemkin intended it, he wrote, "to signify a coordinated plan of different actions aiming at the destruction of essential foundations of the life of national groups, with the aim of annihilating the groups themselves."[9] For Lemkin this coordinated plan had a technique that cut across eight dimensions or "fields." Genocide is accomplished in the *political* field by destroying institutions of self-government; in the *social* field "by the abolition of local law and local courts"; in the *cultural* field by prohibiting or destroying language, art, music, and other forms of cultural identity; in the *economic* field by the coordinated destruction of the foundations of economic existence and the upward distribution of wealth; in the *biological* field by assuming a policy of depopulation of the oppressed race and normalizing intergenerational violence between the races; in the field of *physical existence* by "racial discrimination in feeding" (I would add drinking), endangering health by prohibiting basic necessities, and mass killings; in the *religious* field by interfering with religious influences; and in the field of *morality* by creating "an atmosphere of moral debasement" within the group.[10] Even non-lethal acts that undermine the personal security, liberty, health, and dignity of members of a group constitute genocide, according to Lemkin's original framing, if they help weaken the group's viability.[11]

In *A Little Matter of Genocide,* author Ward Churchill reveals that Raphaël Lemkin's original draft submitted to the UN Secretariat proposed a far more expansive classification. Acts or policies that aimed at "preventing the preservation or development" of "racial, national, linguistic, religious or political groups" would also be considered genocidal, along with a range of "preparatory acts," including "all forms of propaganda tending by their systematic and hateful character to provoke genocide, or tending to make it appear as a necessary, legitimate, or excusable act."[12]

Churchill also documented how, during negotiations over the wording, the United States sought to influence both the definitional ambiguity and legal timidity of the final document so as to move it more in line with American imperialism, both at home and abroad, effectively tempering the Convention's original mandate and Lemkin's aspiration.[13] With few exceptions, Churchill wrote, there has been a general dilution of the meaning and elimination of criteria included in the term *genocide*. This conceptual retrenchment has served the sovereign purposes of all United Nations member states, which immediately had second thoughts about the broader implications of such far-reaching pronouncements on their own genocidal tendencies on the heels of the Nuremburg Trials. With few exceptions, the "remarkable disinterest in the topic of genocide" by the scholarly community has all but sealed the fate of a significant theoretical construct and restricted a deep social problem to a moment in history.[14]

Scholars have noted that the UN General Assembly's insertion of the word *intent* in the Convention was equally problematic in that this framing inevitably ran up against the "burden of proof" problem: the intent to commit genocide is, on its face, virtually impossible to prove. Also, confining this form of racism to hostile and intentional acts effectively has limited how we understand genocide, directing our attention to the pathologies of individuals while overshadowing the political ideologies, the systems of government, and a "civilized" society that normalizes the premature death of a particular group. Lastly, the notion of intentionality serves to eclipse the seemingly "ordinary" and even "rational" origins of modern-day genocide. Everything that rendered the Holocaust possible, Polish sociologist and philosopher Zygmunt Bauman wrote, was "normal—in the sense of being fully in keeping with everything we know about our civilization, its guiding spirit, its priorities, its immanent vision of the world—all of the proper ways to pursue human happiness together with a perfect society."[15]

To better understand what genocide is and is not, the few social scientists who have studied the matter have steered clear of the all-too-easy notion of intentionality and argued that genocide is a problem of our modern rational society, not the intent of madmen and psychopaths. "It was the rational world of modern civilization," Bauman wrote, "which made the Holocaust thinkable."[16] Moreover, Bauman and others argue that the Holocaust was not a hiccup of barbarism in an otherwise civilized and civilizing process; rather, modern civilization was the Holocaust's *necessary* condition.[17] This sober description of the modern bureaucratic mode of rationalization reminds us just how ethically blind our highly advanced and rational, civilized society has become. The "twisted road to Auschwitz," to paraphrase Bauman, was—in the last resort—the product of routine bureaucratic procedures: a means-ends calculus and the balancing of budgets, "earnest efforts to find rational solutions to successive 'problems,' as they arose."[18] Today, none of the societal conditions that made Auschwitz and the other Nazi death camps possible has disappeared; on the contrary, they have been refined over time, making the social production of small wars and invisible genocides an inescapable feature of neoliberal orthodoxy.

Defining genocide as a sociological concept, Helen Fein wrote that "social scientists have been reticent to define genocide because of fear of backlash and because, as a phenomenon, genocide is difficult to define categorically, often cloaked in normative and prescriptive agendas."[19] How, Fein asked, do we explain the sociology of what is not observed sociologically?[20] We can, she suggested, relate this conundrum both to the phenomenon of collective denial and to the inadequacy of social theory that glosses over or takes for granted the prevalence of state violence. In an effort to both expand and frame genocide from a sociological perspective and in a manner consistent with the Convention on Genocide's definition, Fein defined *genocide* as "sustained purposeful action by a perpetrator to physically destroy a collectivity directly or indirectly, through interdiction of the biological and social reproduction of group members, sustained regardless of the surrender or lack of threat offered by the victim."[21] In Flint and Detroit, purposeful action, enforced and condoned by the state of Michigan, not only stripped away Black assets and democratic autonomy but poisoned Black residents as well. Austerity policies in Michigan formed the *necessary* condition that resulted in the Flint water crisis and rationalized Detroit's water shutoffs. Both were the result of routine bureaucratic procedures carried out by a self-selecting cadre of political elites determined to balance the budgets of "problemed" cities. The only thing missing was the label, and only Monica Lewis-Patrick was up to the task.

Figure 21. Strategizing at the We the People of Detroit headquarters. We the People of Detroit 2019a.

IMAGINE A DAY WITHOUT WATER

October 12, 2017, marked the third annual Imagine a Day Without Water, an event dedicated to advocacy and awareness of water insecurity in the United States. With the water crisis in Flint still going on, this day provided an opportunity for Detroit and Flint activists to hold a press conference to draw attention to their efforts to ensure safe and affordable water in their communities. The meeting took place in the basement of the Berston Field House on Saginaw Street. "This is a historic building for Black people," reflected Debra Taylor, cofounder of We the People of Detroit. "My dad and my uncle played baseball here back in the forties and the fifties. There is a lot of history [here]. . . . This was the side of the town where Black people could live back then too." They might have been able to live in the neighborhood, but they could swim in the Berston Field House pool only on Wednesdays, as the park managers maintained segregation until the 1940s. Nevertheless, Taylor felt that holding the meeting here was fitting. In attendance were Lyndava Williams, cofounder and program director of the youth organization Raise It Up; Gwendolyn Winston and Stacy Stevens from the Race2Equity Healing Stories Project at the Michigan Roundtable for Diversity and Inclusion; Monica Lewis-Patrick and Debra Taylor; Angela Stamps, program coordinator for Kentakee Athletic and Social Clubs; and Juani Olivares from the Genesee County Hispanic Latino Collaborative—all women of color. Also joining this star-studded group of Black artists, activists, and intellectuals was Ariana Hawk, the mother of Sincere Smith, the boy—two years old at the time and covered with facial rashes—featured on the cover of *Time* Magazine's article "The Poisoning of an American City."[22]

After introductions and a poetry reading, Angie Stamps from Kentakee approached the podium. Kentakee Athletic and Social Clubs provides a bicycle maintenance program and an after-school curriculum for participating youth. "I only have two or three minutes," she regretted, to talk about the Michigan Civil Rights Commission report on the Flint water crisis, "and the report is 138 pages. It is a long read, but it was a tough read because I have been studying history for a number of years, and particularly African American history here in the United States, . . . and after reading this report . . . I felt like it was 1895, 1872, or even 1693 . . . it was the same [racist] principles at work but just in a different form." Ms. Stamps chose those moments in history carefully: 1896 was the year the Supreme Court decided *Plessy v. Ferguson*, establishing the doctrine of "separate but equal" among Blacks and whites in public facilities. In 1862 President Abraham Lincoln signed the Homestead Act, allotting 160 acres of land to "anyone" who could pay $1.25 per acre and cultivate it for five years. European immigrants and land speculators were given millions of acres of land, while Native Americans, Blacks, and non-European immigrants were excluded. What was clear to this student of American history is how little has changed in the racial structure of American democracy over the past four hundred years.

For activists like Angie Stamps, current policies of austerity are nothing but consistent with a long history of genocidal tendencies in this country. Slavery may have been abolished and *Plessy v. Ferguson* overturned, but violent aspects of these previous forms of structural racism live on in its present form—racialized austerity. According to austerity's principles, commonsense accounting practices and the privation imposed by standard decision-making processes further entrench two unequal societies, those with rights to water and access to health care, quality education, housing, and employment, and those without.

For those people gathered in the basement of the Berston Field House, the pages of African American history tell a story of exploitation, premature death, and erasure—genocide—rooted in routine bureaucratic procedures, mundane polices, and means-ends calculations designed to effect financial discipline. Today, as in the past, these activists contend, where you work, live, play, and pray, and whether you're imprisoned or not, is a matter of "what race one belongs to."[23] This framing of environmental justice suggests that we must stretch our analysis to include austerity and other forms of racialized capitalism alongside settler colonialism and genocide. Failing to do so ignores a past, to paraphrase Raphaël Lemkin, aimed at the destruction of essential foundations of the life of African Americans and other people of color—destruction that can end only in their annihilation. Not calling it genocide is perhaps the definitive privilege of white supremacy, as the modern world system of racial capitalism has always depended on slavery, violence, imperialism, and genocide.[24]

Conclusion

USA Today named Detroit's Thanksgiving Parade "Best Holiday Parade in America" in 2022.[1] Earlier the same year, *Time* Magazine selected Detroit in its third annual list of the "World's Greatest Places." The story of Detroit's resilient people, along with a rich heritage of design, innovation, and diversity, ensured that it was part of this prestigious fifty-site worldwide cohort, the website Visit Detroit boasted.[2] Wishing to capitalize on the city's apparent renaissance, local business leaders have once again turned to local taxpayers to subsidize yet another proposal for downtown development, this time with a price tag of $1.5 billion.

The project began in 2013 when the Olympia Development Company, owned by the billionaire Ilitch family,[3] unveiled plans to revive the area between Detroit's midtown and downtown neighborhoods. Their ambitious vision, which included plans for new office space, restaurants, bars, and housing, was named The District Detroit.[4] The entire development was anchored by the Ilitch-owned Little Caesars Arena. To help complete their vision, local leaders handed the billionaire family a huge tax deal in early 2014, just as Detroit slid into the nation's largest-ever municipal bankruptcy. In addition to the tax deal, the city handed the Ilitches land valued between $3 million and $27 million to help with the development of The District Detroit.[5]

In the fall of 2022, the Ilitch family's Olympia Development Company and developer Stephen Ross proposed a new, $1.5 billion development for downtown Detroit. The massive project sought additional public money in the form of $616 million in Transformational Brownfield funds and commercial and residential tax abatements worth $133 million. In addition, public moneys intended for affordable housing and infrastructure, as well as Detroit's public libraries and schools, would be redirected to The District Detroit proposal. The tax revenue loss related to The District Detroit would amount to $226.8 million for Detroit public schools and $5.7 million for libraries.[6] Offering a sobering assessment, the Detroit People's Platform, an organization that fights to "protect, maintain, and empower majority Black Detroit," declared: "When we factor in the interest on bonds, value of public land, and bonus incentives, public investment for these projects will be well over a billion dollars. To put it in perspective, that sum is about Detroit's entire annual general fund." To paraphrase David Harvey, cities like Detroit epitomize the insane side of urbanization "where we are not actually . . . building cities for people to live in. We are building cities for people to invest in."[7]

For years, local advocates like Equitable Detroit Coalition and Detroit People's Platform "have warned that Detroit's celebrated recovery and economic comeback were misguided, concluding that the beneficiary of these economic gains was largely white and wealthier, leaving the majority of Black Detroiters behind"[8] Meantime in Black Detroit the city's water shutoff moratorium was scheduled to end on December 31, 2022. We the People of Detroit predicted that 120,000 Detroit households (approximately 300,000 Detroiters) were in jeopardy of getting their water shut off. They have set up a water hotline to help residents navigate these new policies.

Speaking in Washington, DC, in the spring of 2021, President Joe Biden highlighted the Flint water crisis in an effort to engender support for his administration's "Once in a Generation" infrastructure plan. "Everybody remembers what happened in Flint," the president said, and "there's hundreds of Flints all across America." And, while the latter may unfortunately be true, I argue in this book that not everybody knows or remembers what really happened in Flint—or Detroit, for that matter—and that most of what we now know about the environmental racism that unfolded in these cities is being retold to us by outsiders or other experts of one sort or another. For example, on the ninth anniversary of the Flint water crisis's beginning, Virginia Tech professor Marc Edwards suggested that hyperbolic messaging from the news media, celebrities, and even parents may have contributed to an increase in the number of Flint children who entered special education programs. Some in the community see this article and the study behind it as not only accusatory but insulting: yet another incursion from the from the outside, branded as science, used to demean and harass the majority-Black residents in Flint. Let's not forget that this same expert launched an unsuccessful lawsuit against three of the water activists for publicly disputing his brand of citizen science. Nine years after the state of Michigan intentionally poisoned a majority-Black city, nine years after residents began collecting extensive data and having and recording substantive conversations documenting the consequences of living with lead poisoning, the media continue to defer to the opinions of outsiders who discount the true violence of this modern-day Tuskegee experiment.

These two recent examples underscore the fact that patterns of racialized austerity—the same patterns that justified the poisoning and water shutoffs for thousands—continue to prevail in Michigan. Activists circulated a picture, taken in 2015 at the height of the Flint water crisis and Detroit water shutoffs, showing Mike Duggan, Rick Snyder, and Dan Gilbert sitting together at a table (fig. 22). One activist wrote: "A picture is worth a thousand words. One man poisoned a whole city, one man cut off water to thousands and one man scammed thousands with toxic predatory lending." To which another activist responded: "Pure Michigan means white Michigan. Pure evil." For many the extraordinary power of these three individuals has come to symbolize the financial fascism that has destabilized their city. They represent willful and reckless abandonment of basic social norms for personal gain. In the struggling cities of Flint and Detroit, their agenda was enabled by blaming and demonizing people of color for the economic problems of the entire state. These three white males epitomize the raw power of particular actors, groups, and their social networks to mobilize both racial capitalism and white supremacy in

Figure 22. Mike Duggan, Rick Snyder, and Dan Gilbert.
Courtesy of Claire McClinton via Facebook.

operationalizing the state's austerity-driven reforms. Flint and Detroit, activists claim, were the beta tests. If this sort of financial discipline can occur in labor-strong Michigan, they warn, it can occur anywhere in the United States. Through it all—lead poisoning, the Legionnaire's disease and hepatitis A outbreaks, water shutoffs, foreclosures, and evictions—the cities of Flint and Detroit never missed a bond payment.

This sort of structural violence was made possible through the strategic elimination of democracy in the state. In a strong democracy, political scientist Benjamin Barber writes, "politics is something done by, not to, citizens."[9] But the weak policies that materialized in Michigan put democracy in abeyance in majority-Black cities and allowed state autocrats to impose their will without any political process for accountability. Michigan's Emergency Manager Law effectively set aside voting rights in Black communities and gave the power of local decision-making authority to one man and his exclusive networks, circumventing the state's entire governing process. The rhetoric of racialized austerity provided a convenient narrative to target Flint, Detroit, and other majority-Black cities in Michigan as new frontiers for economic extraction. This was strategic, involving political and legal reforms that usurped the decision-making power of local government, Black-controlled government, and put it in the hands of the courts, corporate elites, and nonprofits—institutions of white supremacy.

This political and racialized assault was countered, in contrast, with unapologetic and deeply committed activist organizing. As horrible as all of this was, a community organizer told me, what was inspiring was "the coalition of people that came together. I'm sure that some of those people would never [have been] in the same room together. It was diverse and divisive. You had the religious African American pastors, white moms, community activists like Nayyirah Shariff and Claire McClinton." A truly multiracial alliance formed not only to counter this form of state violence but also to provide help to fellow citizens in need of water, health care, food, and housing. Activists worked together with scientists to provide data on the risks of their city's water source. They then communicated those risks to other residents and the wider community. Activists' groups collaborated with academics to document the degree to which this anti-democratic regime was configuring emergent forms of environmental racism through the back door.

. . . . .

On September 8, 2018, the Michigan Environmental Justice Coalition hosted the third Environmental Justice Statewide Summit at the McCree Theater. The event brought together activists, environmental practitioners, citizens, and scholars to talk about what it means for all living beings to have clean and affordable access to water, air, and land. This was an important opportunity not only to reflect on the ongoing environmental injustices in Flint and throughout the state but also to change the dominant narrative in an effort to empower those in the room and outside to take control of our future. The formidable preparation by summit organizers provided food and water and an array of speakers and content that was truly engaging. Thank you, Michelle Martinez, for organizing such an important and powerful event.

"It was better than most," a Flint resident told me.

We've had a bunch of those things in the city. A bunch of meetings, a bunch of rallies. Lots of this, lots of that. A lot of running around. It is hard to actually ascertain what is important until after it is over. And a lot of us are exhausted because you go running around from one thing to the next because you just never know when the decisions are going to be made, where the accurate information is, where you are going to find the thing that you need. The summit provided a platform to help cultivate strategies that might be useful for participants working with neighborhood groups, coalitions or on environmental justice campaigns.

One striking observation about this summit was the people in the room. There was clearly a diversity of expertise—citizen, organizer, professional, academic. But the diversity of experiences was also striking as young activists talked with elders, and professionals collaborated with citizens. We all felt that we had something important to contribute and that, together, we had the power to change our communities and the larger environments in which we live, not just for humans but for all living creatures. I, for one, was taken aback by the mix of idealism, expertise, and capacity in the room.

Taking a turn at the microphone, Monica Lewis-Patrick reminded the attendees, "We are used to making waves out of no wave. That's where we come from. I don't care Black, white, Asian, Hispanic, . . . most of us come from blue-collar folks. You know how to make a pot of greens. You have to mix some greens and cornbread and stretch it. But this is where we are— we are in that stretch moment." As Lewis Patrick suggested, this fight for environmental justice is far from over.

.   .   .   .   .

Problems of water access and affordability in many BIPOC communities will only worsen under the growing effects of climate change. As those who hold the reins of the state's power apparatus continue to reap the excesses of sacrificing the lifeblood of mother earth for profit, "contemporary notions of environmental and social justice largely hinge on how we come to think about water in the twenty-first century," as I've written elsewhere.[10] And, while scholars concede that environmental racism persists, they have put limited effort toward understanding how the processes of racialization are a necessary condition for pursuing and justifying environmental degradation everywhere. It is this persistent violence that compels activists to charge genocide against state institutions. For how else does one characterize the purposeful shutting off and poisoning of thousands? April 25, 2023, marked the ninth anniversary of the

Flint Water Crisis, and as I write, the temporary moratorium on water shutoffs in Detroit is about to end. These water crises continue to make headlines as new research reveals more evidence that the Flint water crisis was no accident, in the true sense. Yet, to date, no official for the state of Michigan or the city of Flint has faced a jury or been convicted. On October 31, 2023, Michigan Attorney General ended its quest to prosecute all public officials for their role in the crisis, after the state Supreme Court shot down efforts to charge former Gov. Rick Snyder, underscoring the legal and political protection afforded to whiteness in this country.[11]

I finish with what I feel are three important social problems that this analysis highlights. First, we can no longer continue to blame people of color for structural problems that disproportionately harm their health and well-being. While Donald Trump blazed a trail to the White House on such hateful rhetoric, we must recognize that this narrative, no matter how powerful it may appear to some, is the real fake news. There are many drawn to this impulse of replacing democracy with fascist sociability, many who have too much invested in an economy and cultural war that undervalues both people and the environment. The viciousness of this form of undemocratic governance is evidenced by the many who are ready to lie, cheat, steal, and poison others to exercise and hold onto their newly established form of power. This rise of societal fascism may have begun with the strategic employment of racial capitalism in Black Michigan. However, it has now creeped into institutions of public education, as evident in measures to omit certain subjects from curricula, the protesting of pride events in school districts, and the removal of books from schools and universities throughout the country. We are also witnessing other social groups rendered vulnerable by this same ideology, as evident in policies restricting the rights of women, immigrants, refugees, and transgender people everywhere.

Second, this book highlights the importance of social movements in mounting struggles for environmental and social justice everywhere. Local grassroots movements have provided care in time of need, education, housing to friends and family, health care, and above all else, empathy and love. We must never forget that simple fact. Third, any possibility of realizing environmental justice in places like Flint and Detroit means opposing financial fascism and other forms of racial capitalism everywhere. In other words, fights for basic human rights like food and water require a strong democracy, not a market solution. If this analysis has shown us anything, it is an ominous warning about what happens when public goods are assailed by private interests. There can be no peace without justice, as activists claim, and "so we better stop acting like we don't know what time it is," because the fight is far from over.

Notes

PREFACE

1. Baldassare, Bonner, Lawler, and Thomas 2022.

2. Philp 2017.

3. Ruble, Carah, Ellis, and Childress 2018.

4. These and other quotations from interviews I conducted for this book are transcriptions of recordings I made.

5. Peck and Whiteside 2016, 247.

6. De Sousa Santos 2014.

7. Harris 1993; Lipsitz 2006, 2011; Moreton-Robinson 2015.

8. Mack and Wrase 2017.

9. London, Fencl, Watterson, et al. 2018; Pannu 2012.

10. Allairea, Wub, and Lallb 2018; Balazs, Morello-Frosch, Hubbard, and Ray 2012; Mascarenhas 2012; Stillo, and MacDonald 2017; Waldron 2018; Zimring 2015.

11. Wilson 2012.

12. Beck 2004.

13. Bellant 2002.

14. Tracey, Bast, and Spinder 2023.

15. We the People of Detroit, retrieved July 15, 2023 from https://www.wethepeopleofdetroit.com/.

16. McGonigal 2015.

17. Although I have intended to protect the anonymity of all participants in this ethnography, I have also given participants the option to have their identity revealed. Jan Worth-Nelson, Ted Nelson, Monica Lewis-Patrick, and Debra Taylor wanted the reader to be clear about their contributions to the book.

18. The title of the symposium was "Toxic Water: The Poisoning of Flint, Shut-offs in Detroit, and the Looming Water Crisis in American Cities."

19. "Flint Water Hearings," Michigan Department of Civil Rights, retrieved July 15, 2023, from https://www.michigan.gov/mdcr/commission/flint-water-hearings#:~:text=After%20a%20year%2Dlong%20investigation,and%20all%20races%20were%20victims.

20. "Complaint Request Letter Sent May 10th, 2018," Flint Complaints.com, retrieved July 16, 2023, from http://flintcomplaints.com/.

21. "Letter to STEM from Academics," July 19, 2018, Flint Accountability, retrieved July 16, 2023, from https://flintaccountability.org/.

INTRODUCTION

1. Pellow 2016; Pellow 2018; Ringquist 2005.

2. Eligon 2016.

3. Flint Water Advisory Task Force 2016.

4. Pauli 2019.

5. Clark 2017.

6. K. Davis 2021.

7. Ranganathan 2016.

8. Pulido 2016.

9. Pulido 2017; Pellow 2018; Pellow 2020.

10. Pellow 2020.

11. Dyson 2018, 58.

12. Mayer 2017, 226.

13. Mayer, 2017.

14. United States Department of Justice Civil Rights Division 2015, 74.

15. King 1968.

16. Lipsitz 2006.

17. Omi and Winant 1994.

18. Gans 2017.

19. Gans 2017, 343.

20. Gilmore 2008.

21. Taylor 2014.

22. Hill Collins 2009; Crenshaw 1991; Davis 2016; Hill Collins and Bilge 2017; Lorde 2007.

23. Lorde 2007, 137.

24. The history of this tradition of collective intelligence and activism is explained in the works of activist scholars and writers W. E. B. Du Bois, C. L. R. James, Franz Fanon, Richard Wright, Cedric J. Robinson, James Baldwin, Audre Lorde, and Patricia Hill Collins, to name only a few.

25. Hartman 2017.

26. Baldwin 1963, 7.

27. Gilroy 1993, 76.

28. Zimring 2015.

29. Zimring 2015, 170.

30. Zimring 2015.

31. Zimring2015, 156.

32. Highsmith 2015, 24.

33. Highsmith 2015.

34. Highsmith 2015.

35. Anderson 2015, 2016.

36. Anderson 2016.

37. Highsmith 2015, 170.

38. Feagin and Elias 2013.

39. As Dr. King wrote in *Where Do We Go from Here: Chaos or Community?* (1968), white backlash is nothing new. "White America has been backlashing on the fundamental God-given and human rights of Negro Americans for more than three hundred years. With all of her dazzling achievements and stupendous material strides, America has maintained its strange ambivalence on the question of racial justice" (87).

40. King 1968, 212.

41. King 1968, 213.

42. King 1968, 141, 139.

43. We the People of Detroit Community Research Collective 2016.

44. Mayer 2017, 5.

45. Neu and Therrien 2003.

46. Fullbrook 2016; Lipsitz 2011.

47. Du Bois (1903) 2014.

48. We the People of Detroit Community Research Collective 2016, 1.

49. We the People of Detroit Community Research Collective 2016, 1.

50. King 1963.

51. Davis 2016.

CHAPTER 1. IN THE SERVICE OF WHITE PRIVILEGE

1. Scott 1998.

2. Melosi 2000.

3. Strang 2004.

4. Mascarenhas 2012; Strang 2004.

5. Zimring 2015.

6. Gutman 2008; Wiltse 2007.

7. Zimring 2015.

8. Eagle Bear quoted in Levin 2016.

9. Taibbi 2017; Zimring 2015.

10. Highsmith 2015.

11. Young and Wheeler 1994, 4.

12. Young and Wheeler 1994, 2.

13. Koeppel 2000.

14. Camp, Dresser & McKee, 2003.

15. Melosi 2000.

16. Young and Wheeler 1994, 2.

17. Chafets1990.

18. Moynihan 1965.

19. Melosi 2000, 179.

20. Melosi 2000.

21. Chafets 1990.

22. Anderson 2016.

23. Chafets 1990, 50.

24. Chafets 1990, 50.

25. Loewen 2005.

26. Nelson et al. 2015; Zimring 2015.

27. Zimring 2015.

28. Nelson et al. 2015; Zimring 2015.

29. D38 borders Woodward Avenue to the west, Chene Road to the east, Larned Street to the south, and E. Canfield Street to the north. The figure is a screenshot taken from the Mapping Inequality website at the University of Richmond's Digital Scholarship Lab, retrieved from https://dsl.richmond.edu /panorama/redlining/#loc=11/42.348/-83.293&city=detroit-mi&area=D21&text= downloads.

30. Taken from HOLC agents' property descriptions in Nelson et al. 2015.

31. Lipsitz 2006. By "deed-restricted," I mean that the homeowner's deed restricts the property's sale and purchase to certain groups of people.

32. Lipsitz 2006; Zimring 2015.

33. Highsmith 2015.

34. Highsmith 2015, 34.

35. Highsmith 2015.

36. Camp, Dresser & McKee 2003; We the People of Detroit Community Research Collective 2016.

37. Melosi 2000.

38. Cunningham 1967; Nino 1970; Norgaard 1994.

39. Many of these suburbs are not on city water or sewer service but rather have their own wells and septic tanks.

40. Melosi 2000.

41. Melosi 2000.

42. Bellant 2002. The account in this paragraph relies mainly on Bellant's article.

43. Kornberg 2016.

44. Loewen 2005; Lamb 2005.

45. Lamb 2005.

46. Lamb 2005.

47. Lamb 2005.

48. Sabaugh quoted in Lamb 2005, 328.

49. Chafets 1990.

50. Hubbard quoted in Chafets 1990.

51. King 1992, 121.

52. King 1992, 121.

53. Kornberg 2016.

54. Kornberg 2016.

55. Kornberg 2016; Pondera and Omstedt 2019.

56. Loewen 2005.

57. Young quoted in Chafets 1990.

58. Kornberg 2016.

59. We the People of Detroit Community Research Collective 2016.

60. Bellant 2002.

61. Kornberg 2016; Pondera and Omstedt 2019.

62. Kornberg 2016; Pondera and Omstedt 2019

63. Kornberg 2016; Pondera and Omstedt 2019.

64. Chafets 1990.

65. Kornberg 2016; Sugrue 2005; Camp, Dresser & McKee 2003.

66. Rector 2016.

67. Recchie et al. 2019.

68. Zeemering 2010.

69. Zeemering 2010.

70. We the People of Detroit Community Research Collective 2016.

71. Bellant 2002

72. Bellant 2002

73. Rector 2016.

74. Constitution of Michigan 1963, Article VII, Section 25.

75. Beck 2004.

76. Kurth 2016.

77. We the People of Detroit Community Research Collective 2016; Bellant 2002.

78. Recchie et al. 2019.

79. We the People of Detroit Community Research Collective 2016.

80. Recchie et al. 2019.

81. Recchie et al. 2019.

82. Recchie et al. 2019.

83. Barron 1984.

84. Young and Wheeler 1994, 2.

85. Bukowski 2011a.

86. Bukowski 2011a.

87. Mayer 2017, 14.

88. Mayer 2017.

89. Mayer 2017.

90. Mayer 2017.

91. Bukowski 2011b.

92. City of Detroit 2008, entry for January 8.

93. Bukowski 2011a.

94. Bukowski 2011a.

95. City of Detroit 2008, entry for January 8.

96. Gross 2016b.

97. Claxton and Hurt 1999.

98. In 2009, Detroit city council member Monica Conyers, the wife of US representative John Conyers, pleaded guilty to taking bribes in exchange for approving Synagro's $1.2 billion sludge deal. She was subsequently sentenced to thirty-seven months in prison. Landman 2011.

99. Bukowski and Jeffries 2010; Landman 2011.

100. Bukowski 2011a.

101. Young and Wheeler 1994, 256.

102. Young and Wheeler 1994.

103. Young and Wheeler 1994, 266.

104. Dykema Gossett PLLC 2015.

105. We the People of Detroit Community Research Collective 2016.

CHAPTER 2. FLINT

I acknowledge Ted Nelson, dear friend, writer, and contributor to the *East Village Magazine*, for the phrase "Flint is the anvil of democracy."

1. Office of the Inspector General 2018.

2. A pseudonym.

3. Pulido 2000; Lipsitz 2006.

4. Kennedy 2016.

5. Under the guidelines in Public Act 72, Brown was not eligible to be emergency financial manager, because he had been an employee of the city within the five years prior to his appointment.

6. Longley 2013.

7. Earley 2014; Guyette 2016.

8. Goodin-Smith 2018.

9. Fonger 2015; Ridley 2012.

10. Lurie 2016.

11. Lurie 2016.

12. Ridley 2012.

13. Ponsot 2017; City of Flint 2017.

14. This tax foreclosure model was an effort to stymie the transfer of fees for delinquent taxes and the value of foreclosed properties to speculators.

15. Robertson 2016a.

16. US Department of Housing and Urban Development 2020.

CHAPTER 3. DEFENDING THE KAREGNONDI

1. Flint Water Advisory Task Force 2016.

2. It is often said that there are two seasons in Michigan, winter and construction

3. Fonger 2019.

4. Fonger 2019a.

5. Tucker, Young, Jackson & Tull, Inc. 2013.

6. Tucker, Young, Jackson & Tull, Inc. 2013.

7. Tucker, Young, Jackson & Tull, Inc. 2013.

8. Hammer 2014.

9. Flint Water Advisory Task Force 2016.

10. A pseudonym.

11. Insightful details about the specific communications between agency staff, departments, and other parties are detailed in the following book and articles: Clark 2017; Egan 2016; Hammer 2014.

12. Flint Water Advisory Task Force 2016, 63.

13. Longley 2010; Hall 2016.

14. Hall 2016.

15. US Attorney's Office, Eastern District of Michigan 2009.

16. Hall 2016.

17. Ruble et al. 2019.

18. Casey-Dunn 2016.

19. Tucker, Young, Jackson, & Tull, Inc 2013.

20. Wright neglected to mention that "for demonstration purposes," the ROWE and LAN report did "not include the cost of repayment of debt incurred for its construction" in the costing of water for the KWA water supply alternative (AECOM et al. 2009, iv). "Regardless of the alternative selected," the ROWE report concluded, "the cost of water will increase with either alternative" (iv). Wright also contracted ROWE and Jones & Henry to coauthor an earlier feasibility study on alternatives to provide water service to the County (Rowe Engineering 2006).

21. Guyette 2017.

22. Wright 2016, 10.

23. Hammer 2014, 2.

24. Hammer 2014; Wright 2016.

25. Wright 2016, 14, 29.

26. Wright 2016, 32.

27. Bonilla-Silva 2010, 2.

28. Wright 2016, 15.

29. Anderson 2016.

30. Anderson 2016.

31. Wright 2016, 5. Wright's argument reminds me of President George W. Bush's buildup to the war on Iraq, during which he and his administration insisted that Iraq was responsible for the attacks on the World Trade Center and the Pentagon on September 11, 2001, in spite of evidence to the contrary. Yet the rhetoric fell on an angry and unsympathetic country, happy to dethrone a man of color for their own benefit.

32. We the People of Detroit Community Research Collective 2016.

33. Guyette 2017; Hammer 2014.

34. Food and Water Watch 2020.

35. Wright 2016, 5; Michigan Municipal League 2014.

36. Wright 2016, 5.

37. Gross 2016a; Kaffer 2016.

38. Hall 2016.

39. Wright 2016, 6.

40. Barron 1984.

41. Longley 2011.

42. Hammer 2014.

43. Goodin-Smith 2019a.

44. Moore 2017.

45. Fonger 2019b.

46. Fonger 2019c.

47. Fonger 2019c.

48. Highsmith 2015, 4.
49. Highsmith 2015, 4.
50. Highsmith 2015, 4.

CHAPTER 4. FOUNDATION COLONIALISM

1. Dolan 2016.
2. Mascarenhas 2017.
3. "About," Uptown Reinvestment Corporation, accessed August 13, 2023, https://uptownreinvestment.org/about-us/.
4. Goodin-Smith 2019b.
5. Mascarenhas 2017.
6. Highsmith 2015, 6.
7. Sapotichne et al. 2015.
8. Minghine 2014.
9. Sapotichne et al. 2015.
10. Pruett 2016.
11. City of Flint Planning and Development and Houseal Lavigne Associates 2013a.
12. "Frequently Asked Questions," Genesee County Land Bank, accessed December 21, 2018, http://www.thelandbank.org/faq.asp.
13. Highsmith 2015, 55.
14. Highsmith 2015; Lipsitz 2006; Massey and Denton 2003.
15. Tony Palladeno Jr. died on Monday, January 10, 2022, at just sixty years of age. I learned so much from this community activist. Everybody knew him, in one way or another. I remember walking with him in the Kearsley Park neighborhood, knocking on people's doors, chatting for hours on the porches of friends and family. I can only imagine how much his presence is missed in Flint. He believed in the city and fought for it with a passion I have rarely witnessed before. He and his wife, Leah, have a plaque dedicated to them in his beloved Kearsley Park.
16. Fonger 2017.
17. Moynihan 1965b.
18. Highsmith 2015, 47.
19. Robertson 2016a.
20. They are Baker College, Charles Stewart Mott Community College, ITT Technical Institute, Kettering University, Ross Medical Education Center–Flint, the University of Michigan–Flint, and Michigan State University–Flint.
21. Bartik and Erickcek 2008.
22. Flint Institute of Arts 2020

23. Harney and Moten 2013, 62.
24. Charles Stewart Mott Foundation 2016.
25. Agyeman 2005; Harvey 2016.

CHAPTER 5. EMERGENCY (AS A PARADIGM OF) MANAGEMENT

1. Alexander 2012; Davis 2016.
2. Guyette 2014d.
3. Felton 2014.
4. Guyette 2014b.
5. "Opinion Regarding Eligibility" 2013, 172.
6. Guyette 2014d.
7. Burns 2013.
8. Nixon 1974, 994.
9. Constitution of Michigan 1963, Article IX, Section 10.
10. Michigan Municipal League 2014.
11. Bach 2014.
12. Michigan Municipal League 2014; Oosting 2014.
13. Oosting 2014.
14. Michigan Municipal League 2014.
15. Energy and Policy Institute n.d.
16. Minghine 2014.
17. Stampfler 2013.
18. Stampfler 2013, 204.
19. Stampfler 2013, 204.
20. Mayer 2017.
21. Scorsone 2014; Mayer 2017.
22. Mayer 2017.
23. Scorsone 2014, 10.
24. Scorsone 2014, 10.
25. Scorsone 2014, 18.
26. Scorsone 2013, 1.
27. Scorsone 2013, 1.
28. Guyette 2014d.
29. Guyette 2014d.
30. Guyette 2014d.
31. Bukowski 2013; Guyette 2014d.
32. Bukowski 2013.
33. Bukowski 2013.
34. Guyette 2014d.

35. Ellman and Merrett 2011.

36. Ellman and Merrett 2011, 368 (emphasis added).

37. O'Connor 1973; Mayer 2017.

38. Mayer 2017, 152.

39. Schimmel 2005.

40. Abowd 2012.

41. Ellman and Merrett 2011, 372.

42. Ellman and Merrett 2011, 372.

43. Constitution of Michigan 1963, Article IX, Section 24.

44. Executory Contracts and Unexpired Leases, 11 U.S.C. § 365.

45. Ellman and Merrett 2011.

46. "Opinion Regarding Eligibility" 2013.

47. "Opinion Regarding Eligibility" 2013, 116. Further citation to this opinion is noted by page in the text.

48. Ellman and Merrett 2011.

49. Guyette 2014b.

50. Turbeville 2013.

51. Turbeville 2013.

52. Guyette 2014b.

53. Police officers and firefighters injured on the job receive as much as $400 (Guyette 2014c).

54. Guyette 2014a.

55. Guyette 2014b.

56. Guyette 2014a.

57. Turbeville 2013, 4.

58. Stampfler 2013; Turbeville 2013.

59. Ernsthausen and Elliott 2019.

60. Guyette 2014a.

61. Tabbi 2013.

62. Guyette 2014a; Rector 2016.

63. Rector 2016.

64. Rector 2016.

65. Gottesdiener 2013.

66. Gruenstein Bocian, Li, and Ernst 2010.

67. Gruenstein Bocian, Li, and Ernst 2010, 8.

68. Tabbi 2013; Guyette 2014c.

69. Guyette 2014d.

70. Perlovsky and DeMarco 2018.

71. Perlovsky and DeMarco 2018.

72. Perlovsky and DeMarco 2018.

73. Molotch 1976.

74. Tabbi 2013.

75. Tabbi 2013.
76. Baker 2011.
77. Baker 2011.
78. Tabbi 2013.

CHAPTER 6. ENVIRONMENTS OF INJUSTICE

1. Goodnough 2016.
2. Hill Collins 2000.
3. Roberts 1997.
4. Roberts 1997.
5. Pellow 2018, 17.
6. Cook 2007.
7. Scheper-Hughes 1996, 890.
8. Abby slipped into a Receivership Transition Advisory Board (RTAB) meeting. As of the end of April 2015, the city of Flint moved from being under the control of emergency manager Gerry Ambrose to being under the RTAB, whose four members were appointed by the outgoing emergency manager. The board's objective was to administer the measures of the emergency manager after his term ended.
9. Vase 2016.
10. Vase 2016.
11. We made several attempts to contact realtors in Flint, but none returned our emails or phone calls.
12. Goodman 2018.
13. Robertson 2016a, 2016b.
14. Vase 2016.
15. Chen et al. 2007.
16. Goodnough 2016.
17. Worth-Nelson and Ford 2018.
18. Worth-Nelson and Ford 2018.
19. Acosta 2018.
20. Bartolomé 1994.
21. Strauss 2016.
22. Highsmith 2015.
23. Wilkinson 2016.
24. Brown 2016.
25. Some 30,000 school-age children currently reside in Flint.
26. "Opinion" 2017.
27. Roberts 1997.

CHAPTER 7. THE WATER IS OFF

1. Azoulay 2019.
2. International Committee of the Red Cross 1977.
3. International Criminal Court 1998.
4. Gross 2017.
5. Office of the UN High Commissioner for Human Rights 2014a.
6. Office of the UN High Commissioner for Human Rights 2014b.
7. Office of the UN High Commissioner for Human Rights 2014b.
8. Johnson quoted in Gross 2017.
9. Zervos quoted in Gross 2017.
10. Gross 2017.
11. Gilmore 2007.
12. Massey and Denton 2003; Gilmore 2007.
13. United Nations General Assembly 1948.
14. Desmond 2017.
15. Desmond 2017.

CHAPTER 8. SHUT OFF AND SHUT OUT

1. Thompson 2015.
2. Agyeman and Zavestoski 2020.
3. Kurth 2016.
4. Figures in this and the following two sentences come from Clark 2014.
5. Although Mike Illich died in 2017, the Illich family and its company, Illich Holdings, are a major business interest and influence in Detroit.
6. Harrison 2019, 2020.
7. Court order quoted in Halcom 2013.
8. Gaist and White 2013.
9. Gaist and White 2013.
10. Helms and Guillen 2014.
11. Heat and Warmth Fund 2018.
12. Associated Press 2013.
13. Daniel 2013.
14. Mascarenhas 2001.
15. Daniel 2013.
16. Mascarenhas 2001.
17. Moratorium NOW! Coalition. 2014.
18. Kroll 2014.
19. Smith 2017.

20. Smith 2017.

21. Details and quotations in this and the following paragraph come from Neavling 2019.

22. Perkins 2017.

23. The suit charges that Quicken "miscalculated income, ignored red flags on loan applications, and created a value-appeals process, which permitted employees to request specific inflated values from appraisers in order to make a loan eligible for FHA insurance." Plaintiff's brief cited in Perkins 2017.

24. Siegel Bernard 2015.

25. Siegel Bernard 2015.

26. Perkins 2017.

27. Perkins 2017.

28. Hudson 2011.

29. In a separate 2016 case, a National Labor Relations Board judge found Quicken guilty of violating labor law by discouraging union organization, among other activities. Halcom 2016; Perkins 2017.

30. Neavling 2015.

31. Perkins 2017.

32. Perkins 2017.

33. MacDonald and Kurth 2015.

34. MacDonald and Kurth 2015.

35. US Department of the Treasury n.d.

36. Detroit Blight Removal Task Force n.d.

37. Data Driven Detroit 2014.

38. Data Driven Detroit 2014.

39. US Department of the Treasury n.d.

40. Petty 2021; Wylie-Kellermann 2020.

41. City of Detroit n.d.

42. Wylie-Kellermann 2020.

43. Petty 2021; Wylie-Kellermann 2020.

44. Harwell 2019.

45. Wylie-Kellermann 2020. Corporations offered businesses multiple incentives to join Project Green Light. For example, Comcast offered 50% off installation. Comcast also has a multisite discount for businesses that have more than one store they would like to bring onto the project. This can be combined with the 50%-off installation deal. See City of Detroit 2020.

46. Anderson 2016.

47. Petty 2021.

48. Rocket Companies 2020.

49. National Advisory Commission on Civil Disorders 1968, 2.

50. National Advisory Commission on Civil Disorders 1968, 1.

51. Bukowski 2016.

52. Bukowski 2016.

53. Eclectablog 2016.

54. See also Guyette 2014c.

55. Higgins 2010. Search on "Detroit Public Schools" in the blog *The Broad Report*, http://thebroadreport.blogspot.com/.

56. Waldman 2019.

57. Associated Press 2009.

58. Aguirre and Martinez 2014.

59. Henry, Reese, and Torres 2013.

60. Baptiste 2014.

61. Waldman 2019.

62. Whitmire 2016.

63. D. Harris 2016.

64. Guyette 2014c.

65. Slater 2014.

CHAPTER 9. WE CHARGE GENOCIDE

1. African American women make up 1.2% of full professors in the United States, though African Americans represent 18% of the population.

2. Churchill 1997.

3. Cruse 1962.

4. Churchill 1997.

5. Patterson et al. 1951., xi.

6. In fact, Samantha Power, US ambassador to the United Nations from 2013 to 2017, and the author of the Pulitzer Prize–winning book, *"A Problem from Hell": America and the Age of Genocide*, writes that the United States "had never in its history intervened to stop genocide"—at home or abroad—"and had in fact rarely even made a point of condemning it as it occurred" ([2002] 2013, xv).

7. United Nations General Assembly 1948, 1. I am struck by the fact that the Trump administration's policy to separate children from their parents seeking asylum in the United States has yet to be referred to as genocide, as its practice is clearly genocidal according to the Convention.

8. United Nations General Assembly 1948.

9. Lemkin 1944, 79.

10. Lemkin 1944, 83, 87, 89.

11. Lemkin 1944, 89.

12. Churchill 1997, 410.

13. Churchill 1997, 410; Costa Vargas 2008.

14. Churchill 1997., 413.

To expand this narrow construct of genocide, Ward Churchill delineated a framework with which to better understand and demarcate the multiple formulations of the genocidal condition. Churchill (1997) suggests that while it may or may not involve killing, per se, genocide is a denial of the right to existence of entire human groups, as homicide is the denial of an individual's right to live. It is understood, Churchill writes, that, historically, genocide has taken three primary forms—physical, biological, and cultural—which usually, but not always, function in combination with one another as a multifaceted phenomenon. Physical genocide, according to Churchill, is defined as killing members of a targeted group(s) by either direct or indirect means, or by some combination of both. "Indirect means are understood to include, but are not restricted to, the imposition of slave labor conditions, . . . denial of fundamental medical attention to group members, and forms of systematic economic deprivation leading to starvation and other deteriorations in the physical well-being of group members" (1997, 432). The second form of genocide, biological, is the prevention of births within the target group(s), directly, indirectly, or both. Direct means are understood to occur with the imposition on group members of involuntary sterilization or abortion. "Indirect means include the imposition of degrading physical and/or psychological conditions leading to marked declines in birthrates, heightened rates of infant mortality, and the like" (433) The third form of genocide, cultural, includes "the destruction of the specific character of the targeted group(s) through destruction or expropriation of its means of economic perpetuation; prohibition or curtailment of its language; suppression of its religious, social, or political practices . . .; forced dislocation, expulsion or dispersal of its members; forced transfer or removal of its children, or any other means" (433).

In an effort to define culpability for the crime of genocide, Churchill (1997) used the analogy of murder and the varying degrees by which murder is understood. Genocide in the first degree refers to cases where evidence of premeditation to commit genocide is present. Genocide in the second degree refers to cases where evidence of premeditation is absent but where perpetrators acted with reckless disregard for the probability that genocide would result from their actions. Genocide in the third degree refers to instances in which genocide derives, however intentionally, from other violations of international law engaged in by the perpetrator(s) (434). This schema puts to rest the idea that there is one absolute and singular definition of genocide that we would all recognize and agree upon. Like the racism on which it is based, genocide has multiple formulations and motivations.

15. Churchill 1997.

16. Bauman 1989, 476.

17. Bauman 1989, 481. This is not to suggest that modern bureaucracy must result in the Holocaust phenomenon; genocide, I argue, need not be a deterministic spectacle; it is a relational outcome.

18. Bauman 1989, 484.

19. Fein 1993.

20. Fein 1993.

21. Fein 1993, 80.

22. Sanburn 2016.

23. Michigan Civil Rights Commission 2017.

24. Fanon 1963, 5. See also Robinson 1983.

CONCLUSION

1. Visit Detroit 2022b.

2. Visit Detroit 2022a.

3. The Ilitch companies include Little Caesars Pizza, Olympia Development, Olympia Entertainment, MotorCity Casino Hotel, numerous real estate holdings, the Detroit Tigers, and the Detroit Red Wings.

4. See The District Detroit, accessed September 5, 2023, https://www .districtdetroit.com/.

5. Perkins 2018.

6. Perkins 2018.

7. Harvey 2016.

8. Equitable Detroit Coalition and Detroit People's Platform 2021.

9. Barber 1984, 133.

10. Mascarenhas 2012.

11. House 2023.

References

Abowd, P. 2012. "Michigan's Hostile Takeover." *Mother Jones,* February 15. https://www.motherjones.com/politics/2012/02/michigan-emergency-manager-pontiac-detroit/.

Acosta, Roberto. 2018. "Flint News: Building Closures Possible If Flint Schools Fail to Meet Partnership Goals." *Michigan Live,* July 24. https://www.mlive.com/news/flint/index.ssf/2018/07/building_closures_possible_if.html.

AECOM; Gannett Fleming, Inc.; Jones and Henry Engineers, Ltd.; Lockwood, Andrews, and Newnam, Inc.; O'Malia Consulting, ROWE Professional Services Company, and Wade Trim, Inc. 2009. *Preliminary Engineering Report: Lake Huron Water Supply, Karegnondi Water Authority.* September. Archived at Floride-Free Flint. Accessed September 23, 2023. https://fluoridefreeflint.files.wordpress.com/2016/02/karegnondi-water-2009-study.pdf.

Aguirre, Adalberto, Jr., and Rubén O. Martinez. 2014. "The Foreclosure Crisis, the American Dream, and Minority Households in the United States: A Descriptive Profile." *Social Justice* 40(3): 6–15.

Agyeman, Julian. 2005. *Sustainable Communities and the Challenge of Environmental Justice.* New York: New York University Press.

Agyeman, Julian, and Stephen Zavestoski. 2020. "From Dumping to Displacement: New Frontiers for Just Sustainabilities." In *Lessons in Environmental Justice: From Civil Rights to Black Lives Matter and Idle No More,* edited by Michael Mascarenhas, 288–305. Thousand Oaks, CA: Sage.

Alexander, Michelle. 2012. *The New Jim Crow: Mass Incarceration in the Age of Colorblindness*. Revised edition. New York: The New Press.

Allairea, Maura, Haowei Wub, and Upmanu Lallb. 2018. "National Trends in Drinking Water Quality Violations." *PNAS* 115(9):2078–2083.

Anderson, Carol. 2016. *White Rage: The Unspoken Truth of Our Racial Divide*. New York: Bloomsbury.

Associated Press. 2009. "Obama: AIG Can't Justify 'Outrage' of Bonuses." March 16. Archived at Cengage Learning. Accessed April 21, 2021, https://college.cengage.com/polisci/resources/students/hmnewsnow/ps_031609_aig_bonuses.html.

Associated Press. 2013. "Hantz Farms Inks Purchase Deal with Orr, State to Clear 1,500 Detroit Lots for Tree Farms." *Crain's Detroit Business,* October 18. https://www.crainsdetroit.com/article/20131018/news01/131019814/hantz-farms-inks-purchase-deal-with-orr-state-to-clear-1500.

Azoulay, Audrey. 2019. "Message from Ms Audrey Azoulay, Director-General of UNESCO, on the Occasion of World Water Day, 22 March 2019." UNESCO, March 22. https://unesdoc.unesco.org/ark:/48223/pf0000367034.

Bach, M. 2014. "See How Much Revenue Sharing Dollars the State Has Diverted from Your Community." *SaveMICity,* April 11. http://www.savemicity.org/see-how-much-revenue-sharing-dollars-the-state-has-diverted-from-your-community/.

Baker, Dean. 2011. *The Origins and Severity of the Public Pension Crisis*. Washington, DC: Center for Economic and Policy Research.

Balazs, Carolina L., Rachel Morello-Frosch, Alan E. Hubbard, and Isha Ray. 2012. "Environmental Justice Implications of Arsenic Contamination in California's San Joaquin Valley: A Cross-Sectional, Cluster Design Examining Exposure and Compliance in Community Drinking Water Systems." *Environmental Health* 11(84):1–12. Retrieved from https://ehjournal.biomedcentral.com/articles/10.1186/1476-069X-11-84.

Baldassare, Mark, Dean Bonner, Rachel Lawler, and Deja Thomas. 2022. *PPIC Statewide Survey: Californians and the Environment*. Public Policy Institute of California, San Francisco. Retrieved from https://www.ppic.org/publication/ppic-statewide-survey-californians-and-the-environment-july-2022/.

Baldwin, James. 1963. *The Fire Next TIme*. New York: Vintage Books.

Baptiste, Nathalie. 2014. "Staggering Loss of Black Wealth Due to Subprime Scandal Continues Unabated." *American Prospect,* October 13. https://prospect.org/justice/staggering-loss-black-wealth-due-subprime-scandal-continues-unabated/.

Barber, Benjamin R. 1984. *Strong Democracy*. Berkeley: University of California Press.

Barron, James. 1984. "Judge Is Critical of Detroit Mayor: Court Chief Drops Out of Case Involving Young After His Remarks Are Published." *New York Times*, September 2. https://www.nytimes.com/1984/09/02/us/judge-is-critical-of-detroit-mayor.html.

Bartik, Timothy J., and George Erickcek. 2008. *The Local Economic Impact of "Eds & Meds": How Policies to Expand Universities and Hospitals Affect Metropolitan Economies*. Washington, DC: Metropolitan Policy Program, Brookings Institution.

Bartolomé, Lilia 1994. "Beyond the Methods Fetish: Toward a Humanizing Pedagogy." *Harvard Educational Review* 64:173–194.

Bauman, Zygmunt. 1989. *Modernity and the Holocaust*. Ithaca, NY: Cornell University Press.

Beck, J. 2004. "Reclaiming our Resources: Imperialism and Environmental Justice." *Race, Poverty, and the Environment* 11(1):38–40.

Bellant, R. 2002. "Water Wars." *Detroit Metro Times*, November 12. https://www.metrotimes.com/detroit/water-wars/Content?oid=2174925.

Bonilla-Silva, Eduardo. *Racism without Racists: Color-Blind Racism and Racial Inequality in Contemporary America*. 3rd Edition. Lanham, MD: Rowman & Littlefield, 2010.

Brown, Emma. 2016. "Lawsuit Alleges Flint Schools Are Failing to Provide Services to Lead-Poisoned Children." *Washington Post*, October 18th. https://www.washingtonpost.com/news/education/wp/2016/10/18/lawsuit-alleges-flint-schools-are-failing-to-serve-lead-poisoned-children/?utm_term=.b9ae552d739a.

Bukowski, Diane. 2011a. "History of the Feikens Enterprise." *Voice of Detroit*, January 6. http://voiceofdetroit.net/2011/01/06/history-of-the-feikens-enterprise/.

Bukowski, Diane. 2011b. "Fight!! To Stop Takeover of Detroit's Water." *Voice of Detroit*,January26.http://voiceofdetroit.net/2011/01/26/stop-takeover-of-detroits-water/.

Bukowski, Diane. 2013. "Detroiters March in Cleveland, Tell Jones Day and Banks 'Get Out.'" *Voice of Detroit*, March 27. https://voiceofdetroit.net/2013/03/27/detroiters-march-in-cleveland-tell-jones-day-and-banks-get-out/.

Bukowski, Diane. 2016. "State War on Detroit Public Schools Continues: Selling Black Children to the Highest Bidder." *Voice of Detroit*, April 24. https://voiceofdetroit.net/2016/04/24/state-war-on-detroit-public-schools-continues-selling-black-children-to-the-highest-bidder/.

Bukowski, Diane, and Z. Jeffries. 2010. "Crooks Testify: Carlyle/Synagro—Murderers, Money Launderers, Drug Traffickers, and Gangsters." *Michigan Citizen*, February 7. Archived at Texas Disposal Policy. Accessed July 23, 2023, https://www.texasdisposalpolicy.com/wp-content/uploads/2018/05

/2-7-10%20Carlyle%20Group%20subsidiary%20in%20Michigan%20
bribery%20trial.pdf.

Bullard, Robert D., Paul Mohai, Robin Saha, and Beverly Wright. 2007. *Toxic Wastes and Race at Twenty, 1987–2007: Grassroots Struggles to Dismantle Environmental Racism in the United States.* Cleveland, OH: United Church of Christ.

Burns, G. 2013. "Gov. Rick Snyder and Detroit EFM Kevyn Orr Met over a U-M Snowball Fight." *Michigan Live,* March 14. https://www.mlive.com/news /detroit/2013/03/gov_rick_snyder_and_detroit_ef.html.

Camp, Dresser & McKee. 2003. "Wastewater Master Plan: Executive Summary, Prepared for Detroit Water and Sewage Department." Boston.

Casey-Dunn, Dan. 2016. "Flint Water Switch Was Not about Cost Savings." *Michigan Policy Wonk* (blog). Institute of Public Policy and Social Research, Michigan State University, East Lansing, June 6. https://ippsr.msu.edu /public-policy/michigan-wonk-blog/flint-water-switch-was-not-about-cost- savings. 2016.

Chafets, Ze'ev. 1990. "The Tragedy of Detroit." *New York Times,* July 29. Retrievedfromhttps://www.nytimes.com/1990/07/29/magazine/the-tragedy-of- detroit.html.

Charles Stewart Mott Foundation. 2016. *2016 Annual Report.* Davison, MI: Riegle Press.

Chen, Aimin, Bo Cai, Kim N. Dietrich, Jerilynn Radcliffe, and Walter J. Rogan. 2007. "Lead Exposure, IQ, and Behavior in Urban 5- to 7-Year-Olds: Does Lead Affect Behavior Only by Lowering IQ?" *Pediatrics* 119(3):e650–e658.

Churchill, Ward. 1997. *A Little Matter of Genocide: Holocaust and Denial in the Americas, 1492 to Present.* San Francisco: City Lights Books.

City of Detroit. 2008. "Journal of the City Council." https://detroitmi.gov/Portals /0/docs/City%20Clerk/2008%20Council.pdf.

City of Detroit. 2020. "Crime Intelligence Unit: Project Green Light Detroit Presentation." August 6. Accessed September 24, 2023, https://detroitmi .gov/sites/detroitmi.localhost/files/2020-08/Facial%20Recog%20and%20 Project%20Green%20Light.pdf.

City of Detroit. n.d. "Project Green Light Map." Accessed April 8, 2021. https:// detroitmi.gov/webapp/project-green-light-map.

City of Flint. 2017. "Statement from Mayor Weaver on Impending Tax Lien Notices Issued in Flint.". <Press release? Date?>.

City of Flint Planning and Development and Houseal Lavigne Associates. 2013a. "Imagine Flint Master Plan: Here's What's Possible." Imagine Flint. Accessed August 13, 2023, https://www.imagineflint.com/.

City of Flint Planning and Development and Houseal Lavigne Associates. 2013b. "Placetype" map. Imagine Flint. Accessed September 23, 2023, https://www.imagineflint.com/maps/a89b61af36134b0d801fd81313f-2b8eb/explore?location=43.025033%2C-83.698659%2C13.00.

Clark, Anna. 2014. "Going without Water in Detroit." *New York Times,* July 3. https://www.nytimes.com/2014/07/04/opinion/going-without-water-in-detroit.html.

Clark, Anna. 2017. *The Poisoned City: Flint's Water and the American Urban Tragedy.* New York: Metropolitan Books.

Claxton, M., and C. Hurt. 1999. "Wasted Dollars, Broken Buildings: Bad Management, Cronyism, Waste School Repair Money." *Detroit News and Free Press,* October 3, 1A–10A.

Constitution of Michigan. 1963. Michigan Legislature. https://www.legislature.mi.gov/(S(1ozhbvqinhtmfpk02pab4v0h))/mileg.aspx?page=getObject&objectName=mcl-Constitution.

Cook, Katsi. 2007. "Environmental Justice: Women Is the First Environment." In *Reproductive Justice Briefing Book: A Primer on Reporductive Justice & Social Change,* edited by Loretta Ross, 62–63. Pro-choice Public Education Project (PEP), SisterSong Women of Color Reproductive Justice Collective. https://www.protectchoice.org/downloads/Reproductive%20Justice%20Briefing%20Book.pdf.

Cooper, Jason. 2014. "Grand Blanc Company Wins Bid for Part of KWA Pipeline Construction." 1470 WFNT, Flint's News Talk, June 12. https://wfnt.com/grand-blanc-company-wins-bid-for-part-of-kwa-pipeline-construction/.

Costa Vargas, João H. 2008. *Never Meant to Survive: Genocide and Utopias in Black Diaspora Communities.* Lantham, MD: Rowman & Littlefield.

Crenshaw, Kimberle Williams. 1991. "Mapping the Margins: Intersectionality, Identity Politics, and Violence against Women of Color." *Stanford Law Review* 43(6):1241–1299.

Cruse, Harold. 1962. "Revolutionary Nationalism and the Afro-American." *Studies on the Left* 2(3).

Cunningham, Roger E. 1967. "Public Control of Land Subdivision in Michigan: Description and Critique." *Michigan Law Review* 66(1, November): 3–80.

Daniel, Pete. 2013. *Dispossession: Discrimination against African American Farmers in the Age of Civil Rights.* Chapel Hill: University of North Carolina Press.

Data Driven Detroit. 2014. "Detroit Blight Removal Task Force Releases Blight Plan and Recommendations Today." Data Driven Detroit, May 27. https://datadrivendetroit.org/blog/2014/05/27/detroit-blight-removal-task-force-releases-report/.

Davis, Angela Y. 2016. *Freedom Is a Constant Struggle: Ferguson, Palestine, and the Foundations of a Movement.* Chicago: Haymarket Books.

Davis, Katrinell M. 2021. *Tainted Tap: Flint's Journey From Crisis to Recovery*. Chapel Hill: University of North Carolina Press.

De Sousa Santos, Boaventura. 2014. *Epistemologies f the South. Justice against Epistemicide*. Boulder, CO: Paradigm.

Desmond, Matthew. 2017. *Evicted: Poverty and Profit in the American City*. New York: Broadway Books.

Detroit Blight Removal Task Force. n.d. "Our Mission." Accessed December 17, 2020. http://www.timetoendblight.com/.

Dolan, Matthew. 2016. "Foundations Pledge Nearly $125M to Flint Recovery." *Detroit Free Press*, May 11. https://www.freep.com/story/news/local/michigan/flint-water-crisis/2016/05/11/foundations-pledge-nearly-125m-to-flint-recovery/84180758/.

Du Bois, W. E. B. 1999 [1903]. *The Souls of Black Folk: Authoritative Text, Contexts, Criticism*. Edited by Henry Louis Gates Jr. and Terri Hume Oliver. New York: W. W. Norton.

Dykema Gossett PLLC. 2015. Executive Summary: City of Detroit, Detroit Water and Sewerage Department Sewage Disposal System Revenue Bonds, Series 2015. Lansing, MI.

Dyson, Michael Eric. 2018. *What Truth Sounds Like. RFK, James Baldwin, and Our Unfinished Conversation about Race in America*. New York: St. Matin's Press.

Earley, Darnell. 2014. Letter to Ms. Sue McCormick (DWSD), Re: DWSD Water Rates, March 7. Flint, MI: City of Flint.

Eclectablog. 2016. "Detroit Schools Get FIFTH Emergency Manager, Another Overseer with ZERO Background in Education." March 2. https://www.eclectablog.com/2016/03/detroit-schools-get-fifth-emergency-manager-another-overseer-with-zero-background-in-education.html.

Egan, P. 2016. "#x2018;Sweetheart' Bond Deal Aided Flint Water Split from Detroit. *Detroit Free Press*, May 11. https://www.freep.com/story/news/local/michigan/flint-water-crisis/2016/05/11/did-state-give-flint-break-its-water/84238120/.

Eligon, John. 2016. "A Question of Environmental Racism in Flint." *New York Times*, January 21. https://www.nytimes.com/2016/01/22/us/a-question-of-environmental-racism-in-flint.html.

Ellman, J., and D. Merrett. 2011. "Pensions and Chapter 9: Can Municipalities Use Bankruptcy to Solve Their Pension Woes?" *Emory Bankruptcy Developments Journal* 27:365–413.

Energy and Policy Institute. n.d. "Mackinac Center for Public Policy." Accessed August 19, 2023, https://www.energyandpolicy.org/mackinac-center-for-public-policy/.

Equitable Detroit Coalition and Detroit People's Platform. 2021. "Majority Black Detroit Left Behind as Economic Recovery Benefits White and

Wealthy." *Detroit Metro Times,* May 25. https://www.metrotimes.com/news
/majority-black-detroit-left-behind-as-economic-recovery-benefits-white-
and-wealthy-27217522.

Ernsthausen, J., and J. Elliott. 2019. "How a Tax Break to Help the Poor Went
to NBA Owner Dan Gilbert." ProPublica, October 24. https://www
.propublica.org/article/how-a-tax-break-to-help-the-poor-went-to-nba-owner-dan-
gilbert.

Fanon, Frantz. 1963. *The Wretched of the Earth.* New York: Grove Press.

Feagin, Joe, and Sean Elias. 2013. "Rethinking Racial Formation Theory: A
Systemic Racism Critique." *Ethnic and Racial Studies* 36(6):931–960.

Fein, Helen. 1993. *Genocide: A Sociological Perspective.* London: Sage.

Felton, Ryan. 2014. "Bankruptcy Judge OKs Detroit's Plan to Exit Ch. 9
Bankruptcy." *Detroit Metro Times,* November 7. https://www.metrotimes
.com/news-hits/archives/2014/11/07/bankruptcy-judge-to-decide-detroits-
historic-case-today.

Flint Institute of Arts. 2020. "About the FIA." Flint Institute of Arts Accessed
October 8. https://flintarts.org/about/about-the-fia.

Flint Water Advisory Task Force. 2016. *Flint Water Advisory Task Force Final
Report.* Commissioned by the Office of Governor Rick Snyder, State of
Michigan. Lansing, MI.

Fonger, Ron. 2013. "Low Bid Is $24.6 million on Genesee County–Lake Huron
Water Pipeline Intake." *Michigan Live,* updated February 28. https://www
.mlive.com/news/flint/2013/02/low_bid_on_karegnondi_water_pi.html.

Fonger, Ron. 2015. "Judge Orders Flint to Cut Water Rates 35 Percent in
Sweeping Injunction." *Michigan Live,* August 7. Flint. https://www.mlive
.com/news/flint/2015/08/flint_ordered_to_cut_water_rat.html.

Fonger, Ron. 2017. "Activist Says More Recordings on the Way of Official Who
Used Racial Slur." *Michigan Live,* June 5, Flint News. https://www.mlive
.com/news/flint/index.ssf/2017/06/activist_says_more_recordings.html.

Fonger, Ron. 2019a. "Former Genesee County Drain Commissioner: We Can't
Afford a New Water Pipeline." *Michigan Live,* January 21. https://www
.mlive.com/news/flint/2010/04/former_genesee_county_drain_co.html.

Fonger, R. 2019b. "Seven Months after New GLWA Water Contract, Flint Still
Has No Seat on Board." *Michigan Live,* January 30. https://www.mlive.com
/news/flint/2018/07/seven_months_after_new_glwa_wa.html. January
30th, 2019.

Fonger, R. 2019c. State Officials, EPA Back Flint Mayor's Plan to Stay on
Detroit Water." *Michigan Live,* January 19. Retrieved from https://www
.mlive.com/news/flint/2017/04/flint_state_officials.html.

Food and Water Watch. 2021. "Stopping the Privatization of a Public Right."
March 2. https://www.foodandwaterwatch.org/2021/03/02/stopping-
privatization/.

Fullbrook, Edward. 2016. *Narrative Fixation in Economics*. London: College Publications.

Gaist, Thomas, and Jerry White. 2013. "A Who's Who of the Conspirators behind the Detroit Bankruptcy: Part Two." World Socialist Web Site, November 19. https://www.wsws.org/en/articles/2013/11/19/detr-n19.html?fbclid=IwAR03aAxn47l8aeadLHwCUFTudsnly8lMIbVtPlmGxwr72yKlLvSSJA1nmeM.

Gans, Herbert J. 2017. "Racialization and Racialization Research." *Ethnic and Racial Studies* 40(3):341–352.

Gilmore, Ruth Wilson. 2007. *Golden Gulag: Prisons, Surplus, Crisis, and Opposition in Globalizing California*. Berkeley: University of California Press.

Gilmore, Ruth Wilson. 2008. "Forgotten Places and the Seeds of Grassroots Planning." In *Engaging Contradictions. Theory, Politics, and Methods of Activist Scholarship*, edited by Charles R. Hale, 31–61. Berkeley: University of California Press.

Gilroy, Paul. 1993. *The Black Atlantic: Modernity and Double Consciousness*. London: Verso.

Goodin-Smith, Oona. 2018. "Flint's History of Emergency Management aAnd How It Got to Financial Freedom." *Michigan Live*, January 16. https://www.mlive.com/news/flint/2018/01/city_of_the_state_flints_histo.html.

Goodin-Smith, Oona. 2019a. "Flint Mayor Karen Weaver Survives Recall Vote with Landslide Victory." *Michigan Live*, January 19. https://www.mlive.com/news/flint/2017/11/flint_mayor_karen_weaver_wins.html.

Goodman, Diane M. 2018. "Flint, Michigan: We Haven't Forgotten You." Elite Learning, by Colibri Healthcare. August 8. https://www.elitelearning.com/resource-center/nursing/flint-michigan-we-havent-forgotten-you/.

Goodin-Smith, Oona. 2019b. "See How $33.4M in Flint Water Crisis Grants, Donations Have Been Spent." *Michigan Live*, May 20. https://www.mlive.com/news/flint/2017/09/see_how_334m_in_flint_water_cr.html.

Goodnough, Abby. 2016. "Flint Weighs Scope of Harm to Children Caused by Lead in Water." *New York Times*, January 30. https://www.nytimes.com/2016/01/30/us/flint-weighs-scope-of-harm-to-children-caused-by-lead-in-water.html.

Gottesdiener, Laura. 2013. "Detroit's Debt Crisis: Everything Must Go; The City Just Suspended Its Payments to Wall Street, but Is This the Beginning of a Resurrection for the City—or an Organ Sale?" *Rolling Stone*, June 20.

Gregerson, John. 2014. "Pipeline Project Takes Crews on a 67-Mile Trek." *Engineering News Record Midwest*, September 22. https://www.enr.com/articles/11094-pipeline-project-takes-crews-on-a-67-mile-trek.

Gross, Allie. 2016a. "Docs Reveal Flint's EM Agreed to Buy $1M Worth of Extra Water from the KWA—This Was Never about Saving Money." *Detroit*

Metro Times, February 27. https://www.metrotimes.com/news-hits/archives/2016/02/27/em-kurtz-agreed-to-spend-over-1m-per-year-more-than-flint-needed-on-water-from-the-kwa-pipeline.

Gross, Allie. 2016b. "Duggan's Legacy Blighted by Questionable Rehab Projects." *Detroit Metro Times,* July 20. https://www.metrotimes.com/news/celebrate-duggans-demolitions-but-lets-not-forget-the-90s-2456040.

Gross, Allie. 2017. "Experts See Public Health Crisis in Detroit Water Shutoffs." *Detroit Free Press,* July 26. https://www.freep.com/story/news/local/michigan/detroit/2017/07/26/detroit-water-shutoffs/512243001/.

Gruenstein Bocian, Debbie, Wei Li, and Keith S. Ernst. 2010. *Foreclosures by Race and Ethnicity: The Demographics of a Crisis.* Washington, DC: Center for Responsible Lending.

Gutman, Marta 2008. "Race, Place, and Play: Robert Moses and the WPA Swimming Pools in New York City." *Journal of the Society of Architectural Historians* 67(4):532–561.

Guyette, Curt. 2014a. Bad Interest Rate Swaps Contribute to Detroit Water Crisis and Financial Crisis." *Detroit Metro Times,* August 6. https://www.metrotimes.com/detroit/water-woes-and-the-swaps-swamp/Content?oid=2214702.

Guyette, Curt. 2014b. "Bankruptcy Costs Detroit Retirees." *Detroit Metro Times,* November 5. https://www.metrotimes.com/detroit/bankruptcy-costs-detroit-retirees/Content?oid=2264682.

Guyette, Curt. 2014c. "The EAA Exposed: An Investigative Report." *Detroit Metro Times,* September 24. https://www.metrotimes.com/detroit/the-eaa-exposed-an-investigative-report/Content?oid=2249513.

Guyette, Curt. 2014d. "Examining the Body of Evidence in Detroit's Bankruptcy Trial: Anatomy of a Takeover." *Detroit Metro Times,* April 1. https://www.metrotimes.com/detroit/examining-the-body-of-evidence-in-detroits-bankruptcy-trial/Content?oid=2144001.

Guyette, Curt. 2016. "Exclusive: Gov. Rick Snyder's Men Originally Rejected Using Flint's Toxic River." *Daily Beast,* January 24, 2016. https://www.thedailybeast.com/exclusive-gov-rick-snyders-men-originally-rejected-using-flints-toxic-river.

Guyette, Curt. 2017. "A Deep Dive into the Source of Flint's Water Crisis: Tunnel Vision. *Detroit Metro Times,* April 19. https://www.metrotimes.com/detroit/a-deep-dive-into-the-source-of-flints-water-crisis/Content?oid=3399011.

Halcom, Chad. 2013. "Federal Oversight of Detroit Water Department Ends after Nearly 36 Years." *Crain's Detroit Business,* March 27. https://www.crainsdetroit.com/article/20130327/NEWS/130329875/federal-oversight-of-detroit-water-department-ends-after-nearly-36.

Hall, B. 2016. "Meet Jeff Wright, the Man Who Poisoned Flint. *West Michigan Politics*, September 8. http://westmipolitics.blogspot.com/2016/09/meet-jeff-wright-man-who-poisoned-flint.html.

Hammer, P. 2014. "The Flint Water Crisis, KWA, and Strategic-Structural Racism." Paper presented at the Michigan Civil Rights Commission Hearings on the Flint Water Crisis, Flint, MI.

Harney, Stefano, and Fred Moten. 2013. *The Undercommons: Fugitive Planning and Black Study*. Brooklyn, NY: Autonomedia.

Harris, Cheryl. 1993. "Whiteness as Property." *Harvard Law Review* 106(8):1710–1791.

Harris, Douglas N. 2016. "DeVos and the Evidence from Michigan." *Education Next*, December 5. https://www.educationnext.org/devos-and-the-evidence-from-michigan/.

Harrison, Jill Lindsey. 2019. *From the Inside Out: The Fight for Environmental Justice within Government Agencies*. Cambridge, MA: MIT Press.

Harrison, Jill Lindsey. 2020. "Regulatory Culture: Racial Ideologies and the Fight for Environmental Justice within Government Agencies." In *Lessons in Environmental Justice: From Civil Rights to Black Lives Matter and Idle No More*, edited by Michael Mascarenhas, 128–146. Thousand Oaks, CA: Sage.

Hartman, Saidiya. 2017. "In the Wake: A Salon in Honor of Christina Sharpe." BCRW: Barnard Center for Research on Women. Retrieved October 29, 2018, from https://bcrw.barnard.edu/videos/in-the-wake-a-salon-in-honor-of-christina-sharpe/.

Harvey, David. 2016. "David Harvey: 'There Is No Way You Can Change the World without Changing Your Ideas!.'" *Lefteast*, December 16. https://www.criticatac.ro/lefteast/david-harvey-interview-2016/.

Harwell, Drew. 2019. "Federal Study Confirms Racial Bias of Many Facial-Recognition Systems, Casts Doubt on Their Expanding Use." *Washington Post*, December 19. https://www.washingtonpost.com/technology/2019/12/19/federal-study-confirms-racial-bias-many-facial-recognition-systems-casts-doubt-their-expanding-use/.

Heat and Warmth Fund. 2018. "Financial Statements, June 30, 2018." Accessed February 5, 2021. https://thawfund.org/wp-content/uploads/2019/01/FINAL-The-Heat-and-Warmth-Fund-6-30-18-YEFS.pdf.

Helms, Matt, and Joe Guillen. 2014. "Saunteel Jenkins Is Leaving Detroit City Council." *Detroit Free Press*, October 17. https://www.freep.com/story/news/local/michigan/detroit/2014/10/17/saunteel-jenkins-leaving-detroit-city-council/17443817/.

Henry, Ben, Jill Reese, and Angel Torres. 2013. "Wasted Wealth: How the Wall Street Crash Continues to Stall Economic Recovery and Deepen Racial Inequality in America." Alliance for a Just Society. May. https://

www.allianceforajustsociety.org/wp-content/uploads/2015/09/Wasted.
Wealth_NATIONAL.pdf.

Highsmith, Andrew R. 2015. *Demolition Means Progress: Flint, Michigan, and the Fate of the American Metropolis.* Chicago: University of Chicago Press.

Hill Collins, Patricia. 2000. *Black Feminist Thought: Knowledge, Consciousness, and the Politics of Empowerment.* Second edition. New York: Routledge.

Hill Collins, Patricia. 2009. *Another Kind of Public Education: Race, Schools, the Media, and Democratic Possibilities.* Boston: Beacon Press.

Hill Collins, Patrica, and Sirma Bilge. 2017. *Intersectionality.* Malden, MA: Polity Press.

House, Kelly. 2023. No convictions for Flint: Attorney general ends water crisis prosecutions. *Bridge Magazine.* https://www.bridgemi.com/michigan-environment-watch/no-convictions-flint-attorney-general-ends-water-crisis-prosecutions.

Hudson, Michael. 2011. "Claims of High Pressure Sales, Fraud at Odds with Quicken Loans' Straight-Shooting Image." Center for Public Integrity, February 4. https://publicintegrity.org/inequality-poverty-opportunity/claims-of-high-pressure-sales-fraud-at-odds-with-quicken-loans-straight-shooting-image/.

International Committee of the Red Cross. 1977. "Article 54: Protection of Objects Indispensable to the Survival of the Civilian Population." International Humanitarian Law Databases. Accessed November 16, 2022, https://ihl-databases.icrc.org/en/ihl-treaties/api-1977/article-54.

International Criminal Court. 1998. Rome Statute of the International Criminal Court. https://www.icc-cpi.int/sites/default/files/Publications/Rome-Statute.pdf.

Jackson, Zoe. 2018. "Flint Cultural Center Details How Arts Millage Money Would Be Spent." *Michigan Live*, July 3. https://www.mlive.com/news/flint/2018/07/flint_cultural_center_addresse.html.

Kaffer, N. 2016. State's Interest in Pushing KWA Project Needs Explanation. *Detroit Free Press*, May 15. https://www.freep.com/story/opinion/columnists/nancy-kaffer/2016/05/15/flint-water-crisis/84296376/.

Kennedy, Merrit. 2016. "Lead-Laced Water in Flint: A Step-by-Step Look at the Makings of a Crisis." *The Two-Way*, April 20. National Public Radio. https://www.npr.org/sections/thetwo-way/2016/04/20/465545378/lead-laced-water-in-flint-a-step-by-step-look-at-the-makings-of-a-crisis.

King, Martin Luther, Jr. 1963. "Read Martin Luther King Jr.'s 'I Have a Dream' Speech in Its Entirety." *Talk of the Nation*, NPR. Updated January 16, 2023. https://www.npr.org/2010/01/18/122701268/i-have-a-dream-speech-in-its-entirety.

King, Martin Luther, Jr. 1968. *Where Do We Go from Here: Chaos or Community?* Boston: Beacon Press.

King, Martin Luther, Jr. 1992. *The Papers of Martin Luther King Jr.* Clayborne Carson, senior editor. Volume 1: *Called to Serve. January 1929–June 1951,* edited by Ralph E. Luker and Penny A. Russell. Oakland: University of California Press.

Koeppel, G. 2000. *Water for Gotham: A History.* Princeton, NJ: Princeton University Press.

Kornberg, D. 2016. "The Structural Origins of Territorial Stigma: Water and Racial Politics in Metropolitan Detroit, 1950s–2010s." *International Journal of Urban and Regional Research* 40(2):263–283.

Kroll, Andy. 2014. "Meet the New Kochs: The DeVos Clan's Plan to Defund the Left." *Mother Jones,* January–February. https://www.motherjones.com /politics/2014/01/devos-michigan-labor-politics-gop/.

Kurth, Joel. 2016. "Detroit Hits Residents on Water Shut-Offs As Businesses Slide." *Detroit News,* March 31. Retrieved from https://www.detroitnews.com /story/news/local/detroit-city/2016/03/31/detroit-water-shutoffs/82497496/.

Lamb, C. M. 2005. *Housing Segregation in Suburban America since 1960: Presidential and Judicial Politics.* Cambridge: Cambridge University Press.

Landman, A. 2011. "Synagro's Shiny New Patina." *Common Dreams,* October 4. https://www.commondreams.org/views/2011/10/04/synagros-shiny-new-patina.

Lemkin, Raphaël. 1944. *Axis Rule in Occupied Europe: Laws of Occupation, Analysis of Government, Proposals for Redress.* Washington, DC: Carnegie Endowment for International Peace.

Levin, Sam. 2016. "Dakota Access Pipeline: Native Americans Allege Cruel Treatment." *The Guardian,* October 30, Environment sec. Retrieved from https://www.theguardian.com/us-news/2016/oct/29/dakota-access-pipeline-native-american-protesters.

Lipsitz, George. 2006. *The Possessive Investment in Whiteness: How White People Profit from Identity Politics.* Philadelphia: Temple University Press.

Lipsitz, George. 2011. *How Racism Takes Place.* Philadelphia: Temple University Press.

Loewen, James W. 2005. *Sundown Towns: A Hidden Dimension of American Racism.* New York: New Press.

London, Jonathan K., Amanda Fencl, Sara Watterson, Jennifer Jarin, Alfonso Aranda, Aaron King, Camille Pannu, Phoebe Seaton, Laurel Firestone, Mia Dawson, and Peter Nguyen. 2018. *The Struggle for Water Justice in California's San Joaquin Valley: A Focus on Disadvantaged Unincorporated Communities.* : Center for Regional Change, University of California, Davis.

Longley, Kristin. 2010. "Genesee County Drain Commissioner Jeff Wright Had Past FBI Encounter in Burton Bribery Probe." *Michigan Live,* May 13. https://www.mlive.com/news/flint/2010/05/genesee_county_drain_commissio_8.html.

Longley, Kristin. 2013. "Flint Reviewing Resigned Public Safety Administrator Barnett Jones' Records." *Michigan Live,* January 12. https://www.mlive .com/news/flint/2013/01/flint_reviewing_resigned_publi.html.

Lorde, Audre. 2007. *Sister Outside.* Berkeley, CA: Crossing Press.

Lurie, Julia. 2016. "While Lead Flowed through the Pipes, Flint Residents Paid America's Most Expensive Water Bills." *Mother Jones,* February 17. http:// www.motherjones.com/environment/2016/02/while-lead-flowed-through-taps-flint-had-most-expensive-water-nation.

MacDonald, Christine, and Joel Kurth. 2015. "Gilbert, Quicken Loans Entwined in Detroit Blight." *Detroit News,* July 1. https://www.detroitnews .com/story/news/special-reports/2015/07/01/quicken-loans-blight-dilemma /29537285/.

Mack, Elizabeth A., and Sarah Wrase. 2017. "A Burgeoning Crisis? A Nation-wide Assessment of the Geography of Water Affordability in the United States." *PLOS ONE:*1–19.

Mascarenhas, Michael. 2001. "Farming Systems Research: Flexible Diversification of a Small Family Farm in South East Michigan." *Agricultural and Human Values* 18(4):391–401.

Mascarenhas, Michael. 2012. *Where the Waters Divide: Neoliberalism, White Privilege, and Environmental Racism in Canada* Lanham, MD: Lexington Books.

Mascarenhas, Michael. 2017. *New Humanitarianism and the Crisis of Charity: Good Intentions on the Road to Help.* Bloomington: Indiana University Press.

Massey, Douglas S., and Nancy A. Denton. 2003. *American Apartheid: Segregation and the Making of the Underclass.* Cambridge, MA: Harvard University Press.

Mayer, Jane. 2017. *Dark Money: The Hidden History of the Billionaires behind the Rise of the Radical Right.* New York: Anchor Books.

McGonigal, Mike. 2015. "The Water Warrior: Monica Lewis-Patrick, Community Activist." *Detroit Metro Times,* June 16.

Melosi, M. V. 2000. *The Sanitary City: Environmental Services in Urban America from Colonial Times to the Present.* Pittsburgh: University of Pittsburgh Press.

Michigan Civil Rights Commission. 2017. The Flint Water Crisis: Systemic Racism through the Lens of Flint. Report of the Michigan Civil Rights Commission.

Michigan Municipal League. 2014. "New Analysis Tallies the Impact of Revenue Sharing Diversion on Key Outstate Michigan Urban Areas." Press release, March 18. Accessed August 21, 2014, https://www.mml.org /newsroom/press_releases/2014-3-18-statewide-revenue-sharing.html.

Minghine, Anthony. 2014. "The Great Revenue Sharing Heist." Michigan MunicipalLeague,February.https://mml.org/advocacy/advocacy-great-revenue-sharing-heist/.

Molotch, H. 1976. "The City as a Growth Machine: Toward a Political Economy of Place." *American Journal of Sociology* 82(2):309–332.

Moore, K. 2017. Mayor Recommends City of Flint Stay with Great Lakes Water Authority as Primary Water Source." Press release. City of Flint, April 18. https://www.cityofflint.com/2017/04/18/mayor-recommends-city-of-flint-stay-with-great-lakes-water-authority-as-primary-water-source/.

Moratorium NOW! Coalition. 2014. "Who Is Veolia?" Moratorium Now! Coalition to Stop Foreclosures, Evictions, and Utility Shutoffs, September 18. https://moratorium-mi.org/veolia/.

Moreton-Robinson, Aileen. 2015. *The White Possessive: Property, Power, and Indigenous Sovereignty.* Minneapolis: University of Minnesota Press.

Moynihan, Daniel P. 1965a. "Employment, Income, and the Ordeal of the Negro Family." *Daedalus* 94(4):134–159.

Moynihan, Daniel. 1965b. "The Negro Family: The Case For National Action." US Department of Labor, March. https://www.dol.gov/general/aboutdol /history/webid-moynihan.

Murphy, Shannon. 2011. "State Revenue Sharing Cuts Reshape City Governments in Michigan." *Michigan Live,* October 16. https://www.mlive.com /news/2011/10/state_revenue_sharing_cuts_res.html.

National Advisory Commission on Civil Disorders. 1968. *U.S. Riot Commission Report: What Happened? Why Did It Happen? What Can Be Done?* New York: Bantam Books.

Neavling, Steve. 2015. "Billionaire Dan Gilbert Calls Motor City Muckraker 'Dirty Scum' over Surveillance Story." *Motor City Muckraker,* April 27. http://motorcitymuckraker.com/2015/04/27/billionaire-dan-gilbert-calls-motor-city-muckraker-dirty-scum-over-surveillance-story/.

Neavling, Steve. 2019. "Two Years In, Detroit's QLine falls Far Short of Expectations: A Streetcar Named Disaster?" *Detroit Metro Times,* May 1. https:// www.metrotimes.com/detroit/two-years-in-detroits-qline-falls-far-short-of-expectations/Content?oid=21552552.

Neu, Dean, and Richard Therrien. 2003. *Accounting for Genocide: Canada's Bureaucratic Assault on Aboriginal People.* New York: Zed Books.

Nelson, Robert K., LaDale Winling, Richard Marciano, N. D. B. Connolly, and Edward L. Ayers. 2023. *Mapping Inequality: Redlining in New Deal America.* Richmond, VA: Digital Scholarship Labe, University of Richmond. Retrieved from https://dsl.richmond.edu/panorama/redlining/#loc= 11/42.348/-83.293&city=detroit-mi&area=D21&text=intro.

Nino, Ronald F. 1970. "A Comparative Analysis of Michigan's Subdivision Control Act and Critique." Master's thesis, School of Urban Planning and Landscape Architecture, Michigan State University, East Lansing.

Nixon, Richard M. 1974. *Public Papers of the Presidents of the United States: Richard M. Nixon, 1972.* Washington, DC: Best Books.

Norgaard, Kurt Jay. 1994. "Impacts of the Subdivision Control Act of 1967 on Land Fragmentation in Michigan's Townships." PhD dissertation, Department of Agricultural Economics, Michigan State University.

O'Connor, J. 1973. *The Fiscal Crisis of the State*. New York: St. Martin's Press.

Office of the Inspector General. 2018. *Management Weaknesses: Delayed Response to Flint Water Crisis*. Washington, DC: US Environmental Protection Agency.

Office of the UN High Commissioner for Human Rights. 2014a. "Detroit: Disconnecting Water from People Who Cannot Pay—An Affront to Human Rights, Say UN Experts." June 25. https://www.ohchr.org/EN/NewsEvents /Pages/DisplayNews.aspx?NewsID=14777.

Office of the UN High Commissioner for Human Rights 2014b. "Joint Press Statement by Special Rapporteur on Adequate Housing as a Component of the Right to an Adequate Standard of Living and to Right to Non-discrimination in This Context, and Special Rapporteur on the Human Right to Safe Drinking Water and Sanitation Visit to City of Detroit (United States of America) 18–20 October 2014." October 20. https://www.ohchr .org/EN/NewsEvents/Pages/DisplayNews.aspx?NewsID=15188.

Omi, Michael, and Howard Winant. 1994. *Racial Formation in America*. 2nd edition. New York: Routledge.

Oosting, J. 2014. "How Michigan's Revenue Sharing 'Raid' Cost Communities Billions for Local Services." *Michigan Live*, March 30. https://www.mlive .com/lansing-news/2014/03/michigan_revenue_sharing_strug.html.

"Opinion." 2017. D.R. v. Michigan Department of Education. Case No. 16-13694 (E.D. Mich. S. Div.).

"Opinion Regarding Eligibility." 2013. In re City of Detroit, Michigan, Debtor. Case No. 13-53846 (Bankr. E.D. Mich. S. Div.). https://www.mieb.uscourts .gov/sites/mieb/files/city-detroit-13-53846/docket1945.pdf.

Pannu, Camille. 2012. "Drinking Water and Exclusion: A Case Study from California's Central Valley." *California Law Review* 100(1):223–268. Retrieved from https://www.jstor.org/stable/41346406.

Patterson, William L., Richard O. Boyer, Howard Fast, Yvonne Gregory, Oakley Johnson, John Hudson Jones, Ruth A. Jones, Leon Josephson, Stetson Kennedy, and Elizabeth Lawson. 1951. *We Charge Genocide: The Historic Petition to the United Nations for Relief from a Crime of the United States Government against the Negro People*. New York: Civil Rights Congress.

Pauli, Benjamin. 2019. *Flint Fights Back: Environmental Justice and Democracy in the Flint Water Crisis*. Cambridge, MA: MIT Press.

Peck, Jamie, and Heather Whiteside. 2016. "Financializing Detroit." *Economic Geography* 92(3):235–268. doi: 10.1080/00130095.2015.1116369.

Pellow, David Naguib. 2016. "Toward a Critical Environmental Justice Studies: Black Lives Matter as an Environmental Justice Challenge." *Du Bois Review: Social Science Research on Race*:1–16.

Pellow, David Naguib. 2018. *What Is Critical Environmental Justice?* Medford, MA: Polity Press.

Pellow, David Naguib. 2020. "Black Lives Matter as an Environmental Justice Challenge." In *Lessons in Environmental Justice: From Civil Rights to Black Lives Matter and Idle No More,* edited by Michael Mascarenhas, 306–321. Thousand Oaks, CA: Sage.

Perkins, Tom. 2017. "On Dan Gilbert's Ever-Growing Rap Sheet, and Corporate Welfare." *Detroit Metro Times,* August 30. https://www.metrotimes.com/news /on-dan-gilberts-ever-growing-rap-sheet-and-corporate-welfare-5257860.

Perkins, Tom. 2018. "Big Promises for a Thriving Urban Core in Detroit Vanish in a Swath of Parking Lots." *The Guardian,* October 8. https://www .theguardian.com/us-news/2018/oct/08/detroit-the-district-redevelopment-ilitch-companies.

Perlovsky, Ilya, and Tom DeMarco. 2018. *Overview of the Taxable Municipal Market.* Boston: Fidelity Capital Markets, 2018.

Petty, Tawana. 2021. "Detroit: On a Journey to Be Seen—After Struggling for Decades against Pervasive Narratives and Disinvestment, Detroiters Are Making Policy Work for Them." *Data For Black Lives Blog,* March 5. https:// blog.d4bl.org/detroit-on-a-journey-to-be-seen-2/.

Philp, Drew. 2017. "No Water for Poor People: The Nine Americans Who Risked Jail to Seek Justice." *The Guardian,* July 20. https://www.theguardian.com /us-news/2017/jul/20/detroit-water-shutoffs-marian-kramer-bill-wylie-kellermann.

Pondera, C. S., and M. Omstedt. 2022. "The Violence of Municipal Debt: From Interest Rate Swaps to Racialized Harm in the Detroit Water Crisis." *Geoforum* 132:271–280.

Ponsot, Elisabeth. 2017. "Flint Wants Residents to Pay for Their Poisoned Water—Or Face Losing Their Homes." *Quartz,* May 4.

Power, Samantha. (2002) 2013. *A Problem from Hell: America and the Age of Genocide.* New York: Basic Books.

Pruett, Natalie. 2016. "Rebuild Flint the Right Way: Flint Water Crisis Infra-structure Response Guide." Accessible from "Publications and Portfolio" on Natalie Pruett. Accessed August 13, 2023, https://www.nataliepruett.com.

Pulido, Laura. 2016. "Flint, Environmental Racism, and Racial Capitalism." *Capitalism Nature Socialism* 27(3):1–16.

Pulido, Laura. 2017. "Geographies of Race and Ethnicity II: Environmental Racism, Racial Capitalism, and State-Sanctioned Violence." *Progress in Human Geography* 41(4):524–533.

Pulido, Laura. 2000. "Rethinking Environmental Racism: White Privilege and Urban Development in Southern California." *Annals of the Association of American Geographers* 90(1):12–40.

Ranganathan, Malini. 2016. "Thinking with Flint: Racial Liberalism and the Roots of an American Water Tragedy." *Capitalism Nature Socialism* 27(3):17–33.

Recchie, Anna, Joseph J. Recchie, john a. powell, Laura Lyons, Ponsella Hardaway, and Wendy Ake. 2019. *Water Equity and Security in Detroit's Water and Sewer District.* Berkeley, CA: AAS Institute for a Fair and Inclusive Society. Retrieved from https://belonging.berkeley.edu/detroitwaterequity.

Rector, Josiah. 2016. "Neoliberalism's Deadly Experiment." *Jacobin,* October 21. https://www.jacobinmag.com/2016/10/water-detroit-flint-emergency-management-lead-snyder-privatization/.

Ridley, Gary. 2012. "Lawsuit Filed against Flint by Council President over Water Rate Increases." *Michigan Live,* May 24. https://www.mlive.com/news/flint/2012/05/lawsuit_filed_against_flint_by.html.

Ridley, Gary. 2016. "Engineering Firms 'Botched' Flint Water Studies, Attorney General Says." *Michigan Live,* June 22. https://www.mlive.com/news/flint/2016/06/engineering_firms_botched_flin.html.

Ringquist, Evan. 2005. "Assessing Evidence of Environmental Inequalities: A Meta-analysis." *Journal of Policy Analysis and Management* 24(2):223–247.

Roberts, Dorothy. 1997. *Killing the Black Body: Race, Reproduction, and the Meaning of Liberty.* New York: Vintage Books.

Robertson, Teddy. 2016a. "Feeling a Little Subprime." In *Happy Anyway: A Flint Anthology,* edited by Scott Atkinson, 79–82. Cleveland: Belt.

Robertson, Teddy. 2016b. "What the Flint Housing Crisis Revealed about the True Value of a Neighborhood." *Next City,* July 6. https://nextcity.org/daily/entry/flint-anthology-new-book-excerpt.

Robinson, Cedric J. 1983. *Black Marxism: The Making of the Black Radical Tradition.* Chapel Hill: University of North Carolina Press.

Rocket Companies. 2020. "2020 Rocket Mortgage Classic Generates More than $2.7 Million for Nonprofits, Including More than $2.4 Million for Landmark Digital Inclusion Initiative." September 29. https://www.rocketcompanies.com/press-release/2020-rocket-mortgage-classic-generates-more-than-2-7-million-for-nonprofits-including-more-than-2-4-million-for-landmark-digital-inclusion-initiative/.

Rowe Engineering, Jones & Henry Engineering, and Gannett Fleming. 2006. "Preliminary Report: Long-Term Water Supply for Genesee County. Commissioned by Genesee County Drain Commissioner.

Ruble, Kayla, Jacob Carah, Abby Ellis, and Sarah Childress. 2018. "Flint Water Crisis Deaths Likely Surpass Official Toll." *Frontline,* PBS, July 24. https://

www.pbs.org/wgbh/frontline/article/flint-water-crisis-deaths-likely-surpass-official-toll/.

Kayla Ruble, Jacob Carah, Abby Ellis, and Sarah Childress. 2019. "Transcript: Flint's Deadly Water." *Frontline,* PBS, September 10. PBS. https://www.pbs.org/wgbh/frontline/documentary/flints-deadly-water/transcript/.

Sanburn, Josh. 2016. "The Poisoning of an American City." *Time,* January 21. https://time.com/4188328/the-poisoning-of-an-american-city/.

Sapotichne, Joshua, Erika Rosebrook, Eric A. Scorsone, Danielle Kaminski, Mary Doidge, and Traci Taylor. 2015. "Beyond State Takeovers: Reconsidering the Role of State Government in Local Financial Distress, with Important Lessons for Michigan and its Embattled Cities." MSU Extension White Paper. Institute for Public Policy and Social Research, College of Social Science, Michigan State University, East Lansing, August. ippsr.msu.edu/research/beyond-state-takeovers-.reconsidering-role-state-government-local-financial-distress.

Scheper-Hughes, Nancy. 1996. "Small Wats and Invisible Genocides." *Social Science and Medicine* 43(5):889–900.

Schimmel, L. H., Jr. 2005. "Can Detroit's Problems Be Corrected by an Emergency Financial Manager?" Mackinac Center for Public Policy, December 5. https://www.mackinac.org/V2005-36.

Scorsone, Eric A. 2013. "Frequently Asked Questions about the New Michigan Local Financial Emergency Law (Public Act 436 of 2012)." Michigan State Extension. January 28. https://www.canr.msu.edu/uploads/236/25914/FAQ-WhyNewLawWasPassed.pdf.

Scorsone, Eric A. 2014. "Municipal Fiscal Emergency Laws: Background and Guide to State-Based Approaches." Working paper 14-21. Mercatus Center, George Mason University. https://www.mercatus.org/research/working-papers/municipal-fiscal-emergency-laws-background-and-guide-state-based-approaches.

Scott, James C. 1998. *Seeing like a State: How Certain Schemes to Improve the Human Condition Have Failed.* New Haven, CT: Yale University Press.

Siegel Bernard, Tara 2015. "Justice Department Sues Quicken Loans over Mortgages." *New York Times,* April 24. https://www.nytimes.com/2015/04/24/your-money/justice-department-sues-quicken-loans.html?mcubz=1.

Slater, Tom. 2014. "The Resilience of Neoliberal Urbanism." *openDemocracy,* January 28. https://www.opendemocracy.net/en/opensecurity/resilience-of-neoliberal-urbanism/?fbclid=IwAR1oG_kwHhxgiEfo3jPKmaO6S3EO-T3iekTny4jqyrbMrY-qX5GwpsKj3W4w.

Smith, Jeff. 2017. "We're Rich and We Do What We Want: A DeVos Family Reader." *Grand Rapids Institute for Information Democracy,* December 4. https://griid.org/2017/12/04/were-rich-and-we-do-what-we-want-a-devos-family-reader/.

Stampfler, Michael. 2013. "Emergency Financial Management of Cities by the State: A Cure or Simply 'Kicking the Can Down the Road'?" *Journal of Law in Society* 14:235–243.

Stillo, F., and G. J. MacDonald. 2017. "Exposure to Contaminated Drinking Water and Health Disparities in North Carolina." *American Journal of Public Health* 107:180–185.

Strang, Veronica. 2004. *The Meaning of Water.* Oxford: Berg.

Strauss, Valerie. 2016. "A Sobering Look at What Betsy DeVos Did to Education in Michigan—And What Whe Might Do as Secretary of Education." *Washington Post,* December 8. https://www.washingtonpost.com/news/answer-sheet /wp/2016/12/08/a-sobering-look-at-what-betsy-devos-did-to-education-in- michigan-and-what-she-might-do-as-secretary-of-education.

Taibbi, Matt. 2017. *I Can't Breathe: A Killing on Bay Street.* New York: Spiegel & Grau.

Tabbi, Matt. 2013. "Looting the Pension Funds: All across America, Wall Street Is Grabbing Money Meant for Public Workers." *Rolling Stone,* September 26.

Taylor, Dorceta. 2014. "The State of Diversity in Environmental Organizations: Mainstream NGOs, Foundations, and Government Agencies." University of Michigan, School of Natural Resources and Environment, Ann Arbor.

Thompson, Derek. 2015. "The Richest Cities for Young People: 1980 vs. Today." *The Atlantic,* February 15. https://www.theatlantic.com/business/archive /2015/02/for-great-american-cities-the-rich-dont-always-get-richer /385513/.

Tracey, Ben, Andy Bast, and Chris Spinder. 2023. "New York Investors Snapping Up Colorado River Water Rights, Betting Big on an Increasingly Scarce Resource." Accessed March 27, 2023. https://www.cbsnews.com/news /new-york-investors-snapping-up-colorado-river-water-rights-betting-big- on-an-increasingly-scarce-resource/?fbclid=IwAR0Dmx8HSt5XjJG7F0266 gLPxZq8MQ6g_ud-pyV9ESLg8s_wmQxHwIoBV9I.

Tucker, Young, Jackson, & Tull, Inc. 2013. "City of Flint Water Supply Assessment: Final Report, for Submittal to State of Michigan, Department of Treasury. Detroit, February.

Turbeville, W. C. 2013. "The Detroit Bankruptcy." Demos, November. https:// www.demos.org/sites/default/files/publications/Detroit_Bankruptcy- Demos.pdf.

US Attorney's Office, Eastern District of Michigan. 2009. "Former Synagro Executive Sentenced in Bribery Scheme Related to Detroit Sludge Contract." Press release, November 30. Archived at The FBI: Federal Bureau of Investigation. https://archives.fbi.gov/archives/detroit/press-releases/2009 /de113009.htm.

US Department of Housing and Urban Development. 2020. "Neighborhood Stabilization Program Data." https://www.huduser.gov/portal/datasets/NSP .html.

US Department of the Treasury. n.d. "Hardest Hit Fund (HHF)." accessed August 29, 2023. https://www.treasury.gov/initiatives/financial-stability /TARP-Programs/housing/hhf/Pages/default.aspx.

United Nations General Assembly. 1948. "Article II of the Convention on the Prevention and Punishment of the Crime of Genocide, Approved by the United Nations General Assembly Resolution 260 A(III) of 9 December 1948." Human Rights Web. Accessed August 28, 2023, http://www.hrweb .org/legal/genocide.html.

United States Department of Justice Civil Rights Division. 2015. *Investigation of the Ferguson Police Department*. Washington, DC: Department of Justice.

Vase, Kathryn. 2016. "You Can Buy a House in Flint for $14,000." CNN, March 4. https://money.cnn.com/2016/03/04/real_estate/flint-housing-water-crisis/index.html.

Visit Detroit. 2022a. "Time Selects Detroit in World's Greatest Places List. July 12. https://visitdetroit.com/media/press-releases/.

Visit Detroit. 2022b. "USA Today Announces America's Thanksgiving Parade® Presented by Gardner White as the Number One Holiday Parade in America." December 16. https://visitdetroit.com/media/press-releases/.

Waldman, Annie. 2019. "How Teach for America Evolved into an Arm of the Charter School Movement." *ProPublica,* June 18. https://www.propublica .org/article/how-teach-for-america-evolved-into-an-arm-of-the-charter-school-movement.

Waldron, I. 2018. *There's Something in the Water: Environmental Racism in Indigenous and Black Communities.* Black Point, Nova Scotia: Fernwood Books.

We the People of Detroit. 2019a. "Our People." Accessed September 4, 2023, https://www.wethepeopleofdetroit.com/our-people.

We the People of Detroit. 2019b. "What We Do: Community Coalition Building." Accessed May 24, 2023. https://www.wethepeopleofdetroit.com/.

We the People of Detroit Community Research Collective. 2016. *Mapping the Water Crisis: The Dismantling of African-American Neighborhoods in Detroit.* Volume 1. Detroit.

Whitmire, Richard. 2016. "Ed Reform Battle in Los Angeles." *Education Next* 16(4).https://www.educationnext.org/ed-reform-battle-in-los-angeles-charter-schools/.

Wilkinson, Mike. 2016. "Betsy DeVos and the Segregation of School Choice." *Bridge Magazine,* November 29. https://www.bridgemi.com/talent-education/betsy-devos-and-segregation-school-choice.

Wilson, William Julius. 2012. *The Truly Disadvantaged: The Inner City, the Underclass, and Public Policy.* 2nd edition. Chicago: University of Chicago Press.

Wiltse, Jeff. 2007. *Contested Waters: A Social History of Swimming Pools in America.* Chapel Hill: University of North Carolina Press.

Worth-Nelson, Jan, and Harold C. Ford. 2018. "Flint Community Schools Facing Make-or-Break Challenge under State Partnership Agreement." *East Village Magazine,* August 22.

Wright, J. 2016. "The Flint Water Crisis, DWSD, and GLWA: Monopoly, Price Gouging, Corruption, and the Poisoning of a City." Written Testimony to the Michigan Department of Civil Rights Flint Water Crisis Hearings. Michigan Department of Civil Rights, Detroit.

Wu, Nicholas. 2017. "The Uncomfortable Truths of Home." *Princeton Correspondents on Undergraduate Research,* November 27. https://pcur.princeton.edu/2017/11/the-uncomfortable-truths-of-home/.

Wylie-Kellermann, Bill. 2020. "Tracked but Not Seen: The Fight against Racist Surveillance." *Sojourners,* March.

Young, Coleman Alexander, and Lonnie Wheeler. 1994. *Hard Stuff: The Autobiography of Mayor Coleman Young.* New York: Viking.

Zeemering, E. S. 2010. "Guiding Regionalism and Reform from the Court: Judge John Feikens." *Public Administration Review* (September–October):792–800.

Zimring, Carl A. 2015. *Clean and White: A History of Environmental Racism in the United States.* New York: New York University Press.

Index

Founded in 1893,
UNIVERSITY OF CALIFORNIA PRESS
publishes bold, progressive books and journals
on topics in the arts, humanities, social sciences,
and natural sciences—with a focus on social
justice issues—that inspire thought and action
among readers worldwide.

The UC PRESS FOUNDATION
raises funds to uphold the press's vital role
as an independent, nonprofit publisher, and
receives philanthropic support from a wide
range of individuals and institutions—and from
committed readers like you. To learn more, visit
ucpress.edu/supportus.